People of the Finger Lakes Region

The Heart of New York State

Emerson Klees

By Emerson Klees

Photography by C. S. Kenyon

Friends of the Finger Lakes Publishing, Rochester, New York

For information, write:

Friends of the Finger Lakes Publishing
P. O. Box 18131
Rochester, New York 14618

Library of Congress Catalog Card Number 95-61561

ISBN 0-9635990-6-2
Printed in the United States of America
9 8 7 6 5 4 3 2 1

Cover design by Dunn and Rice Design, Rochester, NY
Book design by Seneca Mist Graphics, Ithaca, NY.
Designer, Dru Wheelin/ Production by Mary Lash.

Preface

People of the Finger Lakes Region: The Heart of New York State is a collection of biographical sketches of people from the Finger Lakes Region. The Heart of New York State is bounded by the I-390 Expressway in the West, the New York State Thruway in the North, the I-81 Expressway and Route 13 in the East, and Route 17, the Southern Tier Expressway, in the South. The scenic Finger Lakes Region is comprised of fourteen counties, 264 municipalities, and 6,125 square miles.

This book contains sixty biographical profiles of people who were either born in the Finger Lakes Region, spent some of their formative years in the area, or distinguished themselves while living in the region. There are ten sketches in each of six categories:

Pioneers / Reformers

Entrepreneurs / Industrialists

Organizers / Notables

Philanthropists / Statesmen

Leaders / Visionaries

Engineers / Change Agents

This book contains some material reprinted from *Persons, Places, and Things In the Finger Lakes Region* and *Persons, Places, and Things Around the Finger Lakes Region.*

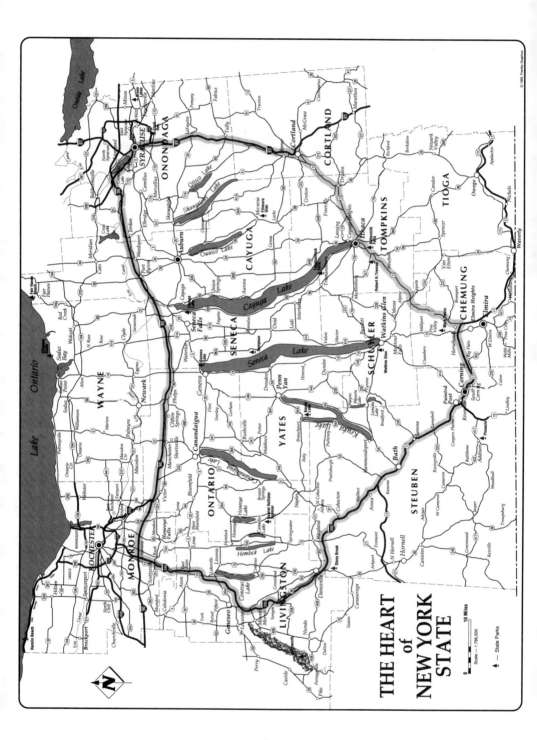

THE HEART
of
NEW YORK
STATE

Scale — 1:798,500

10 Miles

▲ — State Parks

List of Photographs

Front Cover

1. Statue of Elizabeth Blackwell, Hobart / William Smith Colleges, Geneva
2. Clara Barton Red Cross Chapter No. 1, Dansville
3. Statue of Red Jacket, Red Jacket Park, Penn Yan
4. Mark Twain's Octagonal Study, Elmira College
5. Birthplace of Millard Fillmore, Fillmore Glen State Park, Moravia
6. Glen Iris Inn, Letchworth State Park
7. "Zim" House, Horseheads
8. Statue of Mary Jemison, Letchworth State Park
9. The Historic Grandin Building, Palmyra

Back Cover

Aerial view of Keuka Lake, looking north

Elizabeth Blackwell Reading Room, Geneva

Table of Contents

PEOPLE OF THE FINGER LAKES REGION

PAGE NO.

Chapter 6   Engineers / Change Agents

St. Matthew's Episcopal Church, Moravia

Prologue

"There is properly no history, only biography."
—Ralph Waldo Emerson, *Essays: First Series [1841]. History.*

EARLY HISTORY OF THE FINGER LAKES REGION

Indian Migration into the Region

The first inhabitants of the region were the Algonkian Indians who migrated from Asia six thousand years ago. They crossed the Bering Strait, traveled south along the Pacific coast, turned eastward, and reached New York State about 4000 BC. Some historians divide the Algonkians into subcultures, such as the Lamokas (3500 BC) with their long, narrow skulls, and the Laurentians, who migrated south from Canada. Laurentian skulls, with indications of broad faces, foreheads, and noses, have been found on Frontenac Island in Cayuga Lake. A third group, the Woodland Culture, which flourished until about AD 1000, raised crops and were noted fishermen. One of their campsites was excavated at the northern end of Owasco Lake, near Auburn.

About AD 1300, the Iroquois, who had been living along the Mississippi, Ohio, and Missouri Rivers, began to move to the Northeast because of food shortages. The aggressive Iroquois forced the Algonkians out of central New York State. Another Iroquois tribe moved into Canada and split into two groups. One group turned south and became the Onondaga Nation; the other group, who was defeated in Canada, also moved south, settling in the Mohawk Valley. The second group divided again and became the Mohawk and Oneida Nations.

The three strongest nations of the Iroquois Confederacy were the Senecas, the "Keepers of the Western Door"; the Onondagas, keepers of the council fire in the Syracuse area; and the Mohawks, the "Keepers of the Eastern Door." The Cayugas and the Oneidas were the lesser nations of the confederacy, which the five nations of the Iroquois formed in 1570 for mutual defense purposes. In 1722, the Tuscaroras moved north from the Carolinas and joined the Iroquois Confederacy, making it the Confederacy of Six Nations.

The Sullivan Campaign

In 1778, white settlers were massacred by Indians in Wyoming (Wilkes-Barre), Pennsylvania, and Cherry Valley, New York, causing considerable unrest in the region. About the same time, the British tried to convince their Indian allies, four of the six nations of the Iroquois Confederacy, to attack General Washington's Colonial Army from the west. As a result, Congress authorized General Washington to form the Sullivan Expedition on February 27, 1779. Initially, Washington offered the command of the expedition to General Gates, because of his seniority and rank. However, Gates was not one for danger and long marches, so he declined. He wrote to Washington: "The man who undertakes the Indian service should enjoy youth and strength, requisites I do not possess. It therefore grieves me that your Excellency should offer me the only command to which I am utterly unequal."

Washington then chose thirty-nine-year-old Major General John Sullivan, who had distinguished himself in the battles of Brandywine, Germantown, Trenton, Princeton, and particularly in leading the bayonet charge at Butt's Hill. Sullivan's army assembled at Easton, Pennsylvania, stopped at Wyoming, Pennsylvania, to correct some supply problems, and marched on to Tioga Point, now Athens, Pennsylvania. Another element of the expedition started from Schenectady, commanded by Brigadier General James Clinton, Sullivan's second-in-command. They built 212 boats and moved up the Mohawk River to Canajoharie, where they carried the boats overland to Otsego Lake. They built a dam at Cooperstown, raised the level of Otsego Lake by two feet, and proceeded south to meet Sullivan at Tioga Point. Sullivan's men built Fort Sullivan at Tioga Point and waited for Clinton's forces to arrive.

Clinton arrived in late August, and both elements of the expedition marched on to Newtown, five miles south of Elmira. They were met there by a force of one thousand to fifteen hundred men, comprised of Canadian Rangers, Tories, and Indians. The force opposing Sullivan was commanded by the Mohawk chief, Joseph Brant, who had been educated by Eleazar Wheelock, founder of Dartmouth College. Sullivan's army of over three thousand routed Brant's force, partly because some of the Colonials worked in behind Brant's men waiting in ambush. This was the only staged battle of the campaign. The expedition's next encampment was at Horseheads, where on the return journey, Sullivan's men shot thirty to forty worn-out pack horses. Later, the Indians lined the sun-bleached horse skulls along the trail, giving the town of Horseheads its name.

Sullivan's expedition moved through the Finger Lakes Region causing considerable destruction, particularly around Cayuga and Seneca Lakes. Of the six major lakes, Keuka Lake was the only one not visited by Sullivan's men. The army reached as far west as the Genesee River; they marched by the northern ends of Canandaigua, Honeoye, and Hemlock Lakes and the southern end of Conesus Lake. Sullivan sent a detachment to Conesus Lake to scout the Indian settlement at Genesee Castle. Fifteen of the twenty-four men in the scouting party were killed; Lieutenant Thomas Boyd and Sergeant Michael Parker were tortured, mutilated, and killed. Sullivan's men found their bodies at Genesee Castle, a settlement of 128 houses between Cuylerville and the west bank of the Genesee River.

On the expedition's return through the region, Colonel Peter Gansevoort was sent to Albany with a detachment of 100 men, who passed through the sites of Auburn and Skaneateles. At the close of the expedition, Sullivan reported that he had destroyed forty Indian villages, 160,000 bushels of corn, large quantities of other crops, and many acres of orchards. He also destroyed the most advanced Indian culture that existed up until that time. However, he had complied with Washington's order: "It is proposed to carry the war into the heart of the country of the Six Nations, to cut off their settlements, destroy their next year's crops ... lay waste all the settlements around, so that the country may not only be overrun but destroyed." General Sullivan accomplished the goals of removing the British threat from the west and of stopping the Six Nations from making war as a confederation.

General Sullivan returned to New Hampshire, where he was elected to Congress and served as Governor. He was president of the New Hampshire convention that adopted the U.S. Constitution. In 1789, President Washington appointed him judge of the U.S. District Court of New Hampshire. He died in 1795 at the age of fifty-four.

The Phelps-Gorham Purchase and Early Settlement

Until 1786, Western New York was a part of Massachusetts, as granted in its Royal Charter. A convention was held at Hartford, Connecticut, that year to resolve conflicting claims to the land west of Seneca Lake. Massachusetts was granted the "pre-emption" right to sell the land, and New York State was granted the right of sovereignty to govern the region, which was almost entirely populated by the six nations of the Iroquois Confederacy. Two speculators, Oliver Phelps and Nathaniel Gorham, offered to buy the pre-emption rights to the region from the Commonwealth of Massachusetts, set aside the Indian claims, have the land surveyed, and sell lots to settlers. Massachusetts was willing to sell since the Commonwealth was burdened with Revolutionary War debts.

Nathaniel Gorham, who was born in Charlestown, Massachusetts, on May 27, 1738, was a delegate to the Continental Congress in 1782-83 and 1785-87 and was elected President of the Continental Congress in June, 1786. He was influential in obtaining ratification of the U.S. Constitution in Massachusetts. Oliver Phelps, born in Windsor, Connecticut, in 1750, served in the commissary department of the Continental

Army. After the war, Phelps was elected to the Connecticut State Assembly, the State Senate, and was appointed to the Governor's Council. He settled in Canandaigua, served as the first judge of Ontario County, and represented the district in Congress in 1803-05.

The treaty signed by the Iroquois Confederation at Buffalo Creek on July 8, 1788, conveyed 2,600,000 acres of land to the Phelps and Gorham Company for $5,000 and an annuity of $500 forever. The parcel of land extended from the Pennsylvania border along a line near Geneva to Sodus Bay on Lake Ontario in the east, and to the Genesee River in the west. It included a small parcel west of the Genesee River bordering on Lake Ontario.

In 1788, Colonel Hugh Maxwell was delegated to survey the "pre-emption line," the eastern boundary of the purchase. Either due to error or fraud, this line was run further to the west than it should have been. This erroneous line placed Geneva to the east of the purchase and caused Oliver Phelps to locate his land office in Canandaigua rather than Geneva, his original choice. A new survey was made in 1792 by Benjamin Ellicott; the triangular space between the new line and the old line contained 85,896 acres and was called the "gore."

When the federal government assumed all of the Revolutionary War debts of the states, the value of Massachusett's currency multiplied, and Phelps and Gorham could not pay their debt to the state. They sold all of the available land, 1,267,569 acres, including the gore, to Robert Morris, the "financier of the Revolutionary War," for eleven to twelve cents an acre. Robert Morris immediately sold the land to a group of English capitalists; Sir William Pulteney purchased nine-twelfths interest, William Hornby two-twelfths, and Patrick Colquhoun, one-twelfth. Morris realized a profit of $160,000 from the sale.

Lord Pulteney commissioned Charles Williamson as his agent. Williamson was instrumental in the early development of the region, including the construction of roads, the founding of the first newspaper, and the establishment of the first theatre. He helped to prepare the region for the industrial growth that came with the building of the Erie Canal and the railroads.

The Burned-over District

The Burned-over District is the name applied to Western New York State from the Adirondacks and the Catskills to Lake Erie during the first half of the nineteenth century. The name refers to an area that experienced a large number of religious revivals. The term "Burned-over District" was given to the region between Lake Ontario and the Adirondacks by Charles Grandison Finney, the most dynamic evangelist of his day. In his opinion, early Methodist circuit riders had diverted people from the proper religious instruction that he was attempting to provide.

In his book, *Listen for a Lonesome Drum,* Carl Carmer viewed it as a "Spirit Way:"

> Across the entire breadth of York State, undeviatingly, a hilly strip scarcely twenty-five miles wide invites the world's wonder. It is a broad psychic highway, a thoroughfare of the occult whose great stations number the mystic seven. For where, in its rolling course from east of Albany to west of Buffalo, it has reached one of seven isolated and lonely heights, voices out of other worlds have spoken with spiritual authority to men and women, and the invisible mantles of the prophets have been laid on consecrated shoulders. In no other area of the Western Hemisphere have so many evidences of an existence transcending mortal living been manifest. It is impossible to reckon the number of listeners who on the plateaus of this strange midstate adventure have knelt before seen or unseen supernatural visitants to hear counsel. And the sum of those whose lives have been affected by that counsel, save for the fact that it is in the millions, is incalculable.

Three of the seven instances referred to by Mr. Carmer

occurred in the Finger Lakes Region: Jemima Wilkinson, the Publick Universal Friend, and her community at Jerusalem in Yates County; the Fox sisters and their experiences with spiritualism at Hydeville, near Newark; and the founding of the Mormon religion at Palmyra by Joseph Smith. The other four of the "mystic seven" are: Mother Ann Lee and the Shakers, who had two settlements in the Finger Lakes Region; William Miller, who made predictions of the end of the world, and the Millerites; John Humphrey Noyes and the Oneida Community; and Thomas Harris and the Harrisites at Brocton on the shores of Lake Erie.

In addition to these instances, the Finger Lakes Region was the center of the anti-Masonic movement between 1826 and 1850. It was a hotbed of both the abolitionist and temperance movements, and, most notably, it was the center of the Women's Rights Movement in the United States. In order to understand why this agricultural lake country encountered such restlessness, it is necessary to look at the settlers of the region, where they came from, and the religious background that they brought with them.

Settlement in the Finger Lakes Region began in the late 1780s and was dominated by Yankees from New England. Also, many settlers came up the Susquehanna River from Pennsylvania. Many of the New Englanders had settled first in the Eastern New York counties, and then pulled up stakes and resettled in the lake country. Not many of the pioneers came from Boston or the fertile Connecticut River Valley; many came from the hill country of New Hampshire and Vermont and from other areas of Connecticut.

Many of the settlers from New England were Baptists, Congregationalists, or Methodists. Presbyterians and one branch of the Congregationalists merged in 1801 in the Plan of Union. All of the major denominations, except the Episcopalians, were revivalistic. The Baptists and the Methodists were more emotional and easier for common people to understand than the Presbyterians. From 1815-18, there were six revivals in Rhode Island, fifteen in Connecticut, twenty-one each in New Jersey, Eastern New York, and Pennsylvania, forty-five in Vermont, sixty-four in Massachusetts, and eighty in the Burned-over District.

An increase in religious revivals in 1826 is credited to the influence of Charles Grandison Finney, a truly motivational speaker. This increase in activity continued from 1826 through 1837. Work on the Erie Canal began in 1817, and its completion in 1825 brought significant economic changes to the region. Population growth was phenomenal in the 1820s: Albany grew by 96 percent, Buffalo by 314 percent, Rochester by 512 percent, Syracuse by 282 percent, and Utica by 183 percent. Growth in church congregations came with the growth in population.

In 1831, Finney came to Rochester for a revivalist meeting that was one of the largest up until that time. The three Presbyterian churches did not get along with one another, but they pulled together to bring Finney to Rochester. His sermons included "The Carnal Mind is Enmity Against God" and "The Wages of Sin Is Death." Church membership boomed. The next peak in revivalism came in 1837, a year of recession. Interest in the church always increased in bad times.

The Fox sisters were the most notable examples of spiritualists in the Burned-over District, but there were other examples. In fact, the region had more mediums in 1859 than any other region of the United States. There were twenty-seven in Ohio, fifty-five in Massachusetts, and seventy-one in New York.

The religious fervor of the region burned itself out over the last half of the nineteenth century. However, some of the legacies of the Burned-over District survived into the twentieth century: the Mormon Church; several Adventist denominations, including the Seventh-Day Adventists; two species of Methodism, including the Free Methodists; and some spiritualist groups. The American tradition was enriched by these legacies, which formed a pathway to modern versions of religion.

The Erie Canal

One of the first people to suggest the construction of a canal connecting Lake Erie with the Hudson River was Gouverneur Morris in 1803. In 1810, he was appointed to a commission to plan the canal. James Geddes, a lawyer and surveyor from Syracuse, was employed to survey the prospective route of the canal. On July 4, 1817, construction of the 83-lock Erie Canal along a 363-mile route from Albany to Buffalo began at Rome. The ninety-four mile section of the canal from Rome west to the Seneca River was chosen to be constructed first, because it had a long, flat stretch of favorable terrain requiring only six locks. Also, it was easier to dig than other sections, and the landowners were more receptive.

Governor DeWitt Clinton sent Canvass White to England to study canal-building techniques. White came home and experimented with various types of cements. He discovered a hydraulic cement that would set under water. It was made from limestone that he burned and mixed with sand. This breakthrough saved considerable time and money in constructing the canal. Built with sloping sides, the canal was forty feet wide at the top and twenty feet wide at the bottom, with a towpath along one side. The water was only four feet deep.

The canal builders constructed eighteen aqueducts to carry the canal over rivers and streams, and contended with a difference in elevation of 568 feet between Lake Erie and the Hudson River. Two of the most difficult projects during the construction were digging through rock in the eastern section of the canal near Albany and accommodating a sixty-foot drop in elevation at Lockport. Nathan Roberts solved the problem at Lockport with a double set of five-step locks, one set of locks each for eastbound and westbound traffic.

In 1823, the canal from Rochester to Albany was opened; the cost of shipping a barrel of flour between those two cities dropped from $3.00 to $.75. The full length of the Erie Canal was opened in 1825 with the ceremony-filled Buffalo to Albany cruise of Governor DeWitt Clinton on the *Seneca Chief*. Two barrels of Lake Erie water were transported by the Governor to dump into New York harbor, symbolizing the joining of the two bodies of water. The $7,000,000 spent to build the canal ($2,000,000 over the original estimate) was not considered a good expenditure by the populace. They were proved wrong. The canal was economically successful beyond even Clinton's dreams.

The increase in the use of the canal outstripped its capacity; traffic jams became commonplace. Between 1835 and 1862, many changes were made in the canal to facilitate the increased traffic: the width at the top of the canal was increased from 40 feet to 70 feet, the width at the bottom was expanded from 28 to 56 feet, and the depth was increased from four feet to seven feet. In addition, the waterway was straightened, the number of locks was reduced from 83 to 72, and at most lock locations a double lock was built to allow two-way traffic. By the beginning of the twentieth century, railroads were providing stiff competition for the Erie Canal. Canal managers wanted to take advantage of advanced engineering skills and steam tugboats. Construction began in 1905 to increase lock sizes to 45 feet wide by 328 feet long, reduce the number of locks from 72 to 35, and increase the depth of the canal from 7 feet to 12 feet.

Many of the rivers along the route of the canal that were not utilized during earlier construction were incorporated now, including the Clyde, Oneida, Oswego, Mohawk, and Seneca rivers. The canal system was comprised of the new Erie Canal, the Cayuga-Seneca Canal between Cayuga and Seneca Lakes, the Oswego Canal from Syracuse to Oswego, and the Champlain Canal from Albany to Lake Champlain. It was called the New York State Barge Canal System when it opened in 1918.

The new canal system carried increasing amounts of traffic, but, eventually, efficient railroad freight traffic and truck traffic caused the demise of commercial use of the canal. In the late 1950s, the finishing touches to its death were applied by the completion of the New York State Thruway and the St. Lawrence Seaway, which linked the Great Lakes with the Atlantic Ocean.

Introduction

"The history of the world is but the biography of great men."
—Thomas Carlyle, *Heroes and Hero Worship* [1841].
The Hero as Divinity.

People of the Finger Lakes Region: The Heart of New York State contains biographical sketches of sixty individuals who were either born in the Finger Lakes Region, spent some of their formative years in the area, or distinguished themselves while living in the region. Included among these achievers are authors, industrialists, inventors, philanthropists, reformers, and statesmen. These sixty people are an impressive group that accomplished significant achievements. Those who toiled during the 1800s lived in a time of ferment: the temperance movement, the anti-Masonic movement, religious revivals, the abolitionist movement, and the Women's Rights Movement.

Their accomplishments are even more notable when it is realized that they came from a sparsely populated region. The two largest population centers in the region are Rochester (Monroe County) and Syracuse (Onondaga County), both of which were small villages until the completion of the Erie Canal in 1825. The region had an agrarian economy for the period during which most of these individuals lived. Most of them grew up on farms or in small villages. The population chart on the last page of this introduction indicates just how small a population spawned these men and women.

Inevitably, in choosing sixty achievers from the region, many individuals of high accomplishment are left out. Examples of individuals who might have been selected for this collective biography are:

- Francis B. Carpenter of Homer, President Lincoln's artist who lived in the White House for six months
- Theodore Willard Case of Auburn, pioneer in motion picture sound synchronization and founder of the predecessor of Twentieth Century Fox
- Mary Jane Holmes of Honeoye and Brockport, popular author of thirty-eight sentimental novels over a fifty-year period
- Amory Houghton of Corning, founder of Corning Inc.
- Henry Jarvis Raymond of Lima, founder of the New York *Times* and one of the founders of the Associated Press and the Republican Party

Other individuals who have been omitted from this collection are people who are living and achieving notable accomplishments today. This is another long list from which to choose. However, it is hoped that the sixty people chosen for this book are representative of the most noteworthy achievers of the region.

Population, by Counties, of the Finger Lakes Region
(1790-1980)

Counties	1790	1800	1810	1820	1830	1840	1850	1860	1940	1950	1980	Formed	From
Cayuga	--	15,907	29,843	38,897	47,948	50,338	55,458	55,767	65,508	70,136	79,894	1799	Onondaga
Chemung	--	--	--	--	--	20,732	28,821	26,917	73,718	86,827	97,656	1836	Tioga
Cortland	--	--	8,869	16,507	23,791	24,607	25,140	26,294	33,668	37,158	48,820	1808	Onondaga
Livingston	--	--	--	--	27,729	35,140	40,875	39,546	38,510	40,257	57,006	1821	Genesee, Ontario
Monroe	--	--	--	--	49,855	64,902	87,650	100,648	438,230	487,632	702,238	1821	Genesee, Ontario
Onondaga	--	7,698	25,987	41,467	58,973	67,911	85,890	90,686	295,108	341,719	463,324	1794	Herkimer
Ontario	1,075	15,218	42,032	88,267	40,288	43,501	43,929	44,563	55,307	60,172	88,909	1789	Montgomery
Schuyler	--	--	--	--	--	--	--	18,840	12,979	14,182	17,686	1854	Chemung, Steuben,Tompkins
Seneca	--	--	16,609	23,619	21,041	24,874	25,441	28,138	25,732	29,253	33,733	1804	Cayuga
Steuben	--	1,788	7,246	21,989	33,851	46,138	63,771	66,690	84,927	91,439	99,135	1796	Ontario
Tioga	--	7,109	7,889	16,971	27,690	20,527	24,880	28,748	27,072	30,166	49,812	1791	Montgomery
Tompkins	--	--	--	20,691	36,545	37,948	38,746	31,409	42,340	59,122	87,085	1817	Cayuga, Seneca
Wayne	--	--	--	--	33,643	42,057	44,953	47,762	52,747	57,323	85,230	1823	Ontario, Seneca
Yates	--	--	--	--	19,009	20,444	20,590	20,290	16,381	17,615	21,459	1823	Ontario
Total	1,075	47,720	138,485	268,398	420,363	499,119	586,144	626,298	1,262,227	1,423,001	1,931,987		

Note: The 1990 census population of the 14-county Finger Lakes Region was 1,976,685.

Jemima Wilkinson House, Jerusalem

Chapter 1

"To know how to say what other people only think, is what makes men poets and sages; and to dare to say what others only dare to think, makes men martyrs and reformers."
—Elizabeth Rundle Charles

Susan B. Anthony

In 1848, Susan B. Anthony's father, Daniel Anthony, moved from Massachusetts to Rochester, New York, where he was a successful farmer and insurance salesman. Two years after the first Women's Rights convention on July 19 and 20, 1848, in Seneca Falls, New York, which was organized by Elizabeth Cady Stanton and Lucretia Mott, another convention was held in Rochester.

Susan was working in Canajoharie, New York, as the girls' headmistress of the Canajoharie Academy and did not attend the convention. However, her father, mother, and sister did; they signed petitions in support of the resolutions. When Susan heard that they had attended the convention and were in agreement with the sentiments, she wrote that, in her opinion, they were getting ahead of the times.

Within two years, Susan was not only informed on the subject of women's rights, but she had discussed the subject with the abolitionists Frederick Douglass and William Lloyd Garrison, who were convinced that the women's rights cause should be pushed. Susan's interest in the movement was sparked by meeting Elizabeth Cady Stanton in Seneca Falls, after an anti-slavery meeting at which Garrison and the English abolitionist, George Thompson, spoke. It was the beginning of a friendship and a working relationship that lasted over a half century. Susan's attention to detail and organizational skills were a perfect match with Elizabeth's strengths as a philosopher and policymaker.

Initially, Susan supported three causes. The order of importance to her were: first, temperance; second, abolition; and third, women's rights. Elizabeth supported all of the liberal causes of the time, but concentrated upon women's rights and, in particular, women's right to vote.

Susan was introduced to the role of women at a Sons of Temperance convention in Albany. She thought that she was attending as a member of the convention until she attempted to make a motion and was told by the chairman that: "Sisters were invited here not to speak, but to listen and learn." That incident motivated Susan to organize the first Women's State Temperance Society in 1852 in Rochester. Elizabeth was elected president of the society, and Susan was elected secretary—a pattern that was repeated over the years.

Susan attended her first women's rights convention in 1852; it was the third National Women's Rights Convention. Elizabeth didn't attend because she was at home awaiting the birth of her fifth child. However, she sent a letter to be read by Susan at the convention. Two thousand delegates attended, including Lucretia Mott, James Mott, and Lucy Stone from New England, who was another of the movement's leaders.

The working relationship between Susan and Elizabeth was displayed by their respective roles in preparing for a speech that Elizabeth gave to the New York State legislature in February, 1854. Elizabeth addressed the right of women to earn and keep their own wages and the right of women to own property in their name. Elizabeth was willing to give the speech; however, with her large, young family, she didn't have the time to prepare it. She sent a plea for help to Susan, and an agreement was reached. Susan and a lawyer friend sympathetic to their cause would do the necessary research of the discriminating laws and would assemble the information, if Elizabeth would prepare and present the speech.

The speech at Albany was well-received. It provided specific examples of the ways in which women were discriminated against and the means by which the law could be changed to address the

discrimination. Susan was well prepared; she obtained six
thousand signatures on the petitions for women's property and
wage reform, as well as four thousand signatures on the petition in
support of women's right to vote. Changes to the law would not
come for another six years in New York. When the changes came,
Susan and Elizabeth knew that they had contributed heavily to
those changes.

Elizabeth's perception of their working relationship was:

> In thought and sympathy we were one, and in the
> division of labor we exactly complemented each
> other. In writing, we did better work together than
> either of us could have done alone. I am the better
> writer, she the better critic. She supplied the facts
> and statistics, I the philosophy and rhetoric, and
> together we have made arguments that have stood
> unshaken through the storms of thirty long
> years.... Our speeches may be considered the
> united product of two brains.

Susan came to Seneca Falls frequently to take care of the Stanton
children so that Elizabeth could prepare a speech or give a speech.
The children loved "Aunt Susan," even though she was a stricter
disciplinarian than their mother.

Susan and Elizabeth differed on priorities during the Civil
War. Elizabeth wanted to concentrate on anti-slavery issues, and
Susan wanted to support both women's rights and abolitionism.
Elizabeth won, but she admitted later that Susan had been right
because the concentration on anti-slavery issues delayed by four
years the activity to force women's rights reforms.

An example of Susan's quick thinking was her exchange of
unpleasantries with Horace Greeley, editor of the New York
Tribune. Greeley asked, "Miss Anthony, you are aware that the
ballot and the bullet go together. If you vote, are you also
prepared to fight?" Susan replied, "Certainly, Mr. Greeley, just as
you fought the last war—at the point of a goose-quill."

As stated in the fifteenth amendment to the Constitution,
which was adopted in 1870, "The right of citizens of the United

States to vote shall not be denied ... on account of race, color, or previous condition of servitude." The suffragists wanted the phrase "or sex" in the fifteenth amendment. However, the phrase wasn't there, so women began to test the interpretation of their rights as citizens. Susan wasn't the first woman to test this interpretation of the fifteenth amendment, but she certainly received more newspaper coverage than any other woman.

On November 1, 1872, Susan and her sisters Guelma, Hannah, and Mary decided to register to vote. The election judges told them that, according to New York State law, they would not be permitted to register. Susan quoted to them from the the amendments to the Constitution and insisted that she, as a citizen, had a right to vote. They were permitted to register. Susan and her sisters voted in the general election on November 5. She received wide newspaper coverage, including articles in the Chicago *Tribune* and the New York *Times*. She realized that she may have broken the law and might be liable for a $500 fine. On November 18, a marshal came to Susan's home and arrested her.

Susan and her sisters were arraigned and their bond set at $500. Her sisters posted the $500 bail, but Susan refused to pay it. Her lawyer, Henry Selden, who did not want to see his client go to jail, paid her bail. Unfortunately, by posting her bail he had, inadvertently, prevented her from appealing to higher courts— potentially as far as the Supreme Court. Posting bail indicated that she was not contesting the lawfulness of her arrest. Susan made many speeches describing what was happening to her, including speeches in Monroe County where her case was to be tried. Because of this, the trial was moved to Ontario County, south of Rochester.

On June 17, 1873, Susan's trial began in Canandaigua, the county seat of Ontario County. Judge Ward Hunt, an inexperienced judge who had just recently been appointed to the bench, was selected to try her case. Selden conducted a skillful defense, pointing out that Susan sincerely believed that she had been given the right to vote by the fourteenth and fifteenth amendments. Judge Hunt refused to let Susan speak in her own defense.

Judge Hunt stated that it didn't matter what Susan's beliefs were; she had broken the law. He took a note from his pocket, turned toward the jury, and read from it. The note concluded with the statement, "If I am right in this, the result must be a verdict ... of guilty, and I therefore direct that you find a verdict of guilty." An incensed Selden reminded the judge that he did not have the right to instruct the jury in that way and demanded that the jury be asked for their verdict. Judge Hunt ignored Selden, instructed the court clerk to record the verdict, and dismissed the jury.

This poor example of justice was widely covered by the press. People who disagreed with Susan's voting sided with her because of this unfair treatment in the courtroom. Judge Hunt's actions were politically motivated. His mentor was Roscoe Conkling, U.S. Senator from New York and a professed foe of the Women's Rights Movement. Selden requested a new trial on the basis that Susan had been denied a fair trial by jury. Judge Hunt denied the request and stated her sentence—a $100 fine. Susan responded: "I shall never pay a dollar of your unjust penalty...." Ultimately, the fine was dropped.

In 1880, Susan and Elizabeth began their monumental project, *A History of Woman Suffrage*. Elizabeth wrote most of the first two volumes; Susan verified the facts and assembled the material. Susan had a major role in preparing volume three because Elizabeth was in England visiting her daughter, Harriet. The last two volumes were edited by Ida Husted Harper; they traced the history of the movement through 1920. Ida was also Susan's biographer; her *Life and Work of Susan B. Anthony* was published in 1898.

Susan never retired from her lifelong efforts to promote women's rights. The International Woman Suffrage Alliance was formed in 1904, and Susan, at the age of eighty-four, was recognized as the leader. At their convention in 1906, she commanded the delegates: "The fight must not stop. You must see that it does not stop." At a dinner in her honor in Washington, D.C., she concluded her comments by stating, "Failure is impossible."

In 1920, the nineteenth amendment to the Constitution was ratified. It included the statement that, "The right of citizens of the United States to vote shall not be denied or abridged by the

United States or by any state on account of sex." It was called the "Susan B. Anthony amendment." Susan was right. Failure was impossible. In 1976, she was honored further by the United States government by the minting of the Susan B. Anthony dollar.

Antoinette Brown Blackwell

Antoinette Louisa Brown, the seventh of ten children of Joseph Brown and Abigail Morse Brown, was born in Henrietta, New York, in May 1825. She became the first ordained woman minister in the United States. Antoinette indicated her interest in religion at an early age when she gave a spontaneous prayer to conclude a family prayer meeting at the age of eight. In the following year, she spoke up about joining the village Congregational Church, at a time when joining the church so young was rare.

The small Henrietta church was a member of the liberal branch of the Congregational Church, which emphasized God's mercy and forgiveness in addition to human goodness and initiative. The orthodox branch of the church believed that humans were morally corrupt, sinful, and dependent upon an all-powerful God, who would condemn them to hell if they did not obey His word.

Antoinette decided that she wanted to be a minister while in her teens. No woman had been ordained as a minister; however, in the 1820s, a Methodist woman had attempted to preach in New York State, but gave in to public opposition. The Quakers, who considered all members to be ministers, permitted all women to speak at worship services, but women were not considered to be leaders of the church community.

Antoinette was active in her Henrietta church and spoke frequently at prayer meetings, where any church member was permitted to speak. She decided to attend the Oberlin Collegiate Institute in Ohio, where her brother William studied theology. Oberlin was the first U.S. college to admit women to take college courses with men. In the spring of 1846, she began her studies at Oberlin.

6

Oberlin had been founded in 1833 by ministers from New England and New York. By the time that Antoinette arrived, the college had developed its own ideology, which was a combination of liberal religion, practical training, and the politics of reform. The spiritual leader of the Oberlin community was professor of theology Charles Grandison Finney, who had impressed Antoinette's parents at a series of revival meetings in Rochester during the winter of 1831. He was a captivating speaker who advocated the dual responsibility of an individual's commitment to God and his or her working toward a better society. He suggested that this dual responsibility should be implemented by applying one's intellect and education to saving individual souls and to improving society. He became Antoinette's mentor.

Antoinette met Lucy Stone, who later became a leader of the Women's Rights Movement, at Oberlin. Stone was older than her classmates and was paying her way through college because her father, who was against higher education for women, refused to give her financial assistance. Stone was a follower of the radical abolitionist, William Lloyd Garrison; she enrolled at Oberlin specifically to learn public speaking skills to use in advocating women's rights and the abolition of slavery.

The women students at Oberlin discovered early that the college had no intention of training them as public speakers. They learned how to write, but they were "excused" from participation in discussions and debates. Oberlin President Asa Mahan advocated the belief that women should be taught how to speak as well as how to write, but he was always outvoted by the faculty. The policy was apparently based on the words of St. Paul: "Let a woman learn in silence with all submissiveness."

In the winter of 1846-47, during Oberlin's lengthy vacation, Antoinette taught at a large private academy in Rochester, Michigan. The experience verified what she already knew: "God never made me for a school teacher." The headmaster encouraged Antoinette to give her first public speech. She spoke in the village church and was pleased that "It was fairly well received by the students and by the community."

Antoinette and Stone became close friends and confidants despite their differences of opinion. Stone was more radical on the subject of abolition, and she had left the Congregational Church because it approved of slavery and was against women speaking in public. Antoinette was disappointed that her closest friend did not agree with her goals:

> I told her of my intention to become a minister. Her protest was most emphatic. She said, "You will never be allowed to do this. You will never be allowed to stand in a public pulpit, nor to preach in a church, and certainly you can never be ordained." It was a long talk but we were no nearer to an agreement at the end than at the beginning. My final answer could only be, "I am going to do it."

Antoinette completed her undergraduate studies at Oberlin in the summer of 1847. She returned home to Henrietta and practiced her public speaking: "I go out into the barn and make the walls echo with my voice occasionally but the church stands on the green in such a way that I have too many auditors when I attempt to practice there. The barn is a good large one however and the sounds ring out merrily or did before father filled it full of hay."

Antoinette returned to Oberlin in the fall to study theology. She felt that she was called to this vocation, and she was motivated to use her intellect, her ability as a public speaker, and her interest in public reform. However, although Oberlin was committed to providing women with a general education, the only profession that it prepared women for was teaching. In the Theology Department, women were welcome to sit in on classes if their goal was self-improvement.

Antoinette's classmate in her theology courses, Lettice Smith, shared her semi-official status in the department. However, everyone knew that Lettice was going to marry her classmate, Thomas Holmes, and become a minister's wife. Lettice, who was a serious student of theology, didn't have much self-confidence and never responded in class. She didn't provide the sounding board off which to bounce ideas that Lucy did. However, Lucy had graduated and had left Oberlin the previous spring.

Initially, Professor Finney didn't call on the women to respond in class, and Antoinette was offended by this. When she questioned him on it, he said that any woman could respond in class, if she wished to. He responded that "though he did not think she was generally called upon to preach or speak in public because the circumstances did not demand it, still there was nothing right or wrong in the thing itself and that sometimes she was specially called to speak."

Antoinette and Lettice were assigned to write essays on the passages in the Bible stating that women should not preach: "Let your women keep silence in the churches, for it is not permitted unto them to speak.... Let the women learn in silence with all subjection. I suffer not a woman to teach, nor to usurp authority over the man, but to be in silence." Antoinette found confirmation of her choice of a profession in the words of the prophet Joel: "And it shall come to pass in the last days, saith God, I will pour out my spirit upon all flesh; and your sons and daughters shall prophesy."

In her essay, Antoinette observed that St. Paul's suggestion that women should learn in silence had been misinterpreted. She suggested that St. Paul only intended to caution against "excesses, irregularities, and unwarranted liberties" in public worship. Professor Asa Mahan selected her essay for publication in the *Oberlin Quarterly Review.*

In the last year of their studies, Oberlin theology students were allowed to preach in area churches, but not to perform any of the sacraments. Antoinette said: "They were willing to have me preach, but not to themselves endorse this as a principle.... They decided, after much discussion, that I must preach if I chose to do so on my own responsibility." Although she was not given official recognition, Antoinette spoke in small churches nearby, usually on the popular subject of temperance.

Upon completion of her theology studies, Antoinette chose not to be ordained at Oberlin. Not only did she think that it would be "a delicate thing" with Oberlin's difference of opinion on women ministers, but also she preferred the usual path of ordination by a local parish that wanted her as a pastor. She cited "an instinctive desire to be ordained in my own church, and a belief that I could one day in the future be ordained by my own denomination which was then the Orthodox Congregational."

Neither Antoinette nor Lettice participated in the graduation exercises. In later years, Antoinette observed: "We were not supposed to graduate, as at that time to have regularly graduated women from a theological school would have been an endorsement of their probable future careers." Their names did not appear in the roll of the theological school class of 1850 until 1908.

Antoinette attended the first "National" Women's Rights Convention in Worchester, Massachusetts, where she spoke to disprove the Biblical argument that women should not speak in public. There she met Lucretia Mott and Elizabeth Cady Stanton, the organizers of the Seneca Falls Convention two years earlier. Antoinette was introduced to many men and women who were active in social reform. She maintained her contacts with those whom she met, but she thought that her cause would probably not be best served by working with organized groups.

Antoinette decided to earn her living as a public speaker, as her friend, Lucy Stone, was doing. Before the advent of radio and television, the lecture circuit or lyceum was an important means of informing and entertaining people. Women speakers were usually paid less than men. Antoinette told the lyceum organizers that "my terms, from principle, are never less that the best prices received by the gentlemen of the particular association where I speak." She found the work to be satisfying, and she consistently received favorable reviews in the local newspapers where she spoke.

Liberal ministers such as William Henry Channing and Samuel J. May invited Antoinette to preach in their churches. Her oldest brother, William, who had initially opposed her desire to preach, invited her to speak in his church in Andover, Massachusetts. She decided that the time had come to pursue her calling, and she began to actively seek a church in need of a pastor.

During one of her speaking tours across New York State, she visited South Butler, in Wayne County. The small Congregational

Church listened to her speak, and then invited her to become their pastor at an annual salary of $300. In the late spring of 1853, she moved to South Butler and began to give two sermons every Sunday, one prepared and the other extemporaneous.

Her responsibilities included pastoral duties, such as visiting the sick, and she felt suited to her role as minister. She observed: "My little parish was a miniature world in good and evil. To get humanity condensed into so small a compass that you can study each individual member opens a new chapter of experience. It makes one thoughtful and rolls upon the spirit a burden of deep responsibility."

Antoinette's friend, Lucy Stone, met Henry Blackwell, the brother of the pioneer doctor, Elizabeth Blackwell, at an abolitionist meeting. Henry fell in love with Lucy and immediately began to court her. Lucy met Henry's older brother, Samuel, and suggested that he visit Antoinette while on his travels. The Blackwell brothers were business partners in Cincinnati. Samuel called on Antoinette while enroute to Boston. Samuel "enjoyed the visit exceedingly." Antoinette observed that "he stayed perhaps a half a day and had a pleasant visit.... He was not handsome." She was preoccupied with her church duties.

Antoinette's church was pleased with her work, and the governing body decided to proceed with her ordination. She already administered the sacraments, but the ceremony would provide public recognition of her ministry. Reverend Luther Lee, a minister from nearby Syracuse whom Antoinette knew from abolitionist meetings, agreed to preach the ordination sermon.

Reverend Lee based his sermon on the text, "There is neither male nor female; for ye are all one in Christ Jesus." He said, "... in the Church, of which Christ is the only head, males and females possess equal rights and privileges; here there is no difference.... I cannot see how the test can be explained so as to exclude females from any right, office, work, privilege, or immunity which males enjoy, hold or perform." He concluded by saying, "All we are here to do, and all we expect to do, is, in due form, and by a solemn and impressive service, to subscribe our testimony to the fact that in our belief, our sister in Christ, Antoinette L. Brown, is one of the ministers of the New Covenant, authorized, qualified, and called of God to preach the gospel of His Son Jesus Christ."

During the winter of 1854, Antoinette's duties began to weigh heavily upon her. Her job was a difficult one, and her responsibilities began to cause her emotional strain. A minister's functions were many and varied. He or she was expected to be tolerant and understanding, but, at other times, authoritative and judgmental. It was difficult for her to be a "father" figure. Her role would have been easier if she had the support of her friends and associates. However, Susan B. Antony, Elizabeth Cady Stanton, and Lucy Stone all disapproved of her church affiliation. They did not perceive Antoinette's ministerial duties as a contribution to the effort of effecting change in women's status.

Antoinette felt isolated:

> It was practically ten years after my ordination before any other woman known to the public was ordained. It was therefore doubly hard for me—a young woman still in her twenties—to adapt myself to the rather curious relationship I must sustain either to home conditions or to those of a pastorate. Personally this was more of an emotional strain than the enduring of any opposition that ever came to me as a public speaker or teacher.

This isolation began to affect her in a very serious way. She began to question her faith, particularly the emphasis on being condemned to eternal damnation unless saved by a stern God, as espoused by some of her congregation. She was more motivated by Charles Grandison Finney's teachings that stressed human goodness and striving to approach moral perfection. In July, 1854, overcome by mental conflict and nervous exhaustion, she returned home to rest.

In January, 1855, Antoinette wrote to Horace Greeley of the New York *Tribune* to inquire if he would help her to hire a hall in New York in which to preach on Sundays, an activity that he and Charles Dana had suggested three years previously. He encouraged her with her "experiment" and suggested that she visit the city's slums and institutions and write articles for the *Tribune* about her experiences.

One of the individuals who helped Antoinette find herself during this difficult time was Samuel Blackwell. She stayed with the Blackwell family when she was in Cincinnati on her lecture circuit. Samuel's five sisters were all achievers: Elizabeth and Emily became doctors, Ellen and Marian were active in the Women's Rights Movement and other reform efforts, and Anna, who lived at the transcendentalist commune at Brook Farm for a while, was a newspaper reporter in Paris. Samuel was used to activist women.

At the end of 1854, Lucy Stone agreed to marry Henry Blackwell if he would agree to devote his efforts to women's rights. Perhaps motivated by his brother's action, Samuel proposed to Antoinette about the same time. Antoinette hesitated, but she considered some of the women that she knew—Lucretia Mott was an example—who had children, husbands, and homes, in addition to careers.

Later, Antoinette observed, "... when the early faith seemed wholly lost and the new and stronger belief not yet obtained, there seemed no good reason for not accepting the love and help of a good man and the woman's appreciation of all else that this implied." After their marriage, she was known as "Reverend Antoinette L. B. Blackwell."

The Blackwells moved to New Jersey; Samuel found a job as a bookkeeper to support the family as the children began to arrive. During the winter and spring of 1859-60, Antoinette rented a hall in New York and preached every Sunday. She was able to balance family and preaching duties, but, due to the finances, the preaching venture was not long-lived.

At the end of the 1860s, Antoinette devoted herself to writing. Her first large published work was *Studies in General Science,* a collection of essays. Her second work, *The Sexes Throughout Nature,* was published in 1875. It was a compilation of essays first published in periodicals. In 1876, she published *The Physical Basis of Immortality,* which was a synthesis of her philosophy. *The Philosophy of Individuality, or the One and the Many,* was published in 1893. Her last two books, *The Making of the*

Universe and *The Social Side of Mind and Action* were published in 1914 and 1915.

Antoinette was drawn to the Unitarian Church. Samuel Blackwell and three of his sisters had joined the Unitarians. In the spring of 1878, she joined the Unitarian Fellowship and asked to be recognized as a minister. In the fall of 1878, the Committee on Fellowship of the American Unitarian Association acknowledged her as a minister.

In 1879, Oberlin College recognized her status by awarding her an "honorary" master of arts degree, the degree that she had earned during three years of study in the Theological Department. One change from her studies thirty years previously was that she no longer stood alone as woman minister. In 1864, Olympia Brown, motivated by Antoinette's talk to her class at Antioch College, was ordained as a Universalist minister. By 1880, almost 200 woman were recognized as ministers, and many held full time-time pastoral jobs.

In addition to her participation in the Women's Rights Movement, Antoinette was also active in the Association for the Advancement of Women (AAW) and the American Association for the Advancement of Science (AAAS). Although she hadn't had the responsibility of a parish for decades, Antoinette considered herself to be a "minister emeritus" during her later years.

In June, 1908, Antoinette was invited to Oberlin College to receive an honorary Doctor of Divinity degree. In introducing Antoinette to Oberlin President Henry Churchill King at the commencement ceremony, Dr. Charles Wager spoke to the audience:

> It is appropriate for the institution that was the first to provide for higher education of women to honor, at its seventy-fifth anniversary, a woman who has eminently justified that daring innovation, a woman who was one of the first two in America to complete a course in divinity, who as preacher, as pastor, as writer, as the champion of more than one good cause, has in the past

conferred honor upon her Alma Mater, and who
today confers upon it no less honor by an old age
as lovely as it is venerable.

Her health began to slip during the spring and summer of
1921. She was at peace with herself. She was ready for death and
looked upon it as a reunion with Samuel and all of her other loved
ones. In late November 1921, at the age of ninety-seven,
Reverend Antoinette L. B. Blackwell, the first woman minister,
died in her sleep.

Elizabeth Blackwell

Elizabeth Blackwell was the first woman graduate
of a medical school in modern times. Her interest
in becoming a doctor was sparked by a significant
emotional event in her early twenties, while
visiting a friend who was dying of cancer. Her friend said to her,
"You are fond of study, Elizabeth. You have health, leisure, and a
cultivated intelligence. Why don't you devote these qualities to
the service of suffering women? Why don't you study medicine?
Had I been treated by a lady doctor, my worst sufferings would
have been spared me."

Elizabeth began to consider the study of medicine. Although
she was happy with her social and family life in Cincinnati, it was
not fulfilling for her; she did not feel challenged. Elizabeth
entered her personal thoughts on the study of medicine in her
diary: "The idea of winning a doctor's degree gradually assumed
an immense attraction for me.... This work has taken deep root in
my soul and become an all-absorbing duty. I must accomplish my
end. I consider it the noblest and most useful path I can tread."

Before she could begin her medical studies, Elizabeth had to
earn the money to pay for them. Her father, Samuel Blackwell,
had passed away at the age of forty-eight, leaving the family in
debt. Elizabeth, her mother, and her brothers and sisters all
worked to pay off the family debts.

Elizabeth taught school in Asheville, North Carolina, and then in Charleston, South Carolina, to earn money for medical school. She sent out applications to medical schools while teaching at Charleston. She was particularly interested in Philadelphia. With its four highly regarded medical schools, she considered it to be the medical center of the U.S.

She sent one of her first inquiries to Dr. Joseph Warrington in Philadelphia. His response was not encouraging; he viewed men as doctors and women as nurses and recommended that Elizabeth pursue a career in nursing. However, he added that "If the project be of divine origin and appointment, it will sooner or later be accomplished." Elizabeth applied to twenty-nine medical schools and received twenty-eight rejections.

In late October, 1847, Elizabeth received an acceptance from the medical school of Geneva College, Geneva, New York. Dr. Benjamin Hale, the president of Geneva College and a very open-minded individual, had recruited an extremely capable dean for the medical school, Dr. Charles Lee. The medical school later became part of Syracuse University, and Geneva College was renamed Hobart College. However, the medical school was thriving when Elizabeth became student number 130.

The circumstances surrounding Elizabeth's acceptance were unusual. Dr. Warrington wrote a letter to Dr. Lee on Elizabeth's behalf. The faculty was unanimously against the admission of a woman to their medical school; however, they didn't want to be responsible for rejecting the highly regarded Philadelphia doctor's request. The faculty turned the decision over to the medical students; they were confident that the students would vote against Elizabeth's admission.

Dr. Lee read Dr. Warrington's letter to the students and informed them that the faculty had decided to let them decide the issue. He instructed them that one negative vote would prevent Elizabeth's admission. The students were enthusiastic about Elizabeth's acceptance, and the one dissenting voice was browbeaten into submission. She received a document composed by the students and signed by class chairman Francis Joel Stratton:

- Resolved—That one of the principles of a
  Republican government is the universal

education of both sexes; that to every branch
of scientific education the door should be
open equally to all; that the application of
Elizabeth Blackwell to become a member of
our class meets our entire approbation; and
in extending our unanimous invitation we
pledge ourselves that no conduct of ours shall
cause her to regret her attendance at this
institution.

- Resolved—That a copy of these proceedings
be signed by the chairman and transmitted to
Elizabeth Blackwell

Elizabeth was overjoyed to receive the acceptance, and she immediately packed and traveled to Geneva. She arrived there on November 6, five weeks into the session. Elizabeth had grown up with brothers, and she was not an overly sensitive young woman; however, she wasn't sure what to expect from her fellow medical students. She dressed conservatively in Quaker style and was well-mannered.

The Geneva community wasn't ready for a female medical student, and, initially, she had difficulty finding a place to live. She moved into a drafty attic room in a boarding house, where she fed wood into a wood-burning stove to keep warm. Eventually, she realized that she was the subject of ostracism. The other boarders were unfriendly at mealtime, the women she passed on the street held their skirts to one side and didn't speak, and one doctor's wife snubbed her openly. Her feelings were hurt by this treatment; she retreated to her room to study.

Her professor of anatomy was Dr. James Webster, who was friendly and sincerely glad to have her in his class. He predicted, "You'll go through the course, and get your diploma—with great eclat too. We'll give you the opportunities. You'll make a stir, I can tell you."

However, within a short time, he tried to prevent her from attending a dissection. He wrote her a note explaining that he was about to lecture on the reproductive organs, and he could not discuss the material satisfactorily in the presence of a lady. He offered her the opportunity for dissection and study of this part of the course in private. Elizabeth was unaware that Dr. Webster had a reputation for being coarse in covering this material; he sprinkled his lecture with humorous anecdotes. The students liked this approach and responded by being somewhat rowdy.

Elizabeth wrote to Dr. Webster to remind him that she was there as a student with a serious purpose; she was aware of the awkward position in which he found himself, particularly "when viewed from the low standpoint of impure and unchaste sentiments." She asked why a student of science would have his mind diverted from such an absorbing subject by the presence of a student in feminine attire. She offered to remove her bonnet and sit in the back row of benches. If the other students desired it, she would not attend the class at all.

Dr. Webster acquiesced and, with Elizabeth in attendance, conducted the class without the usual anecdotes. To Elizabeth, the class was "just about as much as I could bear." She made an entry in her diary: "My delicacy was certainly shocked, and yet the exhibition was in some sense ludicrous. I had to pinch my hand until the blood nearly came, and call upon Christ to keep from smiling, for that would have ruined everything; but I sat in grave indifference, though the effort made my heart palpitate most painfully."

One of the few places open to her for summer work was the Blockley Almshouse in Philadelphia, which cared for two thousand lower class unfortunates. Again, she had to pay for being a pioneer. The resident doctors openly snubbed her and made a point of leaving a ward when she entered it. They made her life difficult by not entering the diagnosis and the notation of the medication used in the treatment on the patient's chart. She had to make many of her own diagnoses. However, her preparation of a thesis on typhus was a major accomplishment; she received many compliments on the thesis from the senior staff physicians.

Elizabeth worked hard upon her return to Geneva. She was a self-disciplined student, who maintained a friendly but impersonal relationship with her classmates. Although she had always received good grades, she approached her final examinations with trepidation. When the results were compiled, Elizabeth had the best academic record in the class. However, the administration of Geneva College vacillated on the precedent of being the first in the United States to award a medical degree to a woman.

Dr. Webster defended her, saying: "She paid her tuition, didn't she? She passed every course, each and every one with honors! And let me tell you, gentlemen, if you hold back, I'll take up the campaign in every medical journal." Elizabeth received her medical degree on January 23, 1849. Her brother, Henry, traveled to Geneva to share the experience with her. She was invited to participate in the academic procession, but she declined "because it wouldn't be ladyllke."

She was the last to be called to receive her diploma from Dr. Hale. In presenting her diploma, he used the word *Domina* in place of *Domine*. Elizabeth replied, "Sir, I thank you. By the help of the Most High, it shall be the effort of my life to shed honor on your diploma."

Henry documented his recollections of the ceremony:

> ... He [Dr. Lee, who gave the valedictory address] pronounced her the leader of the class; stated that she had passed through a thorough course in every department, slighting none; that she had profited to the utmost by all the advantages of the institution, and by her ladylike and dignified deportment had proved that the strongest intellect and nerve, and the most untiring perseverance were compatible with the softest attributes of feminine delicacy and grace, to all of which the students manifested, by decided attempts at applause, their entire concurrence.

As she left the ceremony, the women of Geneva displayed their smiles and friendly faces to Elizabeth. She was pleased to see this change of attitude, but she recorded her true feelings in her diary: "For the next few hours, until I left by train, my room was thronged by visitors. I was glad of the sudden conversion thus shown, but my past experience had given me a useful and permanent lesson at the outset of life as to the very shallow nature of popularity."

Elizabeth returned to Philadelphia to find the same coolness that she had previously experienced. It was clear that she was not going to be given the opportunity to gain the practical medical experience that she needed. She obtained that experience at St. Bartholomews Hospital in London and at La Maternite in Paris. Again, she encountered bias. She was not given access to all departments at St. Bartholomews, and at La Maternite she was considered an aide, not a doctor.

Upon her return to New York, she was unable to find a position at the city dispensaries and hospitals. She opened her own dispensary in Washington Square, where her landlady expressed her displeasure with the lady doctor by refusing to deliver her messages. She lectured on women's health subjects and published two books.

On May 12, 1857, Elizabeth opened The New York Infirmary for Women and Children. Charles A. Dana, Cyrus W. Field, and Horace Greeley were trustees for the infirmary. In 1868, she opened a medical college for women. Her medical college provided medical education for women until 1899, when it was incorporated into the Cornell Medical Center. The New York Infirmary founded by Elizabeth still exists in lower Manhattan as part of the New York Infirmary-Beekman Downtown Hospital.

In 1899, Hobart-William Smith College, the successor to Geneva College, named its first residence hall for women Blackwell House. Elizabeth was a pioneer who encountered many obstacles. She overcame them and made significant contributions to the medical profession.

Amelia Bloomer

Amelia Jenks Bloomer, for whom bloomers were named, was born on May 27, 1818, in the Village of Homer. She was the youngest of four daughters of Ananias Jenks, clothier, and Lucy Webb Jenks. Amelia noted in her journal, "My earliest recollections are of a pleasant home in Homer, Cortland County, New York...." She attended Homer schools and, after graduating at the age of seventeen, accepted a teaching position in the Village of Clyde in Wayne County.

In 1836, Amelia and her family moved to Waterloo, which was the home of her sister, Elvira. In 1837, she became the governess and tutor for the children of a Waterloo family. She met Dexter Bloomer, fell in love, and was married on April 15, 1840. She was pleased that her husband left out the word "obey" in their wedding vows. Her husband was an owner and editor of the Seneca County *Courier*, which was printed weekly in Seneca Falls.

The temperance movement was very active in the first half of the nineteenth century, and speaking out against "demon drink" was a popular pastime. Amelia helped to establish the local temperance society and contributed to its newsletter, *The Water Bucket*. She became an officer of the Ladies Temperance Society and published the society's newsletter, *The Lily*. Later in life, Amelia commented: "*The Lily* was the first paper published and devoted to the interests of women, and, as far as I know, the first one owned, edited, and published by a woman."

Her temperance society activity was her principal interest until 1847, when Elizabeth Cady Stanton moved to Seneca Falls. Elizabeth, Lucretia Mott, and three other women called the first Women's Rights Convention in Seneca Falls on July 19-20, 1848. The announcement of the convention appeared in the Seneca County *Courier* on July 14, 1848:

> The first Women's Rights Convention to discuss the social, civil, and religious conditions and rights of women will be held at the Wesleyan Chapel at Seneca Falls on Wednesday and Thursday current, commencing at ten a.m. During the first day, the meeting will be exclusively for women, who are earnestly invited to attend. The public generally are invited to be present on the second day when Lucretia Mott of Philadelphia will address the convention.

Amelia attended the convention and was impressed with the speakers—particularly with Elizabeth Cady Stanton.

In the spring of 1849, Dexter Bloomer was appointed Postmaster of Seneca Falls, and Amelia accepted the position of Assistant Postmaster. The new Assistant Postmaster considered herself as an example "of a woman's right to fill any place for which she had the capacity." She performed well in the position for the next four years, while continuing to edit and publish *The Lily.* Elizabeth Cady Stanton wrote articles for *The Lily* using the pseudonym "Sun Flower." The newsletter became more militant with the addition of the letterhead, "The Emancipation of Woman from Intemperance, Injustice, Prejudice, and Bigotry."

In 1850, Amelia introduced two people to each other who were to have a significant impact on life in the United States. Amelia wrote in her journal:

> It was in the spring of 1850 that I introduced Susan B. Anthony to Mrs. Stanton. Miss Anthony had come to attend an anti-slavery meeting in Seneca Falls, held by George Thompson and William Lloyd Garrison, and was my guest. Returning from the meeting we stopped at the street corner and waited for Mrs. Stanton, and I gave the introduction which resulted in a life-long friendship. Afterwards, we called together at Mrs. Stanton's house and the way was opened for future intercourse between them.
>
> It was, as Mrs. Stanton says in her history, an eventful meeting that henceforth in a measure shaped their lives. Neither would have done what she did without the other. Mrs. Stanton had the intellectual, and Susan the executive, ability to carry forward the movement then recently inaugurated. Without the push of Miss Anthony, Mrs. Stanton would never have gone abroad into active life, or achieved half she has done; and without the brains of Mrs. Stanton, Miss Anthony

would never have been so largely known to the
world by name and deeds. They helped and
strengthened each other, and together they have
accomplished great things for women and
humanity. The writer is glad for the part she had
in bringing two such characters together.

One of the many conditions that women had to tolerate in the
mid-1800s was a lack of freedom in the style of dress. A woman's
dress was complicated in the 1850s. Under her long skirts, she
wore a cambric petticoat, a plain longcloth petticoat, two flannel
petticoats with scalloped hems, a lined petticoat with a hem that
stood out, and lace-trimmed drawers. Three starched muslin
petticoats usually replaced the flannel petticoats in hot weather.

In January 1851, Dexter Bloomer's successor as editor of the
Seneca County *Courier* wrote an article about women's clothing
in London in which he mentioned that "improvement in the attire
of females was being agitated." He suggested that women's dress
should be less cumbersome and recommended that women wear
Turkish pantaloons with a skirt that reached below the knee.

Amelia responded in *The Lily:* "... now that our cautious
editor of the *Courier* recommends it [wearing pantaloons], we
suppose that there will be no harm in our doing so. Small waists
and whalebones can be dispensed with, and we will be allowed
breathing room; and our forms shall be what nature made them.
We are so thankful that men are beginning to undo some of the
mischief they have done us."

In February 1851, the issue of women's clothing was raised
when Elizabeth Cady Stanton's cousin, Libby Smith Miller,
visited her in Seneca Falls. Libby had just returned from a
honeymoon grand tour of Europe. In Switzerland, she had seen
women in sanatoriums wearing long, full Turkish trousers made
of broadcloth with a short skirt that reached just below the knee.
She made a traveling costume for herself in this style. Her cousin
Elizabeth immediately adopted the style of dress. The two cousins
visited Amelia at the Post Office, and, within a few days, she
donned the new costume.

Amelia wrote an article about the new style of dress and

provided a sketch of it in the next issue of *The Lily*. She had no thoughts of completely adopting the style, of establishing fashion, or of attracting national attention. The New York *Tribune* was the first national newspaper to refer to Amelia's article; that reference was followed by many others. Some praised the costume, but many ridiculed it. Finally, one of the journalists referred to the "Bloomer costume," and the word entered the English lexicon. Amelia tried to give credit to Libby Smith Miller for introducing the style to the United States, but newspaper publicity had established the word "bloomers" for all time.

Soon, half of the mail handled by the Seneca Falls Post Office was addressed to Amelia. Women from all over the country wrote for more information on how to make the costume. The dress became popular with the Women's Rights Movement, and Amelia was invited to England to speak about the costume.

In the spring of 1852, Amelia was elected corresponding secretary of the Women's Temperance Society for the State of New York. In 1853, she lectured at Metropolitan Hall in New York City. Three thousand people bought tickets; many were turned away. She had become a national figure.

In 1855, Dexter Bloomer purchased *The Western Home Visitor,* and the Bloomer family moved to Council Bluffs, Iowa. Amelia edited the newspaper; when she caught the typesetters drinking on the job, she replaced them with female typesetters. She crusaded for the temperance movement and the Women's Rights Movement for her entire lifetime. She died on December 30, 1894.

Matilda Gage

Matilda Joslyn Gage, who was born in 1826, was active in both the anti-slavery and Women's Rights Movements. She was the daughter of a physician from Cicero and was the wife of Henry Hill Gage, a wealthy Fayetteville dry goods merchant. Matilda first attracted the attention of the leaders of the Women's Rights Movement when she asked permission to speak at the Women's

Rights Convention in Syracuse in 1852. Her forceful personality allowed her to make a significant contribution to the movement. The activist, who lived at 210 East Genesee Street in Fayetteville, was elected to the executive committee of the National Woman Suffrage Association upon its founding on May 11, 1869. Elizabeth Cady Stanton was elected president and Susan B. Anthony headed the executive committee.

Matilda, the mother of four children, was a strong-willed individual, and everyone knew her opinions on women's rights. She once wrote: "Women, if you will not be crushed, arise and fight your own battles. Man, your so-called protector, is your worst foe. Experience shows you cannot trust father, nor husband, nor brother, nor son ..." She was prominent in the Women's Rights Movement, but she spoke too softly to be an effective speaker. However, she was an effective organizer and writer.

Elizabeth Cady Stanton's mentor in the Women's Rights Movement, Lucretia Mott, urged Matilda to write a history of the movement. In 1876, Matilda joined in a partnership with Susan and Elizabeth "for the purpose of preparing and editing a history of the woman suffrage movement." Matilda's and Elizabeth's tasks were to "write, collect, and arrange material"; Susan's task was to "secure publication." In November 1880, they began writing the history at Stanton's home in Teaneck, New Jersey. The first volume of *The History of Woman Suffrage* was published in May 1881; the second volume followed in May 1882. Matilda's work on the history was cut short in 1884, when her husband died. Ida Husted Harper, Susan B. Anthony's biographer, wrote a later volume of the work.

Matilda attempted unsuccessfully to vote in 1872. She was the first woman to vote in the school board elections in Fayetteville in 1880, which was forty years before women were granted the right to vote in national elections. This breakthrough came when women property owners convinced a majority of the New York State Legislature that women should have a voice in the activities of the school districts in which they paid taxes.

Matilda left the National Woman Suffrage Association in 1890; she formed a more progressive organization, the Woman's National Liberal Union. In 1893, she wrote a book stating her view on women's rights entitled *Woman, Church and State.* Count Leo Tolstoy wrote her a letter praising the book and commenting that it proved that a woman could think logically. Poor health prevented her from becoming more of a national figure in the Women's Rights Movement.

Matilda's youngest daughter, Maud, married L. Frank Baum, the author of *The Wizard of Oz* and many other books. Maud had to overcome her mother's objections to marry the author. Gage died in 1898 while visiting the Baums. She wrote her own epitaph: "There is a word sweeter than mother, home, or heaven—that word is liberty."

Mary Jemison

Mary Jemison, the "white woman of the Genesee," was born in 1743 on the sailing vessel, *Mary and William*, enroute from Ireland to Philadelphia. Her parents, Thomas and Jane Jemison, settled near Gettysburg, Pennsylvania. In 1758, during the French and Indian War, the Jemison home was attacked by a party of six Indians and four Frenchmen. They killed and scalped the Jemison family and a visiting family. Fifteen-year-old Mary Jemison was spared, but was carried off by the Indians.

The Indians traveled west to Fort Duquesne and traveled down the Ohio River by canoe. Mary was placed in the keeping of two Seneca women who had lost a relative in battle. They adopted Mary as a sister, gave her Indian clothing to replace her tattered dress, and named her Deh-Ge-Wan-Us, which means "Two Falling Voices." Initially, she missed the society in which she was raised, but she adapted well to Indian life. She had numerous opportunities to leave her Indian captors during her lifetime, but she chose to remain with them. Eventually, her light skin and blonde hair were the only things that distinguished her from the other Indian women.

When she was seventeen, Mary's Indian sisters told her that, according to custom, she must marry. Her sisters' choice for a husband for her was Sheninjee, a Delaware chief. Sheninjee's and

Mary's first child was a daughter who died in infancy. Their second child was a son, who was named Thomas for her father.

Mary's two Seneca sisters returned to their home at the Indian settlement at Little Beard's Town on the Genesee River. Sheninjee left on an extended hunting trip and told Mary he would join her at Little Beard's Town. Mary set out on the long eastward journey carrying her nine-month-old son, Thomas. She was accompanied by two foster brothers.

Mary's first home in Genesee country was at Caneadea, which was described by the Senecas as the place "where the heavens lean against the earth." At the end of the long trek, Mary rejoined her Seneca sisters at Little Beard's Town, thirty-five miles north of Caneadea. The following spring, she heard that Sheninjee had been killed. Her second husband was Hiakatoo, a six-foot-tall, sixty-year-old Seneca chief. In battle, Hiakatoo was ferocious. He had a reputation for brutality, but he was always kind to his twenty-four-year-old bride. Hiakatoo and Mary had six children, four daughters and two sons.

Hiakatoo went off to fight General Sullivan's army in 1779. Mary and her children left the village before it was destroyed by Sullivan's men. She moved to the Gardeau Flats, south of Little Beard's Town, and built a cabin. Gardeau, which is now part of Letchworth State Park, was her home for the next fifty years. The Indians were kind to Mary; they gave her four acres of land at Gardeau for raising crops.

At the great Council of Big Tree in 1797, the Senecas settled their land claims with Robert Morris, the financier of the Revolution. Mary told Thomas Morris, the son and agent of Robert Morris, that she had cultivated many areas in the Gardeau Flats; she requested that her tract be expanded. Morris thought he was giving away about 150 acres, but Mary became the owner of almost 18,000 acres (twenty-seven square miles) of scenic Genesee country. It was known as the Gardeau Tract.

Mary sold her land in the Genesee Valley in 1831 and moved to the Buffalo Creek reservation. She attended an Indian mission school and converted to Christianity at the age of eighty-nine. Mary lived to the age of ninety-one. Her sons all met with violent deaths; her daughters cared for her in her old age. She was buried in the cemetery on the Buffalo Creek reservation.

On March 7, 1874, William Letchworth had her remains reinterred on the plateau near Glen Iris with an appropriate ceremony. A monument, sculpted by Henry K. Bush-Brown, was dedicated at Mary's grave site on September 10, 1910. The sculpture is of Mary as a young woman with a papoose on her back, as she looked on her trek back from Ohio. The cottage that Mary had built for her daughter, Nancy, was moved to the Council Grounds near the statue.

Margaret Sanger

Margaret Higgins Sanger, birth control pioneer, was born in 1879 in Corning. She was the sixth of eleven children of Michael Higgins and Anne Purcell Higgins. Michael Higgins was a mason and stone carver who was frequently out of work. He was a strong-willed individual who supported Henry George's single tax concept and who invited Robert Ingersoll, "The Great Infidel," to speak in Corning. His liberal beliefs lost customers, and the family was poor. Anne Higgins, who had seven miscarriages in addition to her eleven children, died of tuberculosis at the age of forty-eight.

Margaret's sister paid her tuition to Claverack College for a year, prior to her completion of nurse's training at the Manhattan Eye and Ear Institute in New York City. She met William Sanger, an architect, while she was in nurse's training; they were married on August 18, 1902. While living in Hastings-on-Hudson, Westchester County, Margaret prepared and presented a course on reproduction to a group of mothers and their children. It was her first experience in a lifetime association with the subjects of birth control and planned parenthood.

The Sangers moved to New York City, where Margaret made speeches for the Socialist newspaper, the *Call,* on the economic problems of the working class poor and the problems of family life. She wrote a series of articles for the *Call,* entitled "What Every Woman Should Know," about the functions of the

28

reproductive organs, the physiology of a woman's body, and venereal disease. Although articles on these subjects are common today, they were not in 1913.

The principal obstruction to publishing this type of article was the Comstock Law of 1873. Anthony Comstock, an official of the U.S. Post Office, had the authority to open mail and to decide if it was obscene. He notified the *Call* that if they published Margaret's article on venereal disease, he would revoke their mailing permit. The next issue of the woman's page of the *Call* was blank except for: "What Every Girl Should Know—Nothing! By Order of the Post Office Department."

Many of the requests for nursing care that Margaret received were from the lower East Side, where many of Manhattan's poor lived. Frequently, she would be asked: "Tell me how to avoid having a baby for a while. We cannot afford one yet." She could tell them preventative measures that the husband could take, but they wanted to know what they personally could do to prevent conception. They didn't believe that Margaret had nothing to tell them.

She collected all of the information on the subject of contraception that she could find. She researched the subject for six months and was surprised at the dearth of information that existed. One of the few sources was a book written over fifty years earlier by a Massachusetts physician. Margaret went to Europe to gather more information.

In 1914, upon her return to New York, Margaret edited and published a magazine entitled *The Woman Rebel.* Its slogan was "No Gods, No Masters," and an early issue contained a statement of a woman's duty: "To look the whole world in the face with a go-to-hell look in the eyes, to have an ideal, to speak and act in defiance of convention." Comstock reviewed his complaints with the Postmaster General and acted quickly to prevent *The Woman Rebel* from being sent through the U.S. Mail.

Margaret also wrote *Family Limitation,* a pamphlet that described contraceptive techniques. She discussed, in a straightforward style, the birth control devices available to women; the text was supplemented with diagrams. Twenty-two printers refused to print the pamphlet. One printer said, "That can never be printed. That's a Sing Sing job." Finally, a printer agreed to print 100,000 of the pamphlet in his off hours, so that his employees wouldn't know about it.

Margaret was notified that she had been indicted by the U.S. Government on nine counts of violation of the Criminal Code. If convicted on all nine counts, she faced forty-five years in jail. She received no notice to appear in court and was then asked why she had not appeared in court. The court gave her lawyer less than a day to prepare her case. She decided to run and to fight another day. Using an assumed name, she traveled to Canada and then to England.

In England, Margaret met Havelock Ellis, essayist, psychologist, and author of the seven-volume work, *The Psychology of Sex*. Ellis had received medical training, had specialized in obstetrics, and was known as a reformer. He had a profound influence on Margaret's thinking. In Holland, she met Dr. Aletta Jacobs, the first woman in Holland to be granted a medical degree. In 1878, Dr. Jacobs established the first birth control clinic in the world. Between 1878 and 1915, birth control clinics were established across Holland.

Before she left for England, Margaret had established the National Birth Control League. She attended a meeting of the league's executive committee upon her return to ask what support she could expect from them during her trial. The president of the league informed her that she would receive no support because they were an organization that obeyed the law. She was told that the goal of the league was to get the laws changed, but that they would not support a person who had broken the law.

The District Attorney and the judge both received many communications supporting Margaret. Nine distinguished Englishmen, including Arnold Bennett and H. G. Wells, sent a letter to President Wilson in her defense:

> We understand that Margaret Sanger is in danger
> of criminal prosecution for circulating a pamphlet
> on birth control problems. We therefore beg to
> draw your attention to the fact that such work as
> that of Mrs. Sanger received appreciation and

circulation in every civilized country except the
United States of America, where it is a criminal
offense....

Hence, not only for the benefit of Mrs. Sanger,
but of humanity we respectfully beg you to exert
your powerful influence in the interests of free
speech and the betterment of the race.

The judge postponed the case three times; finally, Margaret was
notified that the case had been dismissed.

On October 16, 1916, Margaret opened her first birth control
clinic in the Brownsville section of Brooklyn. Over 140 women
visited the center on the first day. On the tenth day of the clinic's
operation, the police impounded her equipment, files, and birth
control literature. Margaret, her sister, and one of her assistants
were taken to jail, where they spent the night before being
released on bail. She and her sister received sentences of thirty
days in the workhouse. Margaret, over the objections of the
matron, gave birth control lectures during her stay in the
workhouse.

Upon her release, Margaret made a movie entitled *The Hand
That Rocks the Cradle.* It was not permitted to be shown to the
public because it contained the words "birth control." She
published a magazine, *The Birth Control Review,* with articles by
Havelock Ellis and H. G. Wells on population-related economic
and social topics. It was the principal publication of the birth
control movement for twenty-three years.

On January 18, 1918, Margaret's appeal in her case involving
the birth control clinic in Brooklyn was upheld by Judge
Frederick Crane of the New York State Court of Appeals. His
decision, which became known as the Crane decision, allowed
clinics to be established to inform women about birth control
techniques.

In 1921, Margaret formed the American Birth Control League
to provide direction and to solicit financial support for the birth
control movement. The league is still in existence as Planned
Parenthood of America. She also established the Birth Control

Clinical Research Bureau, which received referrals from the Birth Control League. In April, 1929, the Research Bureau was raided by the police department, and its records were impounded. It was determined in a hearing that the police had acted without authority.

In 1933, the Post Office seized a package containing birth control devices addressed to the director of the Research Bureau. The director filed charges to force the case to go to trial, and the judge ruled that the Research Bureau should receive their package. The government appealed, but lost their appeal.

The appeals judge ruled that the Comstock Law's "design ... was not to prevent the importation, sale or carriage by mail of things which might intelligently be used by conscientious and competent physicians for the purpose of saving life or promoting the well-being of their patients." On June 10, 1937, the American Medical Association resolved that doctors should be informed of their rights in prescribing contraceptives and in educating the public on the subject.

In 1952, Margaret founded and served as the first president of the International Planned Parenthood Association. She died on congestive heart failure in 1966 at the age of eighty-seven. Two of her statements typify her outlook on life:

> Some lives drift here and there like reeds in a stream, depending on the changing currents for their activity. Others are like swimmers knowing the depth of the water. Each stroke helps them onward to a definite objective.

> Life has taught me one supreme lesson; this is that we must—if we are to really *live* at all ... put our convictions into action.

Elizabeth Cady Stanton

On November 12, 1815, Elizabeth Cady Stanton was born in Johnstown, New York, the fourth of six children of Daniel and Margaret Livingston Cady. Daniel Cady was a lawyer who served in the state legislature, Congress, and as a judge of the New York supreme court. Elizabeth studied Greek, Latin, and mathematics at the Johnstown Academy and graduated from Emma Willard's Troy Female Academy in 1832.

Elizabeth's first encounter with activists was with anti-slavery activists whom she met at Peterboro, New York, at the home of her cousin, Gerrit Smith, a political reformer and staunch abolitionist. Elizabeth met and fell in love with Henry Stanton, an agent of the American Anti-Slavery Society, on one of her visits to Peterboro. On May 1, 1840, they were married in Johnstown; despite the resistance of the Presbyterian minister, the word "obey" was omitted from their marriage vows. Instead of being called Mrs. Henry Stanton (Elizabeth didn't like being called Henry), she combined her family name and her married name. This was not common at the time; it became established practice about 1841.

On their honeymoon, Elizabeth and Henry traveled to London, where Henry attended the World Anti-Slavery Convention. In London, Elizabeth met Lucretia Mott, whose husband, James, was a delegate to the convention. Lucretia Mott made a strong impression on Elizabeth. She was a Quaker minister and a reformer who was active in both the abolitionist and feminist movements.

Lucretia was twenty-two years older than Elizabeth and became her mentor and role model. She encouraged Elizabeth to think independently about religion and individual rights: "When I first heard from her lips that I had the same right to think for myself that Luther, Calvin, and John Knox had, and the same right to be guided by my own convictions, I felt a newborn sense of dignity and freedom." Lucretia and Elizabeth resolved to convene a Women's Rights Convention as soon as they returned home from London. However, this didn't occur for another eight years.

Upon their return home, Henry Stanton read law with Judge Cady. When completed his clerkship in 1842, he joined a Boston law firm. Elizabeth found Boston to be a stimulating city. Garrison and many of the strong-willed abolitionists lived there; it was a home for liberal thinkers. The Stantons entertained frequently; their friends and guests included Ralph Waldo Emerson, Stephen Foster, Nathaniel Hawthorne, James Russell Lowell, and John Greenleaf Whittier. They were happy in Boston, but Henry developed a chronic lung congestion and needed a less humid climate.

In 1847, they moved to Seneca Falls, New York, where Henry resumed the practice of law. Elizabeth had difficulty settling into the small town atmosphere of Seneca Falls after the social-political scene in Boston. The demands of her young, growing family weighed upon her. Henry was busy with his career and was frequently out of town on trips to Albany and Washington. Elizabeth was glad to hear that Lucretia Mott planned to visit her sister in Waterloo, which is just west of Seneca Falls, in July, 1848.

On July 13th, Elizabeth met Lucretia at the home of Jane and Richard Hunt in Waterloo. Lucretia's sister, Martha Wright, and Mary McClintock were also at the Hunt's home that day. Elizabeth was pleased that these four ladies were eager to proceed with the Women's Rights Conference that she and Lucretia had discussed eight years previously. All but Elizabeth were Garrison-type anti-slavery activists. Lucretia Mott was the only one who had experience as a delegate, orator, or organizer. However, they had all attended temperance and anti-slavery conventions. Elizabeth remembered that she "poured ... out the torrent of my long accumulating discontent with such violence and indignation that I stirred myself, as well as the rest of the party, to do and dare anything."

The time was ripe to address the conditions that confronted women in the United States in the mid-nineteenth century. They are difficult to envision today; women were not permitted to vote, to obtain a college education, or to own property, and their wages were turned over to their husbands. In cases of separation and divorce, guardianship of the children was automatically given to the husband. By law, a women's inheritance went to her husband. She was not entitled to the rights given automatically to men of the lowest station, whether they were born in the United States or were immigrants.

The five women called a convention on July 19 and 20 at the Wesleyan Methodist Church in Seneca Falls. A notice appeared in the Seneca County *Courier* announcing a "convention to discuss the social, civil, and religious condition and rights of women." Elizabeth wrote a *Declaration of Sentiments,* which was based on the *Declaration of Independence,* asserting that "all men and women are created equal." The *Declaration of Sentiments,* which was essentially a declaration of women's rights, was the principal document reviewed and was the basis for the resolutions passed at the convention, including:

> *Resolved,* That all laws which prevent women from occupying such as station in society as her conscience shall dictate, or which place her in a position inferior to that of man, are contrary to the great precept of nature and therefore of no force or validity....

> *Resolved,* That woman is man's equal—was intended to be so by the creator, and the highest good of the human race demands that she should be recognized as such....

> *Resolved,* That it is the duty of the women of this country to secure themselves their sacred right to the elective franchise....

The convention was the starting point of the Women's Rights Movement in the United States. Most newspaper columnists ridiculed the convention; however, some editors were sympathetic to the women's cause. Frederick Douglass, in the *North Star,* could see no reason to deny women the right to vote because "right is of no sex." The convention was the beginning of the support from Horace Greeley of the New York *Tribune.*

In March 1851, Elizabeth met Susan B. Anthony while walking home from an anti-slavery meeting in Seneca Falls. Susan never married and was less of an extrovert than Elizabeth. Susan, with her singleness of purpose, became totally dedicated to the Women's Rights Movement. Elizabeth's and Susan's abilities complemented each other. Elizabeth was the policy formulator, effective writer, and expressive speechmaker; Susan's strengths were her organizational ability, her campaigning skills, and her willingness to make campaign arrangements. In later years, Susan B. Anthony's reputation as a women's rights leader superceded that of Elizabeth, because Susan outlived Elizabeth and left in place a strong organization that promoted her memory.

In 1854, Elizabeth spoke to the New York State legislature about the need for changes to the married women's property law. She reviewed some of the points in the *Declaration of Sentiments,* discussed the lack of women's right to vote and to hold office, and cited their inability to earn wages and to inherit from their family. Her speech included a plea for women to be able to own property, to be guardians of their own children, and to be eligible for higher education. In 1860, when the New York State legislature passed a law granting women the right to keep their wages and to be custodians of their own children, Elizabeth knew that she had contributed to its passage.

In 1869, Elizabeth and Susan founded the National Woman Suffrage Association. Susan was elected secretary; Elizabeth was elected president, a position that she held for twenty-one years. However, Elizabeth's strong stands on women's rights weren't for everyone. In late 1869, a group of conservative suffragists formed a rival organization, the American Woman Suffrage Organization. The new organization, comprised mainly of New Englanders, was led by Lucy Stone.

In November 1888, Elizabeth attempted unsuccessfully to vote in Tenafly, New Jersey; Susan had tried to vote in 1872 and had also failed. Elizabeth convinced Senator Aaron Sargent that year to introduce a women's suffrage amendment to supplement the Fifteenth Amendment to the Constitution. It failed passage in 1888 and in every session of congress until it was adopted in 1920, eighteen years after Elizabeth's death.

In 1890, the two major women's suffrage organizations were joined. Elizabeth was elected president, Susan was elected secretary, and Lucy Stone became head of the executive committee of the combined National American Women Suffrage Association. Elizabeth presided over the new organization for two years and then turned over the reins to Susan.

Elizabeth Cady Stanton was a dynamic leader who, denied entrance to college because she was a woman, was, to a large extent, self-educated. She never gave up in her quest for the right of women to vote. On October 25, 1902, the day before she died, she wrote a plea to President Theodore Roosevelt for his support in obtaining women's right to vote. Ida Husted Harper, the author and editor, observed that Elizabeth was the main philosopher, publicist, and politician for the Women's Rights Movement, and that "If the intellect of Elizabeth Cady Stanton had been possessed by a man, he would have had a seat on the Supreme Bench or the Senate of the United States, but our country has no rewards for great women."

Marcus Whitman / Narcissa Prentiss

On September 4, 1802, Marcus Whitman, the third son of Beza and Alice Whitman, was born in Rushville. The Whitmans were settlers from New England. Whitman's father died in 1810, and his mother remarried. The eight-year-old went to New England to live with relatives to complete his schooling. His first career choice was the ministry, but he didn't have the money to pay for divinity school.

Whitman returned to Rushville and was apprenticed to the village doctor. He was licensed to practice medicine after a year of medical school at Fairfield, Herkimer County. He practiced in small towns in Pennsylvania and in Ontario, Canada, re-entered Fairfield medical school for additional medical education, and received his M. D. degree at the age of twenty-nine.

Dr. Whitman returned to the Finger Lakes Region and established a medical practice in the town of Wheeler. He was at services in the Wheeler Church one day in 1835 when Reverend Samuel Parker, a Congregationalist minister who had served among the Indians in St. Louis, spoke to raise money and volunteers for missionary work with the Native Americans. Reverend Parker told of the four Flathead Indians who had traveled from the Oregon Territory to St. Louis to obtain bibles to take back to their tribe. Dr. Whitman was moved by Reverend Parker's talk. He decided to become a medical missionary and to work with the Indians in the West.

Stephen Prentiss, a businessman and a Steuben County judge, was one of Dr. Whitman's friends in nearby Prattsburg. Judge Prentiss' daughter, Narcissa, was moved by the same talk by Reverend Parker that she heard in Angelica, Allegany County, where her parents had moved in 1833. Narcissa, who taught in district schools in nearby Belmont, wrote to the Mission Board to ask if women could serve as missionaries. She was told they could, if they were married.

Reverend Parker told Dr. Whitman of Narcissa's interest in missionary work with the Indians. Dr. Whitman already knew that the Mission Board preferred married men to unmarried men. Dr. Whitman and Narcissa participated in a whirlwind courtship, and, by late 1835, when Dr. Whitman left with the Reverend Parker for the West, he and Narcissa were engaged.

Rev. Parker and Dr. Whitman joined a caravan of trappers traveling from St. Louis to the Green River, a tributary of the Colorado River. Dr. Whitman was deeply influenced by the trip and decided to return to the East to organize a party of missionaries to travel beyond the Rocky Mountains to the Oregon Territory. Upon his return, Dr. Whitman met with an acquaintance from Wheeler, Reverend Henry Spalding. Rev. Spalding and his plain, quiet wife, Eliza, agreed to join the missionary party, even though Rev. Spalding was one of Narcissa's rejected suitors.

On February 18, 1836, Dr. Whitman and Narcissa were married in the Presbyterian Church in Angelica. In March, they began their trip west. They traveled by sleigh to Hollidaysburg, Pennsylvania, by canal to Pittsburgh, and then by riverboat to St. Louis, where the difficult, overland part of the trip began. At Omaha, they joined a caravan of trappers bound for the Green

River in southern Wyoming. Their company provided protection from the Indians.

The two missionary couples were accompanied across Idaho by two fur traders. Prior to 1835, few travelers followed the trail blazed by Lewis and Clark years before. The Whitmans and the Spaldings encountered real hardships; baggage had to be abandoned, and food was scarce. They converted their wagon into a two-wheeled vehicle, which they had to leave at the Snake River. Finally, they reached the Columbia River country in just over four months and 2,250 miles. Narcissa and Eliza made history as the first white women to cross the Rocky Mountains.

The only inhabitants of the Oregon Territory lived at scattered trading posts. Upon their arrival in the Oregon Territory, Spalding chose his mission site among the friendly Nez Perce Indians. The Whitmans had to locate their mission with the distrustful Cayuse tribe. Dr. Whitman built an adobe home and a sawmill. He also planted crops and an orchard. Both Dr. Whitman and Narcissa learned the Cayuse language and, within three years, established a mission, a farm, and a school.

He administered to the medical and spiritual needs of the Indians, and she taught in the school. The Cayuse were a suspicious tribe; they had killed their own medicine man when his medicine failed to work. Running the mission was a challenge accompanied by risk.

During the winter of 1842-43, Dr. Whitman traveled east with a companion. He wanted to convince the federal government not to barter away the Oregon Territory and to prevent the spreading of English influence until more settlers could migrate from the East and the Midwest. He visited Horace Greeley, editor of the New York *Tribune* and met with government officials in Washington, D. C., including John Spencer of Canandaigua, President Tyler's Secretary of the Treasury.

Whitman led a train of 200 wagons of settlers to the Pacific Northwest when he returned to the Oregon Territory. This was the first of the migrations to the West; it preceded the migrations during the California gold rush of 1849. The Cayuse had burned the sawmill in his absence and had forced Narcissa to move to Fort Walla Walla for safety.

In 1847, an outbreak of measles caused fatalities among the Cayuse. They blamed the white doctor for the deaths in their tribe. Whitman knew that he was in danger. On November 29, 1847, Joe Lewis, a French-Indian half-breed, known as Tomahas by the Indians, came to the Whitman adobe on the pretext of obtaining medicine. He killed Whitman with his tomahawk, shot Narcissa, and then beat her to death. Fourteen of the twenty people at the mission that day were killed, including two children. Three years later, the five ringleaders of the massacre were hanged for their crimes.

When news of their fate reached Washington, D.C., President Polk pressed for passage of a bill granting official territory status to Oregon, which included Oregon, Washington, and part of Idaho. Congress passed the bill; it was law within two months. Whitman was right when he said, "My death will probably do as much for Oregon as my life can." A tall marble monument was erected on the hill near the graves of the Whitmans and their fellow victims. Whitman College at Walla Walla, Washington, has a Narcissa Prentiss Hall on its campus, and the State of Washington named Whitman County in their memory.

Jemima Wilkinson

Jemima Wilkinson was the first American-born woman to found a religious sect. She led a religious community whose members were pioneers in opening Western New York to settlement. Jemima, the eighth of twelve children of Jeremiah Wilkinson and Amey Whipple Wilkinson, was born in Cumberland, Rhode Island, on November 29, 1752. She was named for one of Job's daughters and raised as a Quaker. In her early twenties she was influenced by the New Light Baptists, who emphasized individual inspiration and enlightenment through the Holy Spirit.

In February 1776, she was advised to mend her ways by the Society of Friends. She was chastised for not attending Friends' meetings and for not speaking the Quaker language, with its use of "thee" and "thou." In August 1776, she was disowned by the Smithfield Meeting of the Quakers. She began an intensive meditation and study of the Bible, to the exclusion of all social contacts.

Amey Wilkinson died while giving birth to her twelfth child when Jemima was twelve years old. It was a time of stress for the motherless family. Jemima's sister, Patience, was disowned by the Quakers for giving birth out of wedlock, and two of her younger brothers were disowned for having "frequented trainings for military service and endeavored to justify the same."

Jemima became ill, and it was not clear whether her illness was due to severe emotional stress or was a condition caused by typhus. Dr. Man from Attleboro verified that she had a fever and was seriously ill. In Jemima's opinion, she had died and come back to life; furthermore, she hadn't just come back to life, but she returned as the second coming of Christ. She no longer considered herself to be Jemima Wilkinson; she called herself the Publick Universal Friend or just the Universal Friend. She preached in Connecticut, Massachusetts, and Rhode Island. By 1881, she was preaching in Philadelphia, where her followers included both the well-to-do and the common people.

One individual who heard her preach described her as "straight, well-made, with light complexion, black eyes, round face, and dark chestnut hair." Her style of dress combined some male articles of clothing, such as a hat and collar, with some female articles, for example, a cloth smock that she tied under her chin like a dressing gown. She wasn't a refined or erudite person, but she was confident and sincere. She had a notable memory, which allowed her to recite lengthy sections of the Bible.

Jemima thought about moving her religious followers away from populated areas; she was considering a "wilderness" location. She recommended that they "shun the company and conversation of the wicked world." The sect heard glowing reports about the Finger Lakes Region from members of General Sullivan's 1779 expedition. In 1785, Jemima's brother, Jeptha, explored the region, and Ezekial Shearman traced General Sullivan's route in the following year. Upon Shearman's return, Jemima decided to settle in the Genesee Country, and James

Parker and three other members of the sect were sent to choose a site.

An advance party of twenty-five, led by Parker, established a settlement in 1788 on the Keuka Lake Outlet into Seneca Lake, just west of the present-day Village of Dresden. They were attracted by a waterfall, which they used to power a gristmill and a sawmill. They were the first mills in the region. The Universal Friend joined the settlement in the spring of 1790. The settlement, which was located on a knoll about a mile south of the Keuka Outlet and a mile west of Seneca Lake, was named City Hill. Unfortunately, their site and Geneva to the north of them were both located in the "gore," a disputed triangular area between the incorrect survey line of 1788 and the new line surveyed four years later. This dispute caused Oliver Phelps and Nathaniel Gorham, the speculators who owned the land, to locate their land sales office in Canandaigua, to the west, instead of Geneva, their original choice.

In 1794, the community moved to a six-square-mile site north of Branchport. They named their settlement Jerusalem, which is the name of the town today. The Universal Friend's first house in Jerusalem was a log building to which two log additions were added; the middle building served as the meeting room for the community. The members of the sect subscribed to the practice of celibacy, a rule that cost the community many members. Visitors to the settlement were treated hospitably.

In 1795, the Duke of Rochefoucald-Liancourt passed through the area on his way to Niagara Falls. He observed that "Our plates, as well as the table linen, were perfectly clean and neat. Our repast, though frugal, was better yet in quality than any, of which we had partaken, since out departure from Philadelphia; it consisted of good fresh meat, with pudding, an excellent salad, and a beverage of a peculiar yet charming flavor."

The Universal Friends had a peaceful relationship with the Indians. In 1794, Jemima and some of her followers attended the council at Canandaigua at which the Pickering Treaty was signed with the Iroquois, assuring peace and promoting further settlement of Western New York. She and her followers dined at the home of Thomas Morris, the son of Robert Morris—the "financier of the

Revolutionary War." The Universal Friend addressed the council and was given the name "Shinnewawna gis tau, ge" by the Indians. It meant "A Great Woman Preacher."

A second home was built for Jemima between 1809 and 1815; she lived in this house, which is located on Friend Hill Road off Friend Road, from 1814 until her death in 1819. It fell into disrepair after her death, but has been restored and is now a New York Historic Site. It is a large, three-story rectangular building in the style of a large New England farmhouse. Jemima's bedroom was on the southeast corner of the second floor, with a beautiful view of the west branch of Keuka Lake.

Jemima Wilkinson died on July 1, 1819; the Death Book noted that: "25 minutes past 2 on the clock, the Friend went from here." Her last words were: "My friends I must soon depart—I am going—this night I leave you." Her followers waited three days to see if she would rise again. They placed her on a wooden platform in the basement until they realized they were going to have to bury her. Only two of her followers knew where she was buried. Her religious community did not sustain itself; the last of her followers died in 1874.

Strong individualism was required to lead a group into the wilderness and to successfully establish not one settlement, but two. Historians rank her as one of the outstanding women of the colonial period.

Thomas Watson Homestead, Campbell

Chapter 2

"All great questions of politics and economics come down in the last analysis to the decisions and actions of individual men and women. They are questions of human relations, and we ought always to think about them in terms of men and women—the individual human beings who are involved in them. If we can get human relations on a proper basis, finance and all other complicated aspects of these questions will be easier to solve."

—Thomas J. Watson

William Burroughs

William Seward Burroughs, the inventor of the first practical adding and listing machine, was born on January 28, 1857, in Rochester, New York. His father, a mechanic, moved the family to Lowell, Michigan, when Burroughs was very young. After three years in Michigan, the family moved to Auburn, New York, where Burroughs attended public schools.

Burrough's first job was in a bank, where he learned bookkeeping and accounting. After five years of tedious clerical work, he became bored spending half of his time attempting to avoid making mistakes and the other half looking for mistakes that could not be prevented. He worked hard and frequently toiled through the night adding, checking, and rechecking long lists of numbers. Eventually, his health deteriorated from the strain, and his doctor recommended that he look for another line of work.

In 1882, Burroughs left Auburn and moved to St. Louis, where he became a mechanic in a machine shop. He repaired some machines for Thomas Metcalf, a St. Louis dry goods merchant, and told him of his ideas for an adding machine.

45

Burroughs had been impressed with Dorr Felt's design of a multiple-order key-driven calculating machine that used a ratchet feed motion. Felt had begun producing comptometers in 1887.

In 1888, Burroughs produced his first adding machine, which recorded only the final result of the calculation. He followed this machine with one that printed the numbers being added as well as the total. Burrough's machines were easier to operate than Felt's comptometers. Burroughs began his development effort with funding of only $700. His slogan was "Accuracy is truth filed to a sharp point."

Burrough's first three adding machine designs were unsuccessful. At one point, he threw fifty machines of his most recent model out of a second-story window in St. Louis. He was a perfectionist, but he was also persistent. He worked three days and three nights straight to perfect his design. The main problem with his earlier designs was that the machine performed differently for an operator who pulled the lever slowly than an operator who yanked the lever quickly. He designed a governor mechanism to eliminate the effect of the differences in operators. His solution was a "dash pot," which was a governor mechanism that absorbed the shock of pulling the machine's handle.

On January 21, 1886, the American Arithometer Company was incorporated in Missouri by Burroughs, Metcalf, and two other partners. Metcalf was president and Burroughs was vice-president of the company formed to design and build adding machines. They built 8,000 of their first adding and listing machine, which sold for $475. In 1895, the name of their product was changed from arithometers to Burroughs adding and listing machines, and the first international marketing operation was established in England. In 1898, the first overseas manufacturing facility was opened in Nottingham, England.

Burroughs retired in Citronelle, Alabama, where he died of tuberculosis on September 14, 1898. He was buried in the St. Louis Bellefontaine Center Cemetery. His burial site is marked by a marble shaft inscribed with the words "Under that stately column reposes a man who was noble in poverty, humble in wealth, and great in his benefit to humanity."

In 1905, the company outgrew its facilities in Missouri and

46

moved to Detroit. The name of the company was changed to the Burroughs Adding Machine Company. It became a leader in the design and manufacture of mechanical devices and precision products. During World War II, the company produced the Norden bombsight for the U.S. Army Air Corps and built the electronic memory for the ENIAC, the first electronic automatic computer— developed at the University of Pennsylvania. In 1951, the first Burroughs digital computer was built for the Wayne State University Computation Laboratory. In 1953, the Company's name was changed to the Burroughs Corporation. Eventually, Burroughs merged with Univac to form the Unisys Corporation.

Willis Carrier

Willis Haviland Carrier, the father of air conditioning, was born in Angola, New York, on November 26, 1876. He was the only child of Duane Carrier, a farmer, and Elizabeth Haviland Carrier. Upon his graduation from the Angola Academy in 1894, he could not afford to go to college; instead, he taught school for two years. During the 1896-97 school year he attended Central High School in Buffalo to prepare himself for the competitive examinations for college scholarships.

In the spring of 1897, Carrier won a four-year state tuition scholarship to Cornell University, and a two-year scholarship that helped pay for room, board, books, and expenses. He earned money by mowing lawns, by waiting on tables, and by founding a student laundry in his senior year. In 1901, he graduated from Cornell University with the degree of Mechanical Engineer in Electrical Engineering.

Carrier accepted a position with the Buffalo Forge Company in Buffalo and started work on July 1, 1901. His first assignment was to design a heating plant for the Erie City Boiler Company. He also worked on systems for drying coffee and lumber and on forced draft systems for boilers. He soon realized that there wasn't sufficient empirical data to use in designing these systems. Seat-of-the-pants techniques were resulting in overdesigned systems to ensure the necessary safety factors. He compiled the empirical data needed to create efficient designs. The value of his work was recognized, and he was asked to establish an industrial laboratory to expand his research. His next project was the preparation of data for use in testing and rating heaters.

On his first day of work, Carrier met Irvine Lyle, manager of the New York office of the Buffalo Forge Company. Lyle forwarded a request to Carrier from the Sackett-Williams Lithographing and Publishing Company, who needed to solve a humidity problem. Using dew-point temperature data from Weather Bureau tables, Carrier designed the equipment to solve their problem. His July 17, 1902 drawings represent the first scientific air conditioning system.

Air conditioning provides multiple functions: control of temperature and humidity, air circulation and ventilation, and cleaning of the air. Years later, Carrier gave his definition of air conditioning: "Air conditioning is the control of the humidity of air either by increasing or decreasing its moisture content. Added to the control of humidity are the control of temperature by either heating or cooling the air, the purification of the air by washing or filtering the air, and the control of air motion and ventilation."

Carrier was not satisfied with the design of his first air conditioning systems. He was particularly unhappy with controlling humidity by using salts, which corroded the metal parts of his equipment. He conceived the solution to this problem while waiting for a train in Pittsburgh in late fall, 1902. The temperature was in the low thirties, and he was thinking about the dense fog as he paced the railroad platform.

In later years, Carrier described how the concept of "dew point control" came to him:

> Here is air approximately 100 percent saturated with moisture. The temperature is so low, even though saturated, there is not much actual moisture.... Now if I can saturate air and control its temperature at saturation, I can get air with any amount of moisture I want in it ... drawing the air through a fine spray of water to create actual fog.

By controlling the water temperature, I can control the temperature at saturation. When very moist air is required, I'll heat the water. When very dry is required, that is, air with a small amount of moisture, I'll use cold water to get low temperature saturation. The cold spray will actually be the condensing surface. I certainly will get rid of the rusting difficulties that occur using steel coils for condensing vapor in air. Water won't rust.

On September 16, 1904, Carrier applied for a patent on his invention, "Apparatus for Treating Air"; he was awarded patent no. 808897 on January 2, 1906.

The first customer of equipment with Carrier's new design was the LaCrosse National Bank of LaCrosse, Wisconsin; however, it was only used to wash the air in the ventilating system. Carrier's next installations were in the textile industry. A textile engineer, Stuart Cramer of Charlotte, North Carolina, gave the industry its name when he used the words "air conditioning" in a patent application for a humidifying head in April 1906.

In November 1908, the Carrier Air Conditioning Company of America, a wholly-owned subsidiary of the Buffalo Forge Company, was established. Many of the installations at this time were in tobacco factories. In 1914, although air conditioning sales were substantial, Buffalo Forge decided to get out of the business. They were reacting to the beginning of World War I in Europe. They evaluated their business situation and decided to return to their core business.

As a result of that decision, seven young engineers left the Buffalo Forge Company to form the Carrier Engineering Corporation on June 26, 1915. Carrier was elected president and Lyle became general manager and treasurer. Their first project was the design of improved refrigeration equipment for air conditioning systems.

As the company grew, they needed more factory space. They purchased a plant in Newark, New Jersey, and began to fill orders for department stores and theatres. In July 1925, Carrier won the contract to supply refrigeration equipment for Madison Square Garden. In 1928, they installed air conditioning in the House of Representatives and in the U.S. Senate in the following year. They purchased a second manufacturing plant in Newark and built a new factory in Allentown, Pennsylvania.

In 1930, the Carrier Corporation was formed by merging the Carrier Engineering Corporation with two manufacturing companies. In 1937, the Carrier Corporation centralized five plants in four New Jersey and Pennsylvania cities into one location, the closed factories and offices of the H. H. Franklin Manufacturing Company in Syracuse. The first product developed at the Franklin automobile facility was the popular Weathermaster System, which grew from crude experiments begun in 1928. The Weathermaster design was completed in 1939.

During World War II, Carrier continued to produce air conditioning equipment, but it also manufactured airplane engine mounts, gun sight hoods, tank adapters, and the "Hedgehog," an anti-submarine depth charge device. In the mid-1940s, Carrier reduced his activities with the company because of a heart ailment. In February, 1948, he was made Chairman Emeritus of the Carrier Corporation. He died in New York City on October 7, 1950.

George Dayton

George Draper Dayton, the second oldest child of David Day Dayton, M.D., and Caroline Draper Dayton, was born in Clifton Springs, New York, on March 6, 1857. He was the founder of the Dayton-Hudson Department Store chain in the Midwest. In 1869-70, Dayton attended the seminary at Ovid, and he passed the entrance requirements to Hobart College in 1873. He postponed entering college to work in a coal and lumber yard at Starkey. When the owner of the yard was unable to pay his salary and commissions for his first year of work, he bought the coal and lumber business to secure the money owed to him. His father paid him $2,000 in lieu of attending Hobart College. At the age of seventeen, he was over $7,000 in debt.

During the winter of 1876-77, Dayton worked through the night every other night. The ambitious Dayton worked all of one day, that night, and all of the next day. Then he got a night's sleep and started the cycle over again. By spring, he was ill and had to be attended by his father, a country physician. He slept mornings, afternoons, and evenings while recovering from his illness.

In 1877, he sold the coal and lumber yard and moved to Geneva to work in a lumber yard and saw mill owned by John McKay. Dayton set a goal not to marry until he was twenty-one and had savings of at least $5,000. On December 17, 1878, Dayton and Emma Willard Chadwick were married after waiting until his goals were met. He had known Emma for five years, and he said: "I knew at once what I wanted—in later years she acknowledged she knew at once what she wanted."

In 1883, Dayton sold their house in Geneva and purchased 640 acres of prairie land east of Worthington, Minnesota, with the proceeds. Later, he purchased 160 acres adjacent to his original purchase and developed a 800-acre farm. On April 1, 1883, he became president of the Bank of Worthington. The bank's slogan was "Interest always paid when due; principal according to agreement."

He was president of six corporations during the Panic of 1893. He survived the panic even though many other regional banks failed. Also that year, he participated in his first real estate venture, the building of an eight-story building for physicians and dentists at Nicollet Avenue and Sixth Street in Minneapolis. In 1894, he was elected a trustee of Macalester College. In 1896, Dayton bought a second property on Nicollet Avenue, which he initially expanded by an additional frontage of fifty feet and expanded again to 215 feet in 1918. On July 14, 1902, he moved from Worthington to Minneapolis and founded the mercantile business that bears his name.

In his autobiography, Dayton expressed his views on business: "And so all through the years I have entered into the minutest details as enthusiastically as into the complex problems that puzzle bankers, merchants and successful businessmen who meet and struggle with the intricate questions of the chaotic periods of the present and the past." He concluded that "'There's a divinity that shapes our lives' has certainly been illustrated in my life—and I have come to believe that a higher power has 'opened and closed doorways' for me."

In 1930, the Inter-Racial Service Council awarded its Civic Service Honor Medal to him for "the high integrity of his business standards, his inspiring faith in the city of Minneapolis, the example of his simple Christian life, his public spiritedness in all matters of general welfare, and his financial contributions to spiritual, moral and civic needs." On June 13, 1932, Macalester College conferred Dayton with an honorary LL.D degree. In the following year, Dayton received an honorary D.Litt. degree from Jamestown College.

In later years, he summed up his outlook on life: "I love the details; they are not irksome to me. I enjoy the contacts, the thrills, the surprises, the new problems. And I strive to meet philosophically the disappointments, the losses, the tragedies. The greatest disappointment is that I haven't accomplished more for humanity, for the uplift of the race, for the betterment of the world." Dayton died on February 18, 1938.

George Eastman

George Eastman, founder of the photographic industry, was born in Waterville, New York, on July 12, 1854. He was the third child and first son of George W. Eastman and Maria Kilbourn Eastman. In 1842, Eastman's father established a business school, Eastman's Commercial College, in Rochester. The school prospered in the thriving Erie Canal community, but George W. Eastman didn't move his family from Waterville to Rochester until 1860. George W. Eastman died in 1862, leaving the family in reduced economic circumstances. Maria Eastman had to take in boarders to supplement her meager income. Young Eastman's first job was a part-time job with an insurance agency. He started his first full-time job as junior bookkeeper for the Rochester Savings Bank in April 1874.

The first reference to photography in Eastman's diary was in 1869. His interest began in earnest during the summer of 1877, when he purchased $100 worth of "sundries and lenses," and arranged for a local photographer to teach him "the art of photography." Taking photographs in 1877 was a complex process requiring a considerable amount of equipment. The glass plates had to be exposed in the camera while wet, and development had to be completed before the emulsion dried. He was bothered by the cumbersomeness of the process. He commented, " ... the bulk of the paraphernalia worried me. It seemed that one ought to be able to carry less than a pack-horse load."

Eastman's thinking was given direction when he read an article in the *British Journal of Photography* that provided a formula for a sensitive gelatin emulsion for glass plates that could be used when dry. He spent long hours experimenting until he found a combination of gelatin and silver bromide that had the photographic qualities that he sought. Initially, he experimented to support his hobby of photography, but he soon realized the commercial potential of his effort. He resigned his job at the bank and began to make and market dry plates.

By June 1879, he was manufacturing quality photographic plates and had designed and built equipment for coating them. He sailed to England, the center of the photographic industry at that time, and obtained his first patent on July 22, 1879. On September 9, 1879, his patent attorney, George Selden, submitted an application for him to the U.S. Patent Office for "an Improved Process of Preparing Gelatin Dry Plates for Use in Photography and in Apparatus therefor."

In April 1880, he leased the third floor of a building on State Street in Rochester and began to produce dry plates in quantity. One of the early investors in the Eastman Dry Plate Company was Colonel Henry Alvah Strong, who, with his wife, boarded with Maria Eastman. Strong was a partner in Strong-Woodbury and Company, a successful manufacturer of whips.

During the winter of 1879-80, Eastman formulated four business principles upon which to build his enterprise:
- Production in large quantities by machinery
- Low prices to increase the usefulness of the products

• Foreign as well as domestic distribution
• Extensive advertising as well as selling by demonstration

In 1881, a near-fatal catastrophe struck the business—photographers complained that Eastman dry plates were no longer sensitive and did not capture an image. Customers discovered something that hadn't been realized until then: passage of time lessened the sensitivity of the emulsion on the plate. The New York City distributor had placed the recently received plates on top of the older plates and had sold the new plates before using up the old. By the time the older plates were sold, they had lost their photographic sensitivity. At significant expense for a small company, Eastman recalled all of his plates and replaced them.

Then Eastman received a second staggering blow—he could no longer make a satisfactory emulsion. During many weeks of sleepless nights with his factory shut down, Eastman conducted 469 unsuccessful experiments to produce a usable emulsion. On March 11, 1882, Eastman and Strong sailed for England. In England, they discovered that the problem was due to a defective supply of gelatin received from a manufacturer; it wasn't a problem with the emulsion formula or Eastman's equipment. On April 16th, they returned to Rochester, conducted sixteen more unsuccessful experiments and were successful on the seventeenth try. Eastman learned two lessons from this experience: to test samples of material received and to control the supply, whenever practical.

Eastman searched for a material to replace the fragile, heavy glass as a support for the emulsion. He experimented with collodion, which was made from gun-cotton (nitro-cellulose) and nitric acid. On March 4, 1884, he filed his first patent application for photographic film. Then he worked on a mechanism to hold film in the camera; he designed a roll-holder in a wooden frame.

On October 1, 1882, the Eastman Dry Plate and Film Company was incorporated with $200,000 capital stock. Henry A. Strong was president, and Eastman was treasurer of the new company, which purchased the plant and stock of the Eastman Dry Plate Company. On March 26, 1885, the first commercial film was manufactured by the new company.

Eastman used Dr. Samuel Lattimore, head of the department of chemistry at the University of Rochester, as a consultant. The first chemist hired by Eastman was Henry Reichenbach, one of Dr. Lattimore's assistants. Eastman was too involved with the operation of the business to devote much time to experiments; however, he continued to work on mechanical developments, such as roller mechanisms. On December 10, 1889, a patent for manufacturing transparent nitro-cellulose photographic film was granted to Reichenbach. Joint patents were granted to Eastman and Reichenbach on March 22, 1892, and July 19, 1892.

Another early setback to the company was a serious fire on February 10, 1888, that destroyed most of the interior of the State Street factory and shut it down for two months. Eastman was back in business by April, and by June he had his first camera on the market. He conceived of the name "Kodak" as a trademark for his products. He liked the letter K, the first letter of his mother's maiden name. On September 4, 1888, "Kodak" was registered as a trademark in the United States. The first camera was the "No. 1 Kodak." Eastman explained the origin of the word to the British Patent Office:

> This is not a foreign name or work; it was constructed by me to serve a definite purpose. It has the following merits as a trade mark word:
>
> First: It is short.
> Second: It is not capable of
>   mispronunciation.
> Third: It does not resemble anything in
>   the art and cannot be associated
>   with anything in the art except
>   the "Kodak."

The company continued to expand to meet market demand. In August 1890, the company purchased several farms in the Town of Greece, which were to become Kodak Park, the world's largest film manufacturing complex. Camera and film development continued as Kodak designed and made uncomplicated products that lived up to the slogan "You press the button and we do the rest."

The next challenge that Eastman faced was one that he least expected—employee disloyalty. Reichenbach and two other employees secretly formed a rival company using the film-making formulae and processes of Eastman's company. Eastman investigated the charges and found them to be true. He also found that they had made 39,400 feet of unusable film and had let 1,417 gallons of emulsion spoil. Eastman discharged them.

On November 28, 1889, the Eastman Photographic Materials Company, Ltd., was incorporated in London to represent the company in all areas of the world except the western hemisphere. In December, 1889, the Eastman Company was incorporated in Rochester with $1,000,000 capital to represent the company in the western hemisphere. On May 23, 1892, the name of the Eastman Company was changed to the Eastman Kodak Company and the capitalization was increased to $5,000,000.

In 1912, Eastman established the Eastman Kodak Company Research Laboratories and brought Dr. Kenneth Mees from England to serve as its head. Mees and his chief assistant, S. E. Shepard, who were both graduates of the University of London, made significant contributions to the growth of the company. Motion pictures were introduced in the early 1920s, Kodacolor film was announced in the late 1920s, and many significant film improvements followed. These improvements included Technicolor film, Kodachrome film, and the replacement of nitrate-based film with an acetate-based product.

Eastman never married; he lived alone in his mansion on East Avenue. He was instrumental in the founding of the Eastman School of Music at the University of Rochester and the building of the Eastman Theatre. He gave over sixty million dollars to educational institutions, including the University of Rochester, the Massachusetts Institute of Technology, Hampton Institute, and the Tuskegee Institute. He funded the Eastman Visiting Professorship at Oxford University and gave $5,500,000 to establish dental clinics in Brussels, London, Paris, Rome, and Stockholm.

On March 14, 1932, George Eastman took his own life at his East Avenue home. He left a note which read: "To my friends. My work is done. Why wait? G. E." His death shocked the community. Karl K. Compton, president of the Massachusetts Institute of Technology, wrote in the April 15, 1932, issue of *Science* magazine:

> ... Consider for a moment the full significance of his last words. He had invented the modern photographic plate; he had invented the photographic film; he had made the Kodak a household object throughout the entire world; he had created a business; he had created a great research laboratory which had strikingly fulfilled his faith in it; he had selected certain fields of education, health, and art to which he had devoted his fortune for the benefit of the entire world; he had satisfied his distinctive desires for the excitement of exploration and big game hunting; he had no close relatives; the infirmities of old age had come upon him and were about to master him. He who had always been his own master remained so to the last.

Amory Houghton, Jr.

Amory Houghton, Jr., was born in Cambridge, Massachusetts, in 1837. His father, Amory Houghton, Sr., founded the predecessor companies to Corning, Inc., but it was the son who put the organization on the path to becoming a world-class company. After an early career in coal and lumber, Amory, Sr., invested in Bay State Glass in Somerville, Massachusetts, and founded Union Glass Company there three years later. Amory, Jr., and his brother, Charles, were employees of Union Glass, which manufactured bottles and lamps as well as a line of molded and pressed glass.

In 1864, Amory, Sr., sold his interest in the Union Glass Company and moved to Brooklyn, where he invested in the Brooklyn Flint Glass Company. Amory, Jr., and Charles became stockholders in the company and associates of their father.

In 1866, Elias B. Hungerford of Corning patented a glass window blind with slats of colored glass. He searched for a glass company to manufacturer his inside shutters, but he preferred to have them made in Corning. He knew that Corning would be a good location for a glass company because of its canal and rail transportation, the availability of coal in nearby Pennsylvania, the proximity to markets for glass products, and its supply of workers.

Hungerford suggested to the Houghtons that they move to Corning. They were receptive to his proposal to leave Brooklyn because the cost of living and wages were high, coal and materials were expensive, and a major fire necessitated new construction. Hungerford convinced local investors to contribute $50,000 if the Brooklyn Flint Glass Company would invest $75,000. The $50,000 raised in Corning included $10,000 each from Erastus Corning and Theodore Olcott of the original Corning Company and Joseph Fellows, the agent for the Pulteney Estates. Trustees of the new company, the Corning Flint Glass Company, included Amory Houghton, Sr., Amory Houghton, Jr., and Theodore Wolcott.

In June, 1868, construction began on a T-shaped building that required two-thirds of a million bricks. The building had two 100-foot chimneys, one for each furnace. The Houghtons convinced Hoare & Dailey, a Long Island glass cutting firm, to open a facility in Corning on the second floor of the new building. Corning Flint Glass made the glass blanks and Hoare & Dailey performed the glasscutting and marketed the finished products. Over 100 experienced glassmakers moved from Brooklyn to Corning, and the new factory began the production of glass on October 22, 1868.

By 1869, the new company was headed for financial trouble. The post-Civil War economic boom was waning, competition was keen, and the Houghtons were unable to sell the Brooklyn factory. Competition was principally from larger glass companies, particularly in Pittsburgh, which had most of the the Pennsylvania market for glass. The new company's problems were compounded by the fact that their supply of bituminous coal from Blossburg in the northern tier of Pennsylvania was not suitable for the furnaces in the new Corning plant.

On September 15, 1870, Alexander Olcutt of Corning was appointed receiver for the Corning Flint Glass Company, and Amory Houghton, Sr., retired to his farm in Westchester County. In early 1871, Nathan Cushing, a Boston businessman, bought the firm and appointed Amory Houghton, Jr., manager. The next four years, which included the Panic of 1873, were difficult for the fledgling company. In spite of the country's poor economy, Amory Houghton, Jr., purchased the company on credit from Cushing. In 1875, the company was reorganized and became Corning Glass Works, Inc. Charles Houghton, H. P. Sinclaire, and J. J. Tully were elected partners. Houghton became president and treasurer, Charles was vice president and sales manager, and Sinclaire was elected secretary.

Hoare & Dailey continued to produce cut crystal of the highest quality. In 1870, the glasscutting firm received an order from President Grant for $1,000 worth of glassware. Corning Glass Works supplied the blanks.

Houghton was a strong community supporter who was perceived as a capable business person with integrity. Even in difficult economic times he was able to obtain credit without collateral. Part of the Houghtons' success during this period was due to their capitalizing on the growth of railroads in the country. In 1877, Charles Houghton designed and patented a lens for railroad signals with the bevels on the inside of the lens. Moving the corrugation to the inside surface reduced significantly the buildup of dust, ice, and snow because the outside surface of the lens was smooth. The company began to specialize in glassware for the pharmaceutical industry such as thermometer tubing. The company's business increased dramatically in the 1880s when bulb blanks were required to make Edison's latest product, the electric lamp. Corning Glass Works became the largest producer of light bulb blanks in the country.

Houghton continued to be an active supporter of community activities, both in service and in contributions. He was active in his church and served as member and president of the school board. Amory Houghton, Jr., died on November 5, 1909, at the age of seventy-two. On November 6, the Corning *Daily Journal* paid this tribute to him:

> He listened patiently to the complaints of his employees; he even took time to investigate in small matters so that no injustice might be done. To those employees suffering from disability on account of age or illness, he was especially kind and generous, the only consideration imposed being silence as to the amount of the donation or pension and also as to its donor.
>
> Mr. Houghton took pleasure in making satisfactory and noble use of the means which had been accumulated by the strength of his brain, the industry of his hands, and the steady clearness of his vision. He was a true and staunch friend of those whom he liked or whose opinion he valued.
>
> For many years the most influential citizen of Corning, he never was arrogant, demonstrative or showy in the display of his powers or his resources, but to the end of his days was modest, simple and direct, like all great men. He was a rugged type of man with an inflexible standard of integrity. In business and in private life, he hewed to an unswerving line of honor and honesty and uprightness.

John D. Rockefeller

John Davison Rockefeller, founder of the Standard Oil Company, was born on July 8, 1839, in the Town of Richford, Tioga County. He was the second child of William Avery Rockefeller and Eliza Davison Rockefeller. William Rockefeller was a businessman, a trader, and a salesman for herbal remedies and patent medicines. He was adventuresome, impulsive, outgoing, and intolerant of opposing viewpoints. Eliza was intelligent, frugal, religious, and serene, with a strong belief in common sense and hard work.

In 1843, the Rockefellers moved to the Town of Moravia at the southern end of Owasco Lake. Most of William Rockefeller's income came from horse trading and selling patent medicines. He sold the Moravia property and moved to Owego, where the family lived on River Road opposite Hiawatha Island in the Susquehanna River. John D. Rockefeller attended the River District School and the Owego Academy.

In the summer of 1853, the Rockefeller family moved to Cleveland, Ohio. Young Rockefeller attended Cleveland High School, received his high school diploma in 1855, and then attended Folsom Commercial College. At Folsom's, he learned banking, bookkeeping, business computation, exchange, and mercantile practice. William Rockefeller stressed concentration, dependability, honesty, industriousness, and self-reliance with his sons. He once told a neighbor: "I trade with the boys and skin 'em and I just beat 'em every time I can. I want to make 'em sharp."

Upon graduating from Folsom's, Rockefeller spent several weeks looking for a job, but not just any job. "I did not go to any small establishments ... I was after something big." On September 26, 1855, he accepted a position as bookkeeper and clerk with Hewitt & Tuttle, commission merchants and produce shippers. He didn't even discuss salary: "I cared very little about that." The company "was delightful to me—all the method and system of the office."

Rockefeller learned about jobbers, merchants, railroads, and lake steamships, but particularly about transportation. Fast-growing Cleveland had five railroads serving it in the 1850s. In 1858, Rockefeller was ready for the next level of challenge, and that was to go into business for himself. He found a partner with similar interests, Maurice B. Clark, and they formed a partnership as commission merchants dealing in grain, hay, meat, and sundries. They each contributed $2,000 to the business and opened Clark & Rockefeller on March 18, 1859.

His partner said of Rockefeller, "He was methodical to an extreme, careful as to details and exacting to a fraction. If there was a cent due us, he wanted it. If there was a cent due a customer, he wanted the customer to have it." Rockefeller gave generously to his church. He engaged in considerable self-counseling: "I was afraid I could not stand up to prosperity, and I tried to teach myself not to get puffed up with any foolish notions."

On August 27, 1859, Colonel Edwin Drake opened the first commercial oil well in the United States in Titusville, Pennsylvania. Large quantities of petroleum were shipped to Cleveland, and a number of refineries were built along the Cuyahoga River. Clark & Rockefeller handled consignments of crude oil and kerosene. They knew that there was money to be made in the oil business. Rockefeller observed that drilling for oil was highly speculative, but once you had the oil, it had to be refined. Oil refining was much more of a sure thing than oil exploration and production, and refining costs were low.

Samuel Adams, an English friend of Clark, and two of Clark's brothers joined them in an oil refining business called Andrews, Clark & Company. At this time, the Atlantic & Great Western Railroad opened between the Pennsylvania oil fields and Cleveland, which was already connected to New York City by the Erie Railroad. Later, the New York Central-Lake Shore system opened across northern Ohio and made Cleveland even more of a rail center.

Although Rockefeller was working long hours at the new business, he did not neglect his social life. In March, 1864, he became engaged to Laura Spelman, who was the daughter of a wealthy Cleveland businessman. They were married on September 8, 1864.

Andrews, Clark & Company built their first refinery on Kingsbury run, a tributary of the Cuyahoga River, which was the best location in the Cleveland Area. The three-acre site was on the Atlantic & Great Western Railroad and had barge access to Lake Erie. The site was soon expanded to sixty acres and then to one hundred acres.

Inevitably, strains developed in the partnership of the fast-growing refinery. Rockefeller had disagreements with Clark's brothers who were concerned about expanding too fast. Andrews sided with Rockefeller, but Clark voted with his two brothers. Therefore, Rockefeller came out on the short end of most votes. During the winter of 1865, Rockefeller bought out the Clarks and continued the oil business in the name of Rockefeller & Andrews. In 1866, Rockefeller brought his brother, William, into the partnership and opened a second refinery, the Standard Works, at the head of Kingsbury run.

In 1867, Henry Flagler joined the partnership to deal with the railroad men; he was very effective at his job. Cleveland beat out Pittsburgh as a refining center for several reasons: it had more abundant capital and labor, it was a a larger and more rapidly growing city, and it was closer to western markets. However, Cleveland's main advantage was that it had multiple railroads, whereas Pittsburgh was locked into the Pennsylvania Railroad. Flagler was an expert at playing the Cleveland railroads against one another to hold down transportation costs. This was particularly critical when the bottom fell out of the oil market in 1866 and 1867. Many small refineries went out of business.

In the early 1870s, Rockefeller met with his major competitors in the refining business. He told them to join with Standard Oil to take advantage of economies of scale or they would be forced out of business. When he proposed this, there were many refineries in the Pennsylvania oil region and in New York State, as well as twelve in Philadelphia and twenty-two in Pittsburgh. In the end, oil refining was a virtual monopoly; in April, 1878, Rockefeller refined 33,000,000 barrels a year out of a total of 36,000,000 in the United States. By 1880, Standard Oil refined 95% of the total oil output of the United States.

Allan Nevins analyzed the man in his biography, *John D. Rockefeller*:

> ... to a singular degree it was a career dominated
> by logic and plan. Some of the most famous of
> American lives are full of the unpredictable, the
> fortuitous, and the illogical. Not so with
> Rockefeller. His nature, for all its strength was
> simple; his intellect, never clouded by emotion,
> was direct and analytical; his will, fixed on a few

large purposes, was unwavering. With no great personal magnetism, or versatility, or breadth, he accomplished two epochal tasks; he set an original pattern in the efficient organization of industry, and an equally original pattern in the superintendence of benefactions. He was not a mere rearranger or manipulator of existing forces; he was a creator of new ideas and new systems. By his clarity of thought, keenness of foresight, and strength of purpose, he made his life an important part of the nation's history.

Isaac Merritt Singer

Isaac Merritt Singer, promoter of the sewing machine, was born near Troy, New York, on October 27, 1811. He was the eighth and youngest child of Adam and Ruth Singer. Adam, a cooper and millwright, moved his family to Oswego shortly after Isaac's birth. Isaac did not have a happy childhood; his parents were divorced when he was ten years old. Adam Singer remarried, and young Isaac didn't get along with his stepmother. He left home at the age of twelve, in his words, "without money, without friends, without education, and possessed of nothing but a strong constitution and prolific brain [and without humility, for that matter]."

In 1822, Singer moved to Rochester—which was experiencing a boom due to the construction of the Erie Canal—to live with an older brother. He worked part of the year as a laborer and went to school the remainder of the year. In 1830, he moved to Auburn, where he accepted a job manufacturing lathe-making equipment. He established a nomadic pattern early; it was to become a way of life.

Singer's goal in life was to be an actor. In fact, he was one of those people who was, inherently, an actor. Throughout his life, he frequently talked about his ambition to be on the stage. He was good-looking, over six feet tall, blond-haired, and outgoing. He possessed considerable assertiveness and charisma; he had a knack of winning people over to his viewpoint. These personal qualities served him well in promoting the sewing machine in later years. Women were charmed by him; he instilled trust in people, which a number of his partners lived to regret.

In 1830, Singer joined a group of players in Rochester. His Shakespearean roles with this troupe were his first acting experience. In December 1830, he married Catherine Haley of Palmyra. Catherine was fifteen when they married, and initially they lived with her parents. Singer continued to act but he worked as a woodworker and dry goods clerk in Port Gibson when he wasn't on the stage. In 1835, Singer and his wife moved to New York City, where he accepted a position with Hoe's Press. A year later, he left Hoe's Press and joined a troupe of traveling players as their advance man.

Singer traveled and did odd jobs over the next two years. In 1839, he invented a rock-drilling machine that was powered by horses walking in a circle to turn a crank supported by wooden framework. He patented the invention, sold the patent for $2,000, and returned to his first love, acting. He founded the Merritt Players in Chicago; they stayed together until 1844, when they disbanded in Fredericksburg, Ohio. Singer worked for a press in Fredericksburg, where he developed a machine for carving wooden type for printers. He moved to Pitttsburgh and then to New York City in search of larger markets for his invention, for which he received a patent on April 19, 1849.

The design of the machine was ingenious. A parallelogram device, or pantograph, was used to move the cutter and follow the letter or number being traced. However, Singer's timing was off; wooden type was being replaced with lead type, which could be melted down and reused. Singer was now thirty-eight years old and, by any criteria, couldn't be considered a success. His personal qualities of high motivation and boundless optimism prevented him from settling into a quiet, secure existence. He was a driven man.

In June 1850, George Zieber, a Philadelphia book publisher and jobber, financed a prototype of Singer's machine. In search of customers, they took the prototype to Boston, where they rented a room in Orson Phelps' shop. Phelps manufactured sewing machines that didn't work well and required frequent maintenance. Phelps asked Singer to redesign the machine to make it more reliable. Phelps convinced Singer that there was more money to be made from sewing machines than from typecarving machines.

Singer formed a way of thinking that became his credo in establishing his fortune: "I don't give a damn for the invention, the dimes are what I'm after." Singer redesigned the sewing machine, and he and Phelps applied for a patent. They encountered considerable resistance to their machine from customers who had tried earlier machines and were dissatisfied with them. Singer was in his element when promoting the redesigned machine. He was an actor and an inventor, but he demonstrated clearly that his real strength was as a promoter.

Singer realized that neither he nor Zieber had the necessary financial or legal background required as the business grew. Singer offered Edward Clark, a partner in the law firm of Jordan, Clark and Company, a one-third share of the business for his services. Clark was a vital addition to the business and was the source of many innovations that generated profits for the enterprise.

Clark was effective in dealing with the patent suits for the sewing machine, but he couldn't prevent Elias Howe from winning a suit against them. The design of the sewing machine had evolved from the contribution of many inventors, including Howe. In July, 1854, Singer was directed by the court to pay Howe $15,000 and a royalty of twenty-five dollars per machine.

Clark conceived of the idea of leasing sewing machines with an option to buy; this opened the market to housewives who couldn't afford the purchase price. The I. M. Singer Company expanded its manufacturing and sales to Europe; by 1861, it sold more machines in Europe than in the United States. The I. M. Singer Company was one of the earliest multi-national corporations.

In 1863, Clark and Singer dissolved their partnership, and Singer retired as a wealthy man. Singer and his wife moved to England and built a mansion called the "Wigwam" near Torquay, on the South Devon coast. The Wigwam had a private theatre; Singer never outgrew being an actor. However, he didn't live to see the Wigwam completed. He developed a heart condition, and the combination of a chill and heart problems caused his death on July 23, 1875. He was buried in Torquay cemetery.

Elmer Sperry

Elmer Ambrose Sperry, inventor of the gyroscope, was born in Cincinnatus, Cortland County, on January 1, 1860. He was the only child of Stephen Sperry and Mary Burst Sperry. Sperry's mother died in childbirth, and his aunt, Helen Sperry, raised him for his first seven years. In 1867, Helen married and moved to Virgil; young Sperry moved in with his grandparents. Stephen Sperry had a traveling job, so his parents and his sister were important in the early shaping of his son's values. Before Sperry was ten, his grandparents moved from their farm to the Village of Cortland, and he moved with them.

The arrival of the Syracuse, Binghamton, & New York Railroad in Cortland in the 1850s and the Utica, Ithaca, & Elmira Railroad in the 1870s accelerated the shift of Cortland from an agricultural center to a manufacturing center. The Cortland Normal School, which provided teacher-training and two years of tuition-free college education, opened in 1869. It played a significant role in Sperry's preparation for his life's work. He didn't distinguish himself in the liberal arts courses, but he excelled in the technology courses, particularly in the emerging electrical technology.

Sperry's first invention was an automatically regulated electric generator that supplied constant current despite load variation. One of Cortland's largest companies, the Cortland Wagon Company, provided him with a laboratory and funded his development efforts. The company also helped him to obtain patents for his inventions.

Between 1880 and 1882, he developed a complete arc-light system, which was installed in Chicago. In February 1883, the

Sperry Electric Light, Motor, and Car Brake Company was incorporated in Chicago and capitalized for $1,000,000. The new company's most visible display was the brilliantly lit 300-foot tower of the Board of Trade building. However, the company had many competitors; in August, 1887, it went out of business.

Sperry worked long hours with his struggling business, but he was also active socially. He met and dated Zula Goodman in Chicago. They corresponded frequently when he was away on business trips. Sperry and Zula were married on June 28, 1887.

In October 1888, he founded the Elmer A. Sperry Company. The breadth of his work with the company was impressive. Two of his early inventions were an electric mining machine and an electric locomotive for mine haulage. He also designed a streetcar for a syndicate of Cleveland businessmen. From 1888 to 1890, his development effort spanned electric light and power, mining machinery, streetcars, electric automobiles, batteries, and electrochemistry.

In 1905, the Sperrys moved to Brooklyn, New York, where his electrochemistry work was being done. While living in Brooklyn, Sperry began the work for which he is best known—the development of the gyroscope. In early 1907, he researched all available literature on gyroscopes. He wanted to apply gyroscopes to useful purposes, generally, but his initial interest was the stabilizing effects of the gyroscope.

His first gyroscopic invention was the Sperry marine stabilizer. The U.S. Navy financed the development effort; they wanted gyrostabilizers for their ships. On May 21, 1908, Sperry filed his first patent for a ship's gyroscope. The Navy needed ship stabilizers to provide a stable gun platform for their warships. The complex system of modern naval gunnery is based on Sperry's inventions.

Early in 1911, the first trial of of a gyrostabilizer on an active warship was conducted on the *USS Worden,* a 433-ton destroyer. Carl Norden, who developed the Norden bombsight for World War II, assisted Sperry in this trial. The first gyrostabilizer was fifty inches in diameter and weighed 4,000 pounds. Sperry's next effort was the development of the gyrocompass for the navy, particularly for use in submarines. Trials of the first Sperry gyrocompass were conducted on the 800-ton destroyer, *USS Drayton.*

On April 14, 1910, Sperry established the Sperry Gyroscope Company. The new company's sales grew 50% per year from 1911 through 1914, when World War I caused a significant increase in foreign sales. On one day in 1914, the Sperry Gyroscope Company, which had assets worth $1,000,000, received orders worth $832,000.

During World War I, Sperry designed and manufactured electrical gyroscopes for torpedoes that enabled them to complete long trajectories with accuracy. He also developed aerial torpedoes with automatic gyrocontrol that were effective at a range of thirty-five miles. He worked with Glenn H. Curtiss in developing stabilizers for navy aircraft. Sperry's son, Lawrence, became a test pilot for Curtiss. In 1915, the Secretary of the Navy, Josephus Daniels, appointed Sperry to the Navy Consulting Board.

On July 28, 1926, Sperry resigned as president of the Sperry Gyroscope Company at the age of sixty-six. On April 7, 1930, he suffered a stroke. He died after a gallbladder operation at St. John's Hospital, Brooklyn, on June 16, 1930.

Thomas Watson

Thomas John Watson, the founder of the IBM Corporation, was born on February 17, 1874, in East Campbell, Steuben County. He was the first of five children of Thomas Watson and Jane White Watson. Watson's father was in the lumber business. The family lived in East Campbell until young Watson was seven years old. Subsequently, they lived in Cooper's Plains, Addison, and Painted Post. These moves within Steuben County were driven by the diminishing stands of trees and the competitiveness of the lumber industry.

Watson's father wanted his son to study law, but young Watson didn't want to pursue that career. He applied for a temporary teaching certificate for three years and then enrolled at the Albany Teachers' College. However, one day of teaching changed his mind: "I can't go into a classroom with a bunch of children at nine o'clock in the morning and stay until four."

Watson enrolled at the Miller School of Commerce in Elmira. In May, 1892, he completed the accounting and business courses there and accepted a position as a bookkeeper in Painted Post. He soon decided that "he couldn't sit on a high stool and keep books all my life." He certainly formed opinions quickly about what he didn't want to do.

A neighbor of the Watsons', Willard Bronson, operated a hardware store and a consignment business. He acquired Estey organs, pianos, and sewing machines, and sold them on consignment around the countryside from a wagon. Watson went on the road selling for Bronson; it was the first of his many sales jobs.

He learned the importance of a good appearance and of making a good first impression. He sold for Bronson for two years without a raise in salary and without many kind words from his boss. Bronson was astounded when Watson quit the job after two years. Only then did Bronson offer him a raise. He even offered to sell the business to Watson. Watson's father suggested that he seek opportunity outside the area; he thought that Buffalo might be a good place to look for a job.

Watson accepted a job selling sewing machines for the Wheeler and Wilcox Company. However, after a short time, he was let go. It wasn't because of any shortcoming on his part, but because they didn't need another salesman. C. B. Barron, a co-worker who was let go at the same time, went to work selling shares in the Buffalo Building and Loan Association. Barron invited Watson to join him. He sold shares in the Buffalo Building and Loan Association until Barron ran off with all of the building and loan funds, including Watson's commissions.

Watson applied for a job with the National Cash Register Company. He met the manager of the Buffalo office, John J. Range. Range wasn't interested in hiring him, but Watson persisted. Watson made no sales in the first two weeks, and Range made his disappointment clear. Watson absorbed Range's constructive criticism and, within a year, was one of the most successful National Cash Register salesmen in the East. By the time he was twenty-five, Watson was the top salesman in the Buffalo office.

John Henry Patterson, chief executive of the National Cash Register Company, made the cash register virtually indispensible to businessmen. Then he monopolized its manufacture and distribution. Patterson was a successful manager because he combined paternalism with an emphasis on training. He realized that his salesmen responded to the fear of punishment and the promise of reward. Patterson knew just how hard he could push Watson. He became the prime shaper of Watson's life over the next eleven years.

In the summer of 1899, Patterson selected Watson to be the manager of the Rochester office. Watson moved the sales of the Rochester branch from near the bottom of all the company's offices to sixth from the top within several months. He used some ruthless techniques to beat his main competitor, the Hallwood Company. His performance was followed closely by Hugh Chalmers, the company's general manager, and by Patterson.

The National Cash Register Company had between eighty and ninety-five percent of the sales of new cash registers. However, Patterson wanted to take aggressive action to reduce the impact of the sales of used cash registers. Patterson gave Watson $1,000,000 to set up a company to front for the National Cash Register Company in driving out the used cash register competition in the United States.

Watson established Watson's Cash Register and Second Hand Exchange in Manhattan, undercut the prices of his main competitor, and bought him out. He repeated this activity in Philadelphia and Chicago. He made the second-hand machine business a profitable unit of the company and was offered a position at the company headquarters in Dayton.

Eventually, Chalmers could no longer tolerate Patterson's dictatorial style and, as the number two man in the company, disagreed with some of his non-business decisions. Chalmers was fired, and Watson was made general manager in his place. Patterson went to Europe for two years, and, by the time he returned, Watson had doubled the sales volume (to 100,000 cash registers a year in 1910). The increase in sales was partly due to the redesign of the cash register by Charles (Boss) Kettering; he replaced the manual operation of the cash register with an electric motor. Kettering moved on to General Motors where he designed the self-starter for automobiles.

The company's monopolistic practices in the second-hand cash register business caught up with them. On February 22, 1913, Patterson, Watson, and twenty-eight other company managers were indicted on three counts of criminal conspiracy. They were placed on trial in Cincinnati for restraint of trade and maintaining a monopoly.

While he was awaiting trial, Watson met Jeanette Kittridge of Dayton. Her father was the president of a railroad car manufacturing company. The Kittridges were neighbors and friends of Patterson, and Jeanette was Patterson's choice of a wife for Watson.

On February 13, 1913, Patterson, Watson, and the other managers were found to be guilty as charged. Patterson was released on $10,000 bail, and Watson was released on $5,000 bail. Watson wanted to postpone the wedding until the results of the appeal were known. Jeanette disagreed. She was as strong-willed as he was; together they made a powerful team. Shortly after their marriage, Watson was fired, just as Chalmers had been abruptly terminated earlier. Watson began to look for another job.

Charles Flint had assembled a company called the Computing-Tabulating-Recording Company (CTR) by combining a computing scales company, the Tabulating Machine Company, and a time recorder company. CTR was unprofitable, and Flint was looking for a new manager. He offered the position to Watson; however, Watson was not elected to the board of directors because of the pending appeal of the law suit. On March 13, 1915, the District Court verdict was set aside, and a new trial was granted. No new trial was conducted, and Watson was cleared of any wrongdoing. CTR promptly elected Watson president and general manager of the company.

Watson authorized the redesign of the Hollerith tabulating machine, and the Tabulating Machine Company became the star unit of CTR. From 1914 until 1920, CTR's gross income increased from $4,000,000 to $14,000,000. In 1924, Watson renamed the company International Business Machines (IBM). Watson was appointed chief executive officer and, for the first time, was really in charge of the company.

Unlike many companies, IBM expanded during the Great Depression. By 1940, IBM was still small ($50,000,000 sales per year), but it had become the largest company in the office equipment industry. World War II made IBM a large company. From 1939 to 1945, gross income increased from $40,000,000 to $140,000,000. By 1949, the company was five times larger than it had been in 1939.

In 1952, Thomas Watson, Jr., became president and his brother, Arthur, was appointed general manager of the IBM World Trade Corporation. From 1914 through 1953, assets grew by a multiple of 24 times, employees by 34 times, the data processing business by 316 times, and development expenditures by 500 times.

On May 8, 1956, Thomas Watson, Jr., became chief executive officer of the IBM Corporation. Just over a month later, on June 19th, Thomas Watson, Sr., died of a heart attack.

John North Willys

John North Willys, the second of three children of David Smith Willys and Lydia North Willys, was born on October 25, 1873, in Canandaigua. Willys attended Canandaigua Academy, but he left school at the age of fifteen to operate a laundry with a partner in Seneca Falls. He studied law briefly with an attorney in Canandaigua and from 1896 to 1898 was a traveling salesman for the Boston Woven Hose & Rubber Company. In 1898, he bought the Elmira Arms Company, a bicycle, phonograph, and sporting goods store in Elmira. He specialized in bicycles and became a wholesaler as well as a retailer. By 1900, Elmira Arms had annual sales of $500,000.

He became interested in automobiles around the turn of the century. In 1901, when an Elmira doctor purchased a Pierce

Motorette, Willys went to Buffalo to offer to become an agent for the George N. Pierce Company, manufacturer of bicycles and automobiles. He sold Pierce automobiles as well as the Jeffery Rambler and the American, which was manufactured in Indianapolis. In 1906, he contracted to sell the total production of the Overland Auto Company, another Indianapolis manufacturer. He deposited $10,000 with Overland as security.

Due to poor management and the Panic of 1907, Overland produced few cars that year. Willys traveled to Indianapolis and found that Overland was $80,000 in debt, had virtually no parts inventory, could not pay its employees, and was headed for bankruptcy. He paid the shortfall required to meet the payroll, raised $10,000 to pay the most pressing of Overland's bills, and persuaded the creditors to be patient. He assembled and sold Overlands from the few parts on hand, obtained more supplies on credit, and repeated the process. In 1908, the company, now called Willys-Overland, produced 465 cars, paid off its creditors, and generated a net profit of over $50,000. It was an impressive example of Willys' entrepreneurial skills.

In 1909, the company outgrew the Indianapolis plant and assembled cars in a circus tent. Willys purchased the facilities of the defunct Pope-Toledo Company in Toledo, Ohio, for $285,000. The revenues from selling off the excess equipment and material almost paid for the plant. In 1910, 15,598 Willys-Overlands were sold, and by 1912 only Ford sold more cars than Willys' company. In 1914, Willys acquired the Edwards Motor Car Company, manufacturer of the Edwards-Knight car with a sleeve-valve engine developed by Charles Y. Knight. The four-cylinder car was renamed the Willys-Knight.

In 1914, Willys acquired the Electric Auto-Lite Company, which manufactured automobile generators. He also obtained a controlling interest in the Curtiss Aeroplane & Motor Corporation of Buffalo, the Moline Plow Company, and the Fisk Rubber Company of Chicopee Falls, Massachusetts. By 1915, Willys had 18,000 employees at Toledo and 20,000 at plants in Buffalo, Elyria, Flint, and Pontiac. Production reached a peak in 1916 with sales of 142,779 Willys-Overlands.

One of Willys' greatest innovations was the organizing of the

Guaranty Securities Company on November 8, 1915. The Toledo company was formed to allow cars to be purchased on the installment plan. Up to that time, most cars were paid for upon delivery. When production capacity began to exceed sales, new techniques were required to sell cars, particularly the medium- and high-priced ones. The Guaranty Securities Company offered financing for Dodge, Ford, General Motors, Hudson, Maxwell, Reo, and Studebaker cars, in addition to Willys-Overlands and Willys-Knights. The installment buying concept formed the basis for the General Motors Acceptance Corporation when it was formed in 1919.

Willys built ambulances and trucks for use in World War I, and in 1917 he formed the Willys Corporation as a holding Company for his diversified interests. The company was hurt by a strike at the Toledo plant that resulted in the death of two strikers and injuries to seventy others. No cars were produced at the Toledo facility from the spring of 1919 until year-end. The postwar recession of 1920 caused difficulties for all automobile companies, and Willys-Overland was no exception to the problems of overproduction and excessive inventories.

Willys had left the running of the company to others while he devoted his time to other interests. He had several homes and a $1 million yacht that he turned over to the government during World War I. He collected oil paintings, always with an "eye to the investment value. I only buy pictures that I could sell if I wanted to without loss." When he returned to Willys-Overland, he found that the company had debts of over $50 million. The bankers brought in Walter P. Chrysler at an annual salary of $1 million to turn the company around. One of Chrysler's first moves was to cut Willys' salary from $150,000 to $75,000. When told of the cut by Chrysler, Willys laughed, tossed his head, and said: "I guess we've put our problems in the right man's hands."

While still at Willys-Overland, Chrysler began to devote his turn-around abilities to the struggling Chalmers and Maxwell automobile companies. Chrysler gained control of these two companies along with the services of three key engineers to form the nucleus of his own company, which became the Chrysler Corporation.

Willys took control of Willys-Overland when Chrysler left. Willys accomplished another incredible turn-around:

- Deficits of $20 million in 1920-21 became profits of just under $20 million in 1925
- Cash on hand of under $300,000 in 1922 increased to $20,000,000 in 1925
- A balance sheet deficit of $43 million became a surplus of $25 million in 1925
- Production of 96,623 in 1922 increased to over 215,000 in 1925
- Common stock went from 4 1/2 in 1922 to 35 in 1925.
- Preferred stock increased from 24 to 124 in 1925.
- Domination by bankers became control by management
- The company went from the verge of bankruptcy to third place in the industry

In 1926, the company introduced the Overland Whippet, which sold for $545 to compete with the Model A Ford. In 1928, Willys-Overland sold a record 314,437 cars and had a net profit of $187,233,388. Willys made a substantial contribution to Hoover's presidential campaign that year.

In 1929, Willys sold his 800,000 shares of common stock in Willys-Overland to the Electric Auto-Lite Company for $25 million. He retained his preferred stock and gave up the presidency of the company to become chairman of the board. He took these actions in anticipation of receiving a diplomatic appointment from the Hoover administration. On March 1, 1930, Willys was named Ambassador to Poland. He advised Poland of measures to take to convert their largely agricultural economy to a more industrial economy.

On April 25, 1932, he resigned his ambassadorship to return to the Willys-Overland Company, which was again in financial trouble. The company went into receivership in February, 1933. Willys, the chairman of the board, was named the receiver. He concentrated on the production of the Whippet, the company's lowest cost model. All of his decisions had to be reviewed and approved by the court.

In January, 1935, he assumed the position of president in addition to his duties as chairman. The stress of saving the company began to affect his health. On August 26, 1935, he died of cerebral embolism. The man whose favorite saying was, "Learn to lose without squealing and to win without bragging" would not be around to complete the healing process for Willys-Overland. He was not a technical person; his strengths were in marketing, organizing, and promoting. His principal weakness was in controlling cost.

Willys-Overland became known during World War II for the production of the Jeep. It was rated for a quarter-ton payload and was designed to pull a thousand-pound trailer with its four-cylinder, L-head, 134.2 cubic inch displacement engine. The origin of the name, Jeep, is unclear, but it is thought to have been named for the U.S. Army designation, general purpose vehicle, or GP.

The American Bantam Car Company of Butler, Pennsylvania, provided the original design of the Jeep. Willys-Overland developed the design further, incorporating the running gear of the Willys-Overland automobile. Willys-Overland produced 361,000 of the 660,000 Jeeps produced during World War II. They were also produced by Ford and, in limited numbers, by American Bantam. In 1953, the Kaiser Company gained control of Willys-Overland. In 1970, Kaiser sold out to the American Motors Corporation, which was purchased by the Chrysler Corporation in 1987. The name, Willys, is gone from the U.S. automotive scene, but the heritage of John North Willys remains.

Harriet Tubman House, Auburn

Chapter 3

"Willing and voluntary service to others is the highest duty and glory in human life. . . . The men of talent are constantly forced to serve the rest. They make discoveries and inventions, order the battles, write the books, and produce the works of art. The benefit and enjoyment go to the whole. There are those who joyfully order their lives so that they may serve the welfare of mankind."

—W. G. Sumner

Samuel Hopkins Adams

Samuel Hopkins Adams, the son of Myron Adams, a Presbyterian minister, and Hester Rose Hopkins Adams, was born on January 26, 1871, in Dunkirk, New York. Hester Hopkins was the daughter of Professor Samuel W. Hopkins of the Auburn Theological Seminary. Adams attended public schools in Rochester and attended Hamilton College, the alma mater of his father, grandfather, and five uncles. Upon his graduation from Hamilton, he worked for the New York *Sun* for nine years.

Adams joined the staff of *McClure's Magazine,* where he specialized in writing about public health issues. His series of articles in *Collier's Weekly,* which exposed the quackery of patent medicine, aided in the passage of the first Pure Food and Drug Act. Public health was his speciality, and, although a layman, he was made an associate member of the American Medical Association. He was the first American author to write about medical science.

One of his most popular novels is *Revelry,* which is about the scandals of the Harding administration. It was suppressed in Washington and banned in Philadelphia, but 100,000 copies were sold. His later biography of Harding supported the material in the novel. He wrote a series of detective stories based on a character called Average Jones. He also wrote historical novels and novels such as *The Clarion, Siege,* and *Success,* which exposed urban evils. His favorite subject was idealism overcoming corruption and evil.

In 1946, he received the Critics' Award for his biography of his Hamilton classmate, Alexander Woollcott, the critic and journalist, of whom he said, "I had an affection for Aleck Woollcott, often admiring, sometimes complicated with shuddering." Many of Adams' books were adapted for the screen, including *Men in Her Life*, starring Clara Bow; *It Happened One Night,* with Claudette Colbert and Clark Gable; *The Gorgeous Hussy,* starring Joan Crawford; and *The Harvey Girls,* in 1942. His *Canal Town,* published in 1942, described the construction of the Erie Canal.

One of the last novels he wrote was *Tenderloin,* about life in New York during the time of Diamond Jim Brady. His *Grandfather Stories,* which was published when he was eighty-four, was a Book-of-the-Month selection. It contained many stories reprinted from the *New Yorker.*

Adams spent his summers on Owasco Lake. His grandfather built a home on the lake in 1886, which became Adams' father's home and later became Adams' home. He added onto it and named it Widewaters. His hobbies were antique-collecting, fishing, and tennis. He died at his winter home in Beaufort, South Carolina, on November 16, 1957.

Adams was a dedicated writer who observed: "If I were to repeat my career, I would ask nothing better than the life of a professional writer. It permits freedom of thought, action, and mode of existence, and this in an era in which individual choice, threatened as it is throughout an imperiled world, has never been so precious."

John D. Barrow

 John Dodgson Barrow was born in New York City on November 24, 1824. He was the oldest of ten children of John and Elizabeth Prior Barrow. The family moved to Skaneateles in 1839, when Barrow was fourteen. After a short stay in Skaneateles, he was sent to England to continue his schooling. It was an important move with respect to his career, since he decided to become an artist while he was in England.

He returned to Skaneateles at the age of nineteen, but realized that he would have to relocate to New York City because of the greater opportunities there. Barrow opened a studio in Manhattan in 1856, which was next door to the studio of Charles Loring Elliot, one of America's foremost portrait painters who was also a former resident of Skaneateles. Barrow was greatly influenced by Elliot's style and technique in the portraits that he painted at that time. One of Barrow's most well-known paintings is a portrait of Abraham Lincoln that is owned and displayed by the Chicago Historical Society.

Barrow became interested in landscape painting, partly due to the influence of another friend, George Inness, who was associated with the Hudson River School of art. Inness believed that a landscape painter should have a thorough knowledge of nature. Barrow was known for his blending of the "real" and the "ideal," as well as his effective use of light and shade. Although most of Barrow's paintings depicted the area around Skaneateles, he also painted the Adirondacks, the Delaware Water Gap, Lake George, and the New England scenery of Appledore Island, Keene Valley, and the White Mountains.

Between 1852 and 1879, Barrow's works were shown in nineteen of the Annual Exhibitions of the National Academy. His work was also displayed in exhibitions at the Athenaeum in Boston, the Pennsylvania Academy of Fine Arts in Philadelphia, and the Union League of New York City.

During his time as a professional artist in New York City, Barrow visited his family frequently in Skaneateles. He made many sketches of countryside in the Finger Lakes Region. After about twenty years of painting as a professional artist in New York City, he returned to Skaneateles permanently. Upon his return, he was invited to join the faculty of the Department of Fine Arts at Syracuse University.

Barrow was an active member of the community. He was a

trustee and president of the village, a director of the Skaneateles Library Association, and a vestryman of St. James Episcopal Church. He designed the Civil War memorial in Lake View cemetery.

He was a strong environmentalist who appreciated the natural beauty of the region and was concerned about its preservation. In his 1876 Centennial Address to the village, he said: "Let us not forget our local trusts and duties ... Let us especially remember our lake and its shores ... May we all do something ... so that after another hundred years, our successors shall meet together and rejoice and thank us for what we have done."

Barrow backed up his words with actions. When the Skaneateles Fire Department announced plans to build a firehouse on the shore of the lake in the village, he fought their proposal because it would block the view of the lake. The firemen's counterproposal was to build the firehouse on stilts so the lake could be viewed under the firehouse. Barrow responded by giving the fire department a parcel of his own land, away from the lake, on which they could build their firehouse.

His dream to have an art gallery in Skaneateles in which to display his work was fulfilled in 1900, when an annex to the Skaneateles Public Library was built. The artist financed its construction, and it is the home for over 300 of his paintings. Other Barrow paintings hang in the Everson Museum in Syracuse, the Onondaga County Public Library, and the Onondaga Historical Association.

Barrow also wrote poetry. Two of his published works are *Elliott in Skaneateles* (1897) and *Around Skaneateles Lake* (1907); some of his poems are included in the *Catalog of the John D. Barrow Art Gallery* (1908).

John D. Barrow was one of the "second generation" of American portrait painters upon whose philosophies the Hudson River School was founded. Members of the school did not all have the same style nor did they live in the same area (Frederick Church was one of the few that lived in the Hudson River Region). They had a common interest in depicting spectacular landscapes. They became the country's first coherent art movement and one in which eighteenth-century enlightenment was replaced with nineteenth-century romanticism.

The school was influenced by the English author, Edmund Burke, and the poet, William Wordsworth, who were inspired by nature. Thomas Cole was one of the founders of the Hudson River School in 1825, along with William Dunlap, Asher Duran, and John Trumbull. The "second generation" of American landscape artists flourished in the 1840s.

Thomas Cole's Grand Tour involved trips to the Adirondacks, Appledore Island off the coast of New Hampshire, Lake George, the Maine Woods, Niagara Falls, and the White Mountains in northern New Hampshire. Their mode of operation was to sketch during the summer and paint from the sketches during the winter. This was also the pattern followed by Frederick Church, who used his summers to reflect, to observe, and to gather ideas and material to be expanded upon in his studio during the winter. The goal of the painters of the Hudson River School was "to depict pure landscape in a realistic, convincing manner."

John D. Barrow died at the age of eighty-two at his home in Skaneateles on December 7, 1906. He never married and therefore left no legacy of children; however, he left a rich legacy that is on permanent display in the John D. Barrow Art Gallery in Skaneateles.

Clara Barton

Clarissa Harlowe Barton, founder of the American Red Cross, was born in North Oxford, Massachusetts, on December 25, 1821. She was the youngest of five children born to Stephen Barton, chief town administrator and state legislator, and Sally Stone Barton. Clarissa, who preferred to be called Clara, was raised, to an extent, as an only child, since the next youngest child, Sally, was twelve years older than she was.

Clara's favorite brother was David, who taught her to ride when she was three years old. In July, 1832, she saw her brother fall feet-first from the ridge post of a barn onto a pile of timber in the cellar. He developed a chronic headache, and, as the summer progressed, he contracted a fever. Ten-year-old Clara became her brother's nurse. In her words:

> From the first days and nights of his illness, I remained near his side. I could not be taken away from him, except by compulsion, and he was unhappy until my return. I learned to take all the directions for his medicines from his physicians … and to administer them like a genuine nurse … thus it came about that I was the accepted and acknowledged nurse of a man almost too ill to recover.

Two doctors told the Bartons that their son's condition was hopeless. Clara cheered him up, fed him, bathed him, and read to him. She rarely left his side for two years. Finally, a new doctor, who was a believer in "hydrotherapy," examined David. He moved the young man to his sanatorium and began water therapy. David returned home in three weeks and was fully recovered in six weeks. He owed his life to his little sister, who gave him constant care and the will to live long enough to be cured.

Clara had many relatives who were teachers, and, at the age of seventeen, she passed an oral examination and began to teach school. She was an excellent teacher and was known for her discipline. After teaching for twelve years, she enrolled at the Clinton Liberal Institute to further her education. Upon completion of the program at Clinton, she accepted a teaching position in Bordentown, New Jersey.

She built the enrollment of the Bordentown school up to 600 students, and the Board of Education decided that it was too large a school to be run by a woman. They hired as her superior a young man who was critical of her. Eventually, the emotional strain became intolerable. In 1854, she lost her voice, almost had a nervous breakdown, and resigned her position at the age of thirty-two.

Clara moved to Washington, D.C., to live with her sister, Sally. She worked for the U.S. Patent Office copying documents until 1857, when the incoming Buchanan administration replaced the Superintendent of the Patent Office. She returned to Massachusetts and supported herself by copying documents sent to her in the mail. In 1860, she returned to her job at the Patent Office when President Lincoln began his administration.

At the outbreak of the Civil War, Clara volunteered to help at the Washington Infirmary. She heard that the 6th Massachusetts regiment from Worchester had been attacked by a mob of Confederate sympathizers while traveling through Baltimore. Four men were killed, dozens were wounded, and all their baggage was stolen. They were dressed in winter uniforms and woolen underwear unsuitable for the spring and summer weather in Washington.

Using her own money, Clara furnished the men with summer underwear, eating utensils, food, pots, and pans, as well as handkerchiefs, needles, soap, thread, and towels. She advertised in the Worchester *Spy,* their hometown newspaper, that she would receive and distribute provisions for area servicemen. She received so many items that she had to ask the army quartermaster to warehouse them.

Clara heard that little medical care had been provided to the wounded after the disastrous First Battle of Bull Run. The wounded weren't treated, and they were left without food and water. She offered her services as a nurse, but she encountered resistance. In the 1860s, women weren't considered to be strong enough to deal with conditions at the front. Sense of propriety was an issue. Finally, she received the long-awaited permission from Dr. William Hammond, Surgeon-General of the U.S.: "Miss C. H. Barton has permission to go upon the sick transports in any direction—for the purpose of distributing comforts for the sick and wounded—of nursing them, always subject to the direction of the surgeon in charge."

She was introduced to battlefield nursing at the Battle of Cedar Run in Virginia. She arrived with a wagon load of supplies just as brigade surgeon James Dunn was considering how to treat the wounded without supplies. He called her the "Angel of the Battlefield," a name that stayed with her. Her second battlefield service was treating the staggering casualties of the Second Battle of Bull Run in August, 1862.

At the Battle of Chantilly, she had three sleepless nights in a row; she slept for two hours on the fourth night lying in water from the heavy rains. Returning to Washington, the train carrying the wounded was almost captured by the Confederate cavalry, who burned the station from which they had just departed.

At Antietam, when she arrived with supplies that were vitally needed, brigade surgeon Dunn was using corn husks for bandages. While she was giving a drink of water to a wounded soldier, a bullet passed through her sleeve, and the soldier fell back dead. Another soldier asked her to use his pocket knife to remove a musket ball from his cheek; he couldn't wait for the surgeon. With a sergeant holding the soldier's head, she removed the ball. In 1864, Clara was Superintendent of Nurses for General Benjamin Butler's Army of the James. She organized hospitals and their staffs and supervised their administration.

After the war, Clara collected information on soldiers who were missing in action. As with her nursing jobs, she worked without pay. She located over 22,000 missing soldiers; eventually, she was paid $15,000 for her efforts. In 1868, she was on the verge of a nervous breakdown, similar to her experience in 1854 in Bordentown. She went to Europe to rest and stayed with friends in Switzerland.

Dr. Louis Appia of the Red Cross visited her. He was familiar with her work during the Civil War; he asked why the United States had rejected his offer three times to join the Red Cross. Clara had not heard of the organization founded by Jean-Henri Dunant. After witnessing the bloody Battle of Solferino with 40,000 casualties, Dunant wrote *A Memory of Solferino* in which he proposed the formation of an international relief organization. The Swiss-based organization chose for their symbol a red cross on a white background—the reverse of the color scheme of the Swiss flag. Clara was influenced by Dunant and began to consider forming a relief organization in the United States.

In 1873, Clara returned home. She spent the next four years convalescing from a nervous disorder that caused migraine headaches and periods of blindness. In March 1876, she moved to Dansville, New York, to improve her health at a sanatorium called "Our Home on the Hillside." After a year's rest with wholesome food in a peaceful environment, Clara completely regained her health. She liked Dansville and made many close friends. She bought a home in Dansville and lived there for ten years.

While living in Dansville, Clara worked to bring the United States into the International Red Cross. She discovered that the reason for the resistance in the United States to joining the international organization was because it was considered to be a wartime relief organization. Clara pointed out the need for such an organization in addressing peacetime disasters, such as earthquakes and floods. She went to Washington, D.C., to convince President Garfield's cabinet of the importance of a U.S. role in the international relief organization.

Upon her return to Dansville, the townspeople asked her to help form a local chapter of the Red Cross. On August 22, 1881, the first American chapter of the Red Cross was established in Dansville. The first disaster addressed by the chapter was a Michigan forest fire that took 500 lives and destroyed 1,500 homes. On March 16, 1882, Congress signed the Treaty of Geneva, which made the U.S. a member of the International Red Cross. Clara was appointed as the first president of the American Red Cross. She served in that position until May 1904. She died in Washington, D.C., on April 12, 1912.

Frank Gannett

Frank Ernest Gannett, the third son of Maria Brooks Gannett and Charles Gannett, was born on September 15, 1876, on the family farm on Gannett Hill. Gannett Hill, the highest elevation in West-Central New York, is 1,600 feet above adjacent Canandaigua Lake and 2,200 feet above sea level. One year after Gannett was born, the family moved to the Town of Atlanta, which was then called Blood's Depot. He was educated partly in the public schools and partly tutored at home.

At the age of nine, Gannett, the founder of the Gannett chain of newspapers, had his first job. Not surprisingly, it was delivering papers—for the Rochester *Democrat and Chronicle*. Tenant farming was difficult for Charles Gannett, who had served with General Custer during the Civil War and had ridden with General Phil Sheridan's cavalry through the Shenandoah Valley. When Gannett was twelve, the family moved to a farm in nearby Wallace. Two years later, they moved again, to the the Town of Bolivar. The family was poor, but, by any measure, Gannett had a happy childhood.

Charles Gannett was the proprietor of the Clark House hotel in Bolivar, which thirty years previously had been one of the boom towns in the Bradford oil field. Since Bolivar was outside the circulation area of the Rochester *Democrat and Chronicle,* Gannett delivered newspapers for the Buffalo *News* and the Buffalo *Times.* He began to write articles for the Buffalo *News;* he sold his first article for $1.00. At the age of fifteen, he caught for the town baseball team and played the cornet in the town band.

The Gannett family moved across the state to Oneonta where Charles Gannett was proprietor of the Wilson House hotel. Young Gannett stayed in Bolivar to complete his studies at the Bolivar Academy. He supported himself by bartending at the Newton House, Bolivar's other hostelry. In 1893, he graduated from the Bolivar Academy. The speech that he delivered at the graduation ceremony was entitled "The Press and Public Opinion." He received high marks in more subjects that any other student in the New York State Regents' Examinations that year.

Gannett worked one more year in Bolivar to earn money to attend college. He took a correspondence course from Bryant and Stratton in bookkeeping, a subject that was not offered in high school. He won a $200 a year Cornell University Scholarship that was based on his high marks in a competitive examination. In the fall of 1894, at the age of eighteen, he went to Ithaca to begin his studies at Cornell.

His scholarship paid his tuition, and he supported himself with four jobs: waiting on tables in a student boarding house, operating a laundry route, collecting and delivering for a pants presser, and ushering in Sage Memorial Chapel. He was strongly influenced by hearing many of the finest theologians of the day who spoke in the Sage Chapel. Eventually, he became head usher at the non-sectarian chapel. He also participated in military drill with the Cadet Corps, which was compulsory since Cornell was a land-grant institution. Later, Gannett observed, "There was no leisure in any of my college years."

In the spring of his freshman year, Gannett was elected as his class representative on the board of editors of the Cornell *Sun*, the university's daily newspaper. An editor's annual share of the *Sun's* profits was $200, which allowed him to drop his job of waiting on tables. His assignment as reporter for the *Sun* was covering Cornell President Jacob Schurman's office. Gannett's ability to take shorthand was rewarded one day when Andrew Carnegie spoke to the student body without using a prepared text. The student reporter published every word of Carnegie's speech.

Gannett used the advice that his mother had given him. "Make the most of opportunity and spend less than you earn." He also took the advice of Andrew Carnegie: "Put all of your eggs in one basket, where you can watch them." This financial advice was counter to the popular saying, but Gannett followed it; his single basket was the newspaper business.

Gannett majored in liberal arts, the first two years of which were required courses. The elective courses that he chose during his last two years at Cornell included criminal law, economics, and the psychology of salesmanship. During summers, he peddled the medical compendium, *The Cottage Physician,* in rural areas. He won a sales award his first summer and trained other salesmen during his second summer.

Gannett left the Cornell *Sun* during his junior year for the Ithaca *Journal*, which paid better. He was given a list of names of individuals who were not to be mentioned in the *Journal*, principally because they refused to buy advertising. He disagreed with the business office dictating to the editorial department, a practice that he prevented in the newspapers that he owned later. His byline began to appear in newspapers in Boston, Buffalo, Chicago, New York, Philadelphia, and Syracuse, and he was able to drop his laundry route and his job for the pants presser. Sportswriting was one of his specialities.

In June, 1898, Gannett graduated from Cornell with a Bachelor of Arts degree. He had eighty dollars in his pocket when he enrolled at Cornell; he graduated with savings of $1,000 and joined the news staff the Syracuse *Herald* at a salary of fifteen dollars a week. His motto was "to make myself more useful." He thought that he could make himself more useful by returning to Cornell to take graduate courses in economics, history, and literature and to earn a Master of Arts degree. He moved back to Ithaca and became so involved in reporting that he didn't enroll for the graduate courses.

Gannett's plans were changed by a telegram from Washington, D.C., from Cornell's President Jacob Schurman. Schurman had been appointed by President McKinley as chairman of commission to determine how to govern the Philippine Islands. The United States had become the protectorate of the Philippines as a result of winning the Spanish-American War. Gannett could not turn down the opportunity to be present where news was being made, to travel, and to earn $3,000 a year plus travel expenses as Schurman's secretary.

Schurman and Gannett arrived in the Philippines during the Aguinaldo uprising. Insurgents surrounded Manila, which was still in the control of the U.S. Army and their Philippine allies. Gannett was already an industrious, organized person. However, his working with Schurman, who scheduled his own day in detail and then scrupulously followed it, was a model for the young secretary. He became so efficient in carrying out his duties that he was given the nickname, "Can do." Early in 1900, the Schurman commission finished its work in the Philippines. Gannett took three months to return to the United States via Singapore and the Suez Canal.

Schurman cabled Gannett in London, advising him that there was to be a second commission to the Philippines, whose chairman was William Howard Taft. Schurman had recommended Gannett to Taft as his secretary, and Taft offered him the position. Gannett visited Schurman in Ithaca and was advised to go into the newspaper business as planned and not to take the offered position with Taft. He joined the Ithaca *Daily News* as city editor for fifteen dollars a week.

Two significant changes were occurring at this time in the newspaper business: ethics were improving and new production techniques were being implemented. Newspapers were becoming less sensationialistic and less involved with political party influence. Halftone engravings, high-speed presses, and mechanical typesetters were being used increasingly in the business.

Gannett had been successful in the news side of the business and wanted to gain experience in the management of a newspaper. He became business manager of the Ithaca *Daily News,* in charge of running the paper at a salary of fifty dollars a week. He was appalled at the accounting methods that prevented him from knowing whether he was operating at a profit or a loss. He instituted modern newspaper accounting techniques that were copied by many other newspapers. It became the foundation for the twenty-one newspapers that he ultimately owned and controlled.

Eventually, Gannett became disenchanted with the *Daily News'* dependence upon political advertising. He joined *Frank Leslie's Illustrated Weekly* in New York as a feature editor for fifty dollars a week. It was good experience for him, but he yearned to return to the newspaper business. His return occurred by a chance meeting in the Langwell Hotel in Elmira, where he had lunch between trains while traveling to Ithaca. The Langwell Hotel proprietor, John Causer, knew of Gannett's reputation, and he also knew that a young Elmira newspaperman, Erwin Davenport, was looking for a partner to own and run the Elmira *Gazette.*

The half-interest in the *Gazette* that Gannett wanted to buy was owned by David B. Hill, who had been Mayor of Elmira, Governor of New York, and U.S. Senator. He visited Hill and was asked to stay for three days, probably for Hill to evaluate him. They talked politics for the entire time, and, finally, Gannett was able to bring the subject around to the business at hand. Hill offered the fifty percent interest to Gannett for the same price that Davenport had paid for his half-interest a year previously. Gannett borrowed $2,000 from the Bank of Ithaca and $5,000 from the Bank of Bolivar to add to his savings of $3,000. Hill accepted his note for the remaining $10,000, and Gannett was part-owner of his first newspaper.

Gannett was responsible for the editorials and the news; Davenport managed the business side, including advertising and circulation. The *Gazette's* production equipment was antiquated, but they held it together with bailing wire. Elmira's morning newspaper was the *Advertiser*, and the *Star* was the other afternoon newspaper. The Elmira market could not support two afternoon newspapers. The owners of the *Star* proposed a merger with the *Gazette;* Gannett accepted their proposal.

Although the *Star* was three times the size of the *Gazette,* Gannett proposed that the shares be split fifty-fifty, and the two owners of the *Gazette* and the two owners of the *Star* each received twenty-five percent ownership of the merged *Star-Gazette.* The elder statesman of the *Star* became the president, Davenport continued as business manager, and Gannett and the other *Star* partner shared the editorial and news duties. Gannett worked a fourteen-hour day and stopped by on Sundays to take care of the loose ends. While in Elmira, he realized that if he was going to work at such a furious pace, he had better exercise. Handball became one of his recreational activities.

Gannett's first venture into multiple newspaper ownership was as editor and part owner of the Ithaca *Journal*, for which he had worked as a reporter for $3.00 a hour. The newspaper was owned by two estates, neither of which cared to be active in the newspaper business. Gannett continued to live in Elmira; he traveled to Ithaca on weekends in his Willys-Overland motorcar. His personal politics supporting Woodrow Wilson for President in 1912 were aligned with the Elmira *Star-Gazette,* but he did not impose his views on the Ithaca *Journal,* which favored the candidacy of William Howard Taft.

The *Star-Gazette* was financially successful, but it did not generate enough income to support the four families of the quarter-owners. Initially, they considered buying the Akron *Beacon-Journal,* but Charles Knight decided not to sell. The *Beacon-Journal* became the foundation of the newspaper chain of Charles Knight's son, John S. Knight, who expanded into Chicago, Detroit, and Miami in his early ventures. Gannett and his partners investigated the Rochester newspaper market. The city had five newspapers that were backward in their presentation of the news and lacked modern production facilities.

Rochester had two morning newspapers and three afternoon newspapers, the *Post-Express,* the *Times,* and the *Union and*

Advertiser. The partners decided to buy the *Times* and the *Union and Advertiser* and merge them into the *Times-Union;* however, they needed $250,000 that they didn't have. They borrowed $100,000 from Elmira banks, and Gannett's partner, Copeland, asked for a loan from his friend, John N. Willys. Willys, chairman of the Willys-Overland Motorcar Company who had started his business career in Elmira, didn't give Copeland a loan, but stock certificates in the Fisk Rubber Company instead. The partners used the stock as collateral for a $100,000 bank loan.

Gannett and Davenport moved to Rochester to manage the new acquisitions. Again, Davenport was the business manager and Gannett was responsible for the news and editorials. In the middle of World War I, it was a risky venture. Newsprint was in short supply, and the large orders from major city newspapers were crowding out the orders from smaller papers. However, Gannett had a good relationship with the paper mills. He obtained sufficient newsprint not only for his newspapers, but also for the weekly newspapers in the area as a favor to them.

One of the plums of newspaper publishing was the printing of legal notices for the county. George W. Aldridge, Republican political boss of Monroe County visited Gannett and offered him the printing of the county's legal notices that were worth $50,000 a year in business. However, there were strings attached. Gannett surprised Aldridge by turning down the offer; the young newspaperman wanted to continue to run newspapers that were independent.

Gannett had moved to Rochester in 1918 with few letters of introduction to area notables. One letter of introduction from an Elmira friend was to Mrs. William E. Werner, whose late husband had been a judge of the New York State Court of Appeals. Gannett was captivated by the youngest Werner daughter, Caroline, who was seventeen years younger than he was. The family was surprised by Caroline's interest in someone who had just turned forty with large debts due to his newspaper commitments. Their proposed wedding date of January 26, 1920, was postponed until March 25th due to the widespread flu epidemic.

In 1920, the partners made their third acquisition by buying

Utica's two afternoon papers, the *Herald-Dispatch* and the *Observer,* which they merged into the *Observer-Dispatch.* Initially, they had problems with the new Utica newspaper because none of the partners moved to Utica to help manage it. Eventually it became profitable, largely due to the efforts of Prentice Bailey, the son of the *Observer's* editor.

In 1922, the Rochester *Times-Union,* which had become a profitable enterprise, was faced with its largest challenge— William Randolf Hearst started an afternoon newspaper, the Rochester *Journal,* in direct competition with the *Times-Union.* The *Journal* used all of the big city newspaper techniques and gave away a Ford automobile a day for thirty days in order to gain circulation. Instead of competing with Hearst by using Hearst promotion techniques, Gannett concentrated on improvements to the *Times-Union.* Hearst's next move was an offer to buy out any of Gannett's partners who were interested in selling.

Gannett's partners weren't nearly as aggressive in expanding as he was, and Davenport was bothered by stomach ulcers. The partners had an agreement to sell the other partners their share before selling to an outside party. Gannett realized that the only way to fight Hearst was to buy out his partners and pursue the business aggressively. The 1920s were the time of Gannett's most rapid expansion. His expansion into radio was not as successful as his newspaper ventures. He entered the field too soon and got out too early.

Gannett met George Eastman soon after moving to Rochester and worked well with him. Gannett said: "It was a great experience to have known George Eastman as I knew him." When Gannett's rival, the Rochester *Democrat & Chronicle,* planned to establish a radio station to compete with the one owned by the *Times-Union,* Eastman suggested that they join forces and establish one good station instead of two mediocre ones. The radio station was installed in the Eastman School of Music to broadcast quality music programs.

Gannett continued to expand his newspaper chain. Frank Tripp, his trouble-shooter from Elmira, was a valuable asset in this expansion effort. They didn't always agree on an issue, but they respected each other's judgement. Over a forty-year period,

Gannett acquired twenty-seven newspapers, ten of which he consolidated into five. He sold one newspaper, the Winston-Salem *Sentinel* (his only southern paper), and practically gave one away, the Brooklyn *Eagle,* that was not financially successful. He never established a new newspaper; he always bought existing papers and then improved them.

Gannett placed a heavy emphasis on the value of good auditors, both prior to the purchase and during the early ownership of an acquisition. He ensured that his papers were free from political influence or other interests. His principal goal was to be financially sound. He observed: "No newspaper is really free which is not financially strong. A newspaper editor who is constantly harassed by bill collectors can never produce a great newspaper.... One of the things that has influenced me most in building up a group of newspapers has been the desire to give them financial strength and independence."

In President Roosevelt's second term, Gannett formed the "National Committee to Uphold Constitutional Government" to fight the President's scheme to pack the Supreme Court with additional justices who supported his interests. Gannett served with Republicans on this committee and by 1938 was ready to switch his affiliation from the Democratic Party to the Republican Party.

Gannett became a candidate for the Republican nomination for President in 1940. His rivals for the nomination at the Republican National Convention in Philadelphia were Dewey, Taft, Vandenberg, and Willkie. William W. Wadsworth, Jr., of Geneseo, gave the speech nominating Gannett at the convention. On the first ballot, Dewey received 360 votes, Taft received 129, Willkie 105, and Gannett 33. Willkie won the nomination on the sixth ballot and lost dramatically to President Roosevelt.

The young man from Blood's Depot had come a long way. He did it by being hard-working, honest, responsible, and self-reliant; he didn't curry favor with the powerful and he didn't marry the boss's daughter. From his early days delivering newspapers, to working his way through Cornell, to applying for loans to buy and expand his business, Gannett displayed self-confidence and a sense of responsibility. He was willing to take risks and to trust his partners and key managers. Gannett is an outstanding example of a self-made individual.

John McGraw

John Joseph McGraw, manager of the New York Giants baseball dynasty for thirty years, was born in Truxton, Cortland County, on April 7, 1873. He was the first child of John McGraw, Sr., an Irish immigrant who worked for the Elmira, Cortland & Northern Railroad, and Ellen Comerfort McGraw. In 1884, a diphtheria epidemic raged through the Tioughnioga Valley, and young John McGraw's mother, two brothers, and two sisters died of the disease.

McGraw did the usual chores of a twelve-year-old, but there was much more work to be done around the house after his mother's death. His interest in baseball began when he was eight, and he spent hours hitting stones with a stick. When McGraw was twelve, his father lost patience with having to replace neighbors' windows that had been broken by his son. One night his father attacked him in a rage and punched, slapped, and threw him around the room. McGraw ran upstairs, put his few possessions in a bag, and ran out the front door past his father. He ran across the street to the hotel run by Mary Goddard, a big-hearted widow in her late thirties. Mary had two sons of her own; she treated McGraw as a third son.

McGraw delivered the Elmira *Telegraph* newspaper and sold candy, fruit, magazines, and other sundries on the Cortland-Elmira run of the Elmira, Cortland & Northern Railroad. Soon he had enough money to buy baseballs and the *Spalding Rule Book,* which he memorized. By the time he was sixteen, he was the best player on the Truxton high school team, although he weighed only 105 pounds. That summer he played most positions for the Truxton town team, which was managed by Bert Kenney. However, because of his fast-breaking curve ball, he was the team's star pitcher.

In 1890, Kenney became part-owner and player-manager for

the Olean team in the New York Pennsylvania League. On April 1, 1890, McGraw signed his first professional baseball contract just one week before his seventeenth birthday. Kenny played McGraw at third base because he already had a good pitcher. In his first start, against Erie, McGraw handled the ball ten times at third base and committed eight errors. The lone single that he hit did not make up for his disastrous performance in the field. He hustled and improved his fielding considerably, but it wasn't enough to stay with Olean. In mid-season, he was sent to Wellsville of the Western New York League, where he batted .365 in thirty-four games.

McGraw played ball in Wellsville with Al Lawson, who organized the American All-Stars to play winter ball in Cuba. McGraw spent a number of winters in Cuba and developed a liking for the country and its people. McGraw played shortstop for the All-Stars, who wore bright yellow uniforms. The Cubans loved the small, peppery shortstop who played hard; they called him "El mono amarillo" (the yellow monkey).

In 1891, Lawson signed McGraw to a contract with the Ocala, Florida, Giants for meals, laundry expenses, and a weekly cigar, which he bartered for other commodities. In a game at Gainesville, Florida, McGraw hit three doubles off the Cleveland Indians star pitcher, Cy Young. Teams began to express an interest in him; he accepted a offer to join the Davenport, Iowa, team because they sent him the full advance, and the other teams sent only partial advances (which McGraw kept).

McGraw's play with Davenport was noticed by the Baltimore Orioles of the American Association, and he was asked to join their team during the last half of the 1891 season. In 1892, Baltimore joined the National League. The team was managed by Ned Hanlon, a baseball genius and one of the highest-paid ballplayers in the country. Hanlon was the first to use the hit and run, and he was an advocate of the bunt. McGraw learned much from Hanlon, and he began to hit an endless series of foul bunts to frustrate the pitcher. Within two years, McGraw was the best bunter in the league.

During the summer that McGraw played for Olean, he met Father Joseph Dolan, who supervised athletics at nearby Allegany

College (later renamed St. Bonaventure College to avoid being confused with Allegheny College in Meadville, Pennsylvania). Father Dolan spoke with the young baseball player about the benefits of a college education.

In the winter of 1892-93, McGraw asked Father Dolan if he could take courses without paying tuition and be provided with room and board in return for coaching the college baseball team in the spring semester. Father Dolan agreed, and McGraw spent three academic years with these arrangements. He didn't receive a degree, but he rounded out his limited earlier education and accomplished his objective of self-improvement.

In 1894, the Orioles won their first National League pennant. Baltimore's hysteria was quieted by the Orioles loss in the Temple Cup playoff games against the New York Giants, the team that had placed second in the National League. The Temple Cup games predated the postseason World Series. In 1895 and 1896, the Orioles again won the National League Pennant. One of the team's stars was Willie Keeler who, when asked to what he attributed his success in baseball, replied, "I hit 'em where they ain't."

In 1900, McGraw and his friend and business partner, Wilbert Robinson, played in St. Louis. They both returned to Baltimore for the 1901 and 1902 seasons, where McGraw was player-manager. Robinson, the Orioles' catcher, and McGraw were joint owners of a successful restaurant, bar, bowling alley, and pool hall near the ballpark.

McGraw was asked why he was walked so often. He said: "I shift about, I step from one corner of the box to the other, and I crowd the plate. Again, I stand at the edge of the box and walk into the ball.... I swing and jerk my bat, and all of these little feints rattle the average pitcher." Clark Griffith, a Chicago pitcher who was one of the league's best, said of McGraw, "He simply worries the life out of you.... He stays there fouling the balls off one after another.... When he has had enough fun he gives the ball a dinky little push and it lands safe, you can bet on that." Another player, Frank Selee, said of McGraw, "All things considered, there is no one in his class."

In the late summer of 1902, McGraw moved to New York as

the player-manager of the Giants. By 1904, his second full season with the team, he won his first of ten National League pennants. The rest of the first two decades of the century belonged to the New York Giants; they dominated baseball like no team until the Yankees of the 1920s arrived on the scene. The Polo Grounds, nestled under Coogan's bluff and overlooking the Harlem River, was the home of the first baseball dynasty.

The Giants won consecutive pennants in 1911, 1912, and 1913. In 1918, 1919, and 1920, the Giants finished second in the league. In 1921 and 1922, the team from Coogan's bluff won the National League Pennant and beat their crosstown rivals, the Yankees, in the World Series. The Giants won the National League pennant again in 1923 and 1924, but they were beaten in the World Series. These were McGraw's last pennants, although the Giants placed second in 1925, 1928, and 1931.

McGraw retired in 1932. His last game was as National League Manager in the first All-Star game—at Comiskey Park, Chicago, in July 1933. Connie Mack's American League All-Stars beat him 4-2. Mack was the only manager of that era who was as successful as McGraw was. Mack, the gentleman manager who left the tactical decisions to his team, was the antithesis to the loud-mouthed, rowdy McGraw, the inside manager who even called his pitcher's pitches.

Mack managed the Athletics to nine American League pennants compared with McGraw's ten National League pennants. Mack's teams won five World Series to McGraw's three, but the Athletics also finished last or next to last thirteen times in Connie's fifty-year stint in Philadelphia. McGraw had only one last-place team (1915) and on only one other occasion did one of his teams finish out of the first division (fifth). At a silver anniversary banquet for McGraw, Mack said: "There has been only one McGraw, and there has been only one manager— and his name is McGraw."

In 1933, McGraw was diagnosed as having prostate cancer which had spread to his kidneys and stomach. On February 16, 1934, he was admitted to New Rochelle hospital suffering from uremia. On February 24th, he began to hemorrhage from his intestines and went into a coma. He died the following morning, forty-one days before his sixty-first birthday.

McGraw's widow, referred to as the "first lady of baseball," was left in moderately comfortable circumstances, but not as well-off as might be expected of someone with McGraw's income. He always had enjoyed gambling, particularly on the horses. He never bet more than he could afford to lose, but he liked the "action," the atmosphere, and the anticipation of betting on an unpredictable outcome.

Also, McGraw had the reputation of helping people in need. Frequently, he would spread twenty dollar bills around among the rookie players who were poorly paid. At Aqueduct racetrack one day he talked with an elderly man who had been a horse trainer. The former trainer told McGraw that he would like to go to New Orleans for the winter. McGraw peeled five one-hundred-dollar bills from his roll and gave them to him. He rationalized it to himself; he told the friend who was with him that he had won more from the trainer's tips than he had "loaned" him.

While McGraw was still a player, he encountered a former teammate, a catcher, who had become addicted to morphine and was wandering the streets of Washington as a homeless derelict. McGraw had him admitted to City Hospital in Baltimore and paid for his six-week treatment. A Baltimore reporter saw the catcher at Union Park ballpark, and to him he seemed "like a new man."

McGraw's friends said of him: "He's the toughest loser in the world and the easiest to touch." As a manager, his judgement of a player's ability, "inside" baseball knowledge, tactical decision-making, and insistence on players following his direction were legendary. Rogers Horsby said of him: "When you train under most managers, you merely get yourself in good physical condition. When you train under McGraw, you learn baseball." McGraw was an adversary of umpires; National League umpire Arlie Latham said that McGraw, "eats gunpowder every morning and washes it down with warm blood." Veteran reporter John B. Sheridan observed that, "no man has ever laid the impress of his ego, his psyche, his soul, his animating spirit upon baseball as has John Joseph McGraw." The kid from Truxton definitely made his mark on the national pastime.

John Wesley Powell

John Wesley Powell, explorer of the Grand Canyon, was born in Mt. Morris on March 24, 1834. He was the son of Reverend Joseph Powell, a Methodist minister, and Mary Powell. The Powells immigrated to the United States from England in 1830 to spread the word of Methodism in America. In 1833, they supervised the construction of the the first Methodist church in Mt. Morris. The Powell family moved from Mt. Morris to Ohio and, subsequently, to Wisconsin.

In his teenage years, Powell managed the family farm and taught school to earn college tuition money. He became interested in botany and zoology and had a comprehensive herbarium, a large collection of shells, and a cabinet of reptiles that he collected around the Midwest. He earned a degree in botany and zoology and accepted a teaching position at Hennepin, Illinois.

In the spring of 1861, he responded to President Lincoln's call for volunteers by enlisting as a private with the 20th Illinois. He was commissioned a second lieutenant in the military engineers one month later. He was wounded at the Battle of Shiloh and his right forearm was amputated. He continued to serve with distinction at the Battles of Atlanta, Chattanooga, Meridian, Nashville, and Vicksburg. At the end of the war he was a brevet Lieutenant Colonel and Chief of Artillery of the Army of the Tennessee.

In 1865, Powell became a professor of geology at Illinois Wesleyan University at Bloomington, Illinois. He concentrated on developing methods of instruction and advocated that students, with the teacher serving as guide, should derive principles from observed facts. He favored a balanced approach to learning by supplementing textbook learning with field trips.

In 1867, he led a group of students on an expedition to the Rocky Mountains to collect specimens for museums and to make topological measurements for the Smithsonian Institution. The trip was financed by an endowment from the state legislature for the Museum of the Illinois Natural History Society. In 1868, he led an even larger expedition to the Colorado mountains.

His expedition during the summer of 1869 made him a national figure. His goal was to study the geology and geography of the canyons of the Green River and the Colorado River. He traveled by boat down the Green River Valley and the Colorado River Valley to the Virgin River, just beyond the Grand Canyon in Arizona. Powell led a team of ten men in four small boats through the largest unknown region of the United States. From May 24th to August 31st, they traveled 1,000 miles.

Three men of the party became concerned with dwindling food supplies on the trip and set out on their own. The three men left the Powell expedition at Separation Rapids; they climbed a nearby plateau where they were killed by the Indians. The remaining seven men successfully completed the expedition south of the Grand Canyon. The expedition made Powell a public figure. The combination of his war record, the hardships of the journey, the loss of three men killed by the Indians, and the public's fascination with the exploration of the West, made Powell a national hero.

The expedition made periodic determinations of altitude, latitude, and longitude. They also collected fossils and sampled rock formations, but little scientific knowledge was gained from the expedition. Powell was eager to make another expedition to collect more scientific data. However, he had accomplished two things:

- His paper, "New Tracks in North America," displayed his understanding of the interrelationship of erosion, uplift, vegetation, and water.
- He formed new concepts of drainage and erosion that became the foundation for "new geology," now called geomorphology.

In 1871-72, Powell led a second expedition of the Colorado River Valley that was sponsored by the Department of the Interior. He concentrated on the study of the regional geology and the formulation of concepts about the interaction of land, water, people, and social institutions. Powell wrote three monographs about his expeditions: *Geology of the Uinta Mountains* (1876),

Introduction to the Study of the Indian Language (1877), and *Report on the Lands of the Arid Region* (1878).

Powell's recommendations led to the establishment of the U.S. Geological Survey in 1879. Also that year, he established the Bureau of American Ethnology of the Smithsonian Institution. He served as the director of both agencies from 1881 until 1894. As Director of the U.S. Geological Survey, he initiated the study of ground water, irrigation, soil, flood control and rivers across the country. His interest in the development of the western lands led to the establishment of the Bureau of Reclamation.

In 1888, Powell helped found two societies for the advancement of science, the National Geographic Society and the Geological Society of America. Also, in 1888, he served as president of the American Association for the Advancement of Science. Powell died on September 23, 1902, at Haven, Maine. He was buried at Arlington National Cemetery.

Many of his ideas and his contributions were forgotten after his death. Then, in 1930, Walter Prescott Webb in his book, *The Great Plains*, recalled the important role that Powell had played in effecting reforms in the federal government's land policies. In the 1950s, scientists pointed out the significant part that Powell had played in conservation, the direction of of science in the federal government, and in exploration of the West. Bernard Devoto wrote of Powell: "He was a great man and a prophet. Long ago he accomplished great things and now we are beginning to understand him."

Hal Roach

Hal Roach, the son of insurance and real-estate broker Charles Roach and Mabel Bailey Roach, was born on January 14, 1892, in Elmira, New York. He became a producer, director, and screenwriter, but was known principally as a producer who made an important contribution to American film comedy. He spent his first sixteen years at 309 Columbia Street in Elmira. He was thrown out of parochial school and public school due to his penchant for pranks. He father suggested that he grow up by traveling. He drifted to the West Coast where he sold ice cream from a horse-drawn wagon in Seattle. Then he went north to the Yukon where he became a rural pack-team postman and a failed gold prospector. He also worked as a fish wagon driver, a mule skinner, and a saloon swamper.

Roach traveled to California where he supervised twenty mule-skinners in the construction of a pipeline in the Mohave Desert. In 1912, he began his career in movies as a $5-a-day cowboy extra at Universal Studios. He worked as a bit-part actor, cameraman, writer, and assistant director. Within two years, he was a director and producer. He was never comfortable as a director. He observed:

> I never really cared too much about directing; I did it myself at first because there was no one else, later just to keep my hand in. The first time I directed I felt very unsure of myself; the only thing I knew was that I was probably doing everything wrong. So I told my cameraman not to be afraid to tell me if I made mistakes; he looked very relieved and told me not to worry; it was the first film he'd ever photographed.

One of the most significant experiences that Roach had at Universal Studios was meeting Harold Lloyd. Roach and Lloyd went separate ways upon leaving Universal until Roach inherited $3,000 and sent for Lloyd. In 1915, they began making unsuccessful comedies, borrowing heavily from Charlie Chaplin's work. Lloyd went to work for Mack Sennett at Keystone Studios until Sennett fired him. Roach rehired Lloyd when he and a partner, Dan Linthicum, formed the Rolin Film Company.

Lloyd eventually developed a style of comedy of his own that was distinct from that of Charlie Chaplin. In Roach's words:

> When I broke into this racket, all comics dressed as comics—baggy pants, monkey jackets, big floppy shoes, freak hats, self-cocking eyebrows,

trained performing facial muscles. I had an idea,
and with Harold Lloyd as my raw material, I
experimented with it. I took away his comic
mustache and his grotesque wardrobe and dressed
him instead as a regular human being but wearing
a pair of oversized horn-rimmed glasses which
gave him the slightly owlish appearance of an
innocent-minded, guileless young fellow. Then,
when something devastating befell him, it had the
precious quality of the unexpected, and for
audience reactions was infinitely funnier than if
he'd worn zany makeup.

Roach began to stress the story line and comedy situation—
what he called "construction"—not just visual gags, which
Sennett relied upon so heavily. As a result, Roach's comedies had
much greater appeal than Sennett's work to the increasingly
sophisticated moviegoing audiences of the 1920s and 1930s.
Subsequently, as Roach became more successful, Sennett declined
in popularity. Roach helped to establish the careers of Charlie
Chase, Edgar Kennedy, Harry Langdon, Snub Pollard, and Will
Rogers. The directors of his movies included Frank Capra, Leo
McCarey and George Stevens.

Roach's eighteen-acre studio in Culver City became the
training ground for stars such as Janet Gaynor, Jean Harlow, and
Mickey Rooney. Stan Laurel began working at Roach Studios as a
director and star while Oliver Hardy was a comic foil and bit-part
actor. They appeared as a team in eight films that Roach made for
Pathe in 1927. Roach's move to MGM in the fall of 1927
provided larger budgets and better directors for Laurel and Hardy.
The comedy team, whose genius was recognized by Roach, was
permitted to design their own films; most of the gags were
developed by Laurel.

In 1922, Roach created the "Our Gang" series of comedies
after watching a group of young children frolicking and arguing in
a lumberyard. Their spontaneity captured his attention as possible
subject material for a film series. He insisted that the films be
made with consideration for the children's school and recreation

needs. When one of the young actor's fathers refused to put his son's salary in trust for him, Roach sued the father.

The young actors and actresses were replaced every three or four years. Jackie Cooper and Nanette Fabray began their acting careers in the "Our Gang" series. Roach produced the series for sixteen years and then sold it to MGM, which continued the series for another six years.

In the mid-1930s, Roach realized that two-reel short subjects were being pushed out of the market by the second feature of a double-feature, so he moved to the production of full-length features. Roach, who collaborated with his son, Hal, Jr., was commercially successful with these movies. Two of the movies that he produced during this period were *One Million B.C.,* an innovative special-effects film, and the first screen adaptation of Steinbeck's *Of Mice and Men.* The latter was a poignant movie that retained the content and organization of Steinbeck's book with superb acting by Betty Field and Burgess Meredith.

During World War II, Colonel Roach produced propaganda films and training films for the U.S. Army and the Air Corps. After the war, Hal Roach Studios produced television series such as "The Amos and Andy Show," "The Life of Riley," "My Little Margie," and "Public Defender." In 1955, Roach sold the studio to his son, who was forced out in 1959. His successors filed for bankruptcy shortly afterward; the studio buildings were razed in 1963, and an automobile showroom was built on the site.

Roach was an energetic individual, a flashy dresser, and an avid fisherman and hunter. He owned six airplanes, a boat, and twenty polo ponies. His team won the United States Western Polo Championship four times, and he was a founder and president of the Los Angeles Turf Club.

For forty years, Roach managed Hal Roach Studios where he produced almost 1,000 full-length movies as well as just under 2,000 one-, two-, and three-reel silent and sound short subjects. In 1931, he won his first academy award for "The Music Box," a short subject in which Laurel and Hardy lugged a piano up a staircase. In 1936, he earned his second Oscar for another short subject, "The Bored of Education," with the "Our Gang" cast.

In 1984, he was presented with an Honorary Academy Award

for "distinguished contributions in the motion picture art form." In 1987, an honorary degree was bestowed on Roach by Elmira College, and the Hal E. Roach Theatre Award was established. It is awarded annually to the junior or senior at Elmira College who has demonstrated the potential for a professional career in films or the theatre.

Roach died of pneumonia on November 2, 1992, at the age of 100 in Los Angeles. Elmira commemorates their favorite son on the signs that mark the city limits with the words, "The Birthplace of Hal Roach."

Harriet Tubman

Harriet Ross Tubman, one of eleven children of Harriet Greene and Benjamin Ross, was born in 1820 on a plantation in Dorchester County on the Eastern Shore of Maryland. The plantation on Big Buckwater River, which was owned by Edward Brodas, was 100 miles south of the Mason-Dixon line, sixty miles from Baltimore, and several miles from Bucktown. Harriet's parents were full-blooded Africans of the Ashanti, a West African warrior people.

Harriet, who was called Araminta at birth, was born in a slave cabin with an open fireplace but with no windows or furniture. The family slept on the floor, which was made of clay. When she was five years old, Brodas hired out Harriet to a family named Cook. Mrs. Cook used Harriet to wind yarn. Because she was slow at the job, Harriet was turned over to Mr. Cook, who put her to work tending his muskrat traps. She waded in the cold water of the river with a thin dress and no shoes and eventually developed bronchitis and a high fever. Mr. Cook thought she was faking an illness and returned her to her home plantation where she recovered from bronchitis and a case of measles.

Harriet was hired out again, this time as a baby nurse and housekeeper. She said: "I was so little that I had to sit on the floor and have the baby put in my lap. And that baby was always on my lap except when it was asleep or when its mother was feeding it." When the baby awakened during the night, Harriet was expected to rock it in its cradle to prevent it from crying. If the baby's crying woke up Mrs. Cook, she beat Harriet with a cowhide whip that caused permanent scars on her back and neck.

Harriet was fed scraps from the table and was hungry most of the time. When she was seven, she took a lump of sugar from the sugar bowl. Mrs. Cook saw her take the sugar and got out her whip. Harriet fled the house and lived with the pigs in the pigpen for five days, competing with them for potato peelings and other scraps of food. Finally, she returned to the Cook's home, where she was given a severe beating and sent home to the Brodas plantation.

Harriet was hired out again, this time splitting fence rails and loading wagons with lumber. The heavy work was difficult for her, but she preferred it to being under the thumb of the mistress of a house. In her early teens, she worked as a field hand and saw many examples of cruelty to the slaves on the plantation. Later in life, she said of the the owners and overseers: "They didn't know any better. It's the way they were brought up ... with the whip in their hand. Now it wasn't that way on all plantations. There were good masters and mistresses, as I've heard tell. But I didn't happen to come across any of them."

In 1835, when she was fifteen years old, Harriet saw a slave sneak away from the plantation. The tall black man was followed by the overseer with his whip and by Harriet. The overseer soon caught the runaway slave and asked Harriet to hold the man while he tied him up. She refused. The black man ran away, and Harriet stood in the way of his pursuit. The overseer picked up a two-pound weight and threw it at Harriet. It struck her in the middle of her forehead, fracturing her skull, causing profuse bleeding, and giving her a severe concussion.

Harriet was in a coma for weeks. For the rest of her life, she was affected by severe headaches and "sleeping fits," during which she would fall asleep for a few minutes—sometimes in the middle of a conversation. She was left with a depression in her forehead and a disfiguring scar. While she was in bed recovering, her master brought prospective owners to her bedside in attempts to sell her. No one wanted to buy her, even at the lowest price; she observed: "They said I wasn't worth a penny."

When Harriet had regained her strength, she was hired out to John Stewart, a local contractor. Initially, she worked as a maid in Stewart's home, but she begged him to let her work outdoors with the men. She cut wood, drove a team of oxen, and plowed. Soon she was swinging an ax to cut timber for the Baltimore shipbuilding industry. When work was slack on the Stewart farm, she was allowed to hire herself out to cut and haul wood for neighboring farmers. For this privilege, she paid Stewart fifty dollars a year and was permitted to keep anything she earned above that amount. She managed to put away a small nest egg.

While Harriet toiled at heavy outdoor work, she dreamed of being free. She thought: "I had reasoned this out in my mind; there was one of two things I had a right to, liberty or death; if I could not have one, I would have the other. For no man would take me alive; I should fight for my liberty as long as my strength lasted, and when it came time for me to go, the Lord would let them take me."

In 1844, Harriet married John Tubman, a free black man who lived nearby. Tubman had been born free because his parents had been freed at their master's death. Her husband's freedom didn't change Harriet's slave status. Furthermore, her children would belong to the plantation. The constant threat to slaves in Maryland was to be "sold South," that is, sold to plantation owners from Alabama, Georgia, Louisiana, or Mississippi, where conditions for slaves were much harsher than in states closer to the Mason-Dixon line.

One day Harriet heard that two of her sisters had been sold and were being transported south in chains. She knew of the Underground Railroad and of people who helped slaves escape. She didn't know geography, but she knew enough to follow the North Star to freedom. She tried to convince three of her brothers to come with her, but they were afraid of being captured and punished. She knew that her husband didn't want to travel to the North; in fact, he would have turned her in if he had known that she was leaving.

Harriet left the plantation in the middle of the night with some cornbread, salt herring, and her prized possession, a patchwork quilt. As she left, she sang an old spiritual:

I'll meet you in the morning,
When I reach the promised land,
On the other side of Jordan.
For I'm bound for the promised land.

Harriet went to the house of a woman who was known to help slaves escape. The woman took her in and gave her a slip of paper noting her next stop on the way to freedom. Harriet was so grateful that she gave the woman her quilt. She was tired when she arrived at the next stop early in the morning. The woman opened the door and handed her a broom and told her to start sweeping the yard. At first, Harriet was suspicious; then she realized that no one would question a slave working around the house. The woman's husband put her in his wagon, covered her with vegetables, and took her to the next stop that evening, generally following the course of the Choptank River.

Harriet finally realized that she had crossed the Mason-Dixon line and was in Pennsylvania. Later, she looked back on the event: "When I found that I had crossed that line, I looked at my hands to see if I was the same person. There was such a glory over everything; the sun came like gold through the trees, and over the fields, and I felt like I was in heaven." She was free, but she didn't have any contacts to help her find a job and a place to live. In her words: "I was a stranger in a strange land."

Harriet made her way to Philadelphia where she found a job in a hotel kitchen cooking and washing dishes. She met two of the founders of the Philadelphia Vigilance Committee, James Miller McKim, a white clergyman, and William Still, a freeborn black from Pennsylvania. They needed someone to guide a slave family north from Cambridge, Maryland. Harriet volunteered, but they hesitated letting her go because she might be retained as a slave. When she found out that the family was her sister, Mary, and her brother-in-law, John Bowley, she insisted on going. She bought them to safety in Philadelphia.

In the spring of 1851, Harriet made her second trip south to guide fellow slaves to freedom. This time she guided her brother, James, and two of his friends to freedom. The overseer and the hounds were on their trail. Harriet altered their route by crossing an ice-cold river. None of them could swim, and the men resisted the crossing. She waded out into swift-flowing water up to her chin to prove that they could make it across. If she hadn't changed their route on a hunch, they would have been captured.

On her next trip to Dorchester County, Maryland, she stopped at her husband's cabin and found that he had remarried. Tubman had no interest in traveling north. She brought several slaves back to Philadelphia, being very careful in country in which she was known.

The route northward that Harriet used was through Delaware, waiting until the last moment to cross into Maryland. One reason was that Delaware was the site of the headwaters of many of the rivers that drained through the Eastern Shore into Chesapeake Bay. Secondly, the state's black population in 1860 contained 1,798 slaves out of a total of 21,627. Delaware was the only southern state in which a black was assumed to be free until proved to be a slave.

When she approached a stop on the Underground Railroad, Tubman would hide her "passengers" before she rapped on the door. Then she would announce that she was "A friend with friends." Many of her trips north were via Wilmington, Delaware, the home of Thomas Garrett, a leader of the Underground Railroad movement. He owned a large shoe store where he hid escaping slaves behind a false wall. He provided every slave with a pair of shoes, which for most of them were the first shoes they had owned.

Garrett, a Quaker who became a good friend of Harriet's, aided 2,700 slaves in escaping. He was fined, jailed, and sued, but nothing deterred Garrett form helping those less fortunate than he was—not even the loss of his personal fortune and his shoe business. To the judge who stripped him of his fortune and his business, he said: "Friend, thee hasn't left me a dollar, but I wish to say to thee ... that if anyone knows of a fugitive who wants a shelter, and a friend, send him to Thomas Garrett." William Lloyd Garrison, the Boston abolitionist leader, considered Garrett to be "one of the best men who ever walked the earth."

On September 18, 1850, the passage of the Fugitive Slave Act

111

made helping escaped slaves riskier. United States marshals were empowered to catch runaways and return them to their owners. Anyone assisting a fugitive could be fined $1,000 and sent to jail. Slave catchers were hired to pursue runaway slaves who had thought that they were safe in the North. More slaves were now going to Canada, which was beyond the reach of the Fugitive Slave Act and the slave catchers. Harriet said: "I wouldn't trust Uncle Sam with my people no longer." Eventually, she moved from Philadelphia to St. Catherines, Ontario, where she lived for five years.

In December, 1851, Harriet made her fourth trip south. She guided another one of her brothers and his wife to freedom. When she reached Garrett's home in Wilmington, she added nine more passengers, including a baby. From this trip onward, she carried a sedative to keep baby passengers quiet. Between 1851 and 1857, Harriet made a spring trip and a fall trip to Maryland's Eastern Shore each year. On these trips, she met many of the leaders of the Underground Railroad movement, including John Brown, Frederick Douglass, J. W. Loguen, and Gerrit Smith. Brown called Harriet "General Tubman."

On one of her trips, Harriet had a nervous passenger who panicked and wanted to turn back. Harriet knew that he would be tortured to describe escape methods and "stations" on the road north. She pointed a gun at his head and told him to keep walking, while reminding him that if he were dead he couldn't reveal any information. This occurred more than once on her trips on the railroad.

Harriet frequently stopped at Cooper House in Camden, Delaware, and hid her passengers in a secret room above the kitchen. In Odessa, Delaware, they hid in a concealed loft over the sanctuary in a Quaker meeting house. On many farms, the slaves hid in a "potato hole," a rough vegetable cellar with few amenities. On one occasion Harriet pretended to be reading a book when the slave catchers passed by. One of the men said to the other: "This can't be the woman. The one we want can't read or write."

People began to call Harriet "the Moses of her people." A $12,000 reward was offered for her capture. She made her last journey on the railroad in 1860. In nineteen trips, she led over 300 slaves to their freedom. During the Civil War, she worked with slaves who had been left behind when their owners joined the Confederate Army.

Major General David Hunter was pleased to have Harriet's help with the slaves at Beaufort, South Carolina. She also served as a nurse at Hilton Head, South Carolina, and in Florida. For three years of service to the federal government, she was paid only $200, most of which was used to build a washhouse where she instructed the slave women in doing laundry to support themselves.

During the summer of 1863, Harriet worked as a scout for Colonel James Montgomery, who commanded an African-American regiment. Harriet assembled a network of spies, who notified her which slaves were ready to leave their masters and serve in the Union Army. She was supposed to receive a reward for recruiting slaves to the Grand Army of the Republic. She was owed at least $1,800 for her efforts, but she was never paid.

In 1864, Harriet was exhausted, and her seizures were occurring more frequently. She went to Auburn, New York, to rest and recuperate. While in Auburn, she heard that her husband, John Tubman, had died. In 1867, Harriet's friend, Sarah Bradford, wrote a biography about her and turned over the proceeds of the book, $1,200, to her. Some of the money went to African-Americans who needed food and clothing.

On March 18, 1869, she married Nelson Davis, whom she had met in South Carolina during the war. William H. Seward, Secretary of State in the Lincoln and Johnson administrations, attended her wedding. Seward had obtained some property for Harriet when she first moved to Auburn; they maintained their friendship until he died in 1872.

In 1888, Harriet purchased a 25-acre property at a public auction to establish a home for African-Americans who were ill and needy. She lacked the money to build the home, so she deeded the property to the African Methodist Episcopal Zion Church. The church built the home, but Harriet was unhappy when she heard that it cost $100 to enter it.

Harriet's husband died in 1888. In 1890, Congress approved

pensions for widows of Civil War veterans. Since Davis had served in the Union Army, she was entitled to eight dollars a month, which was increased to twenty dollars a month in 1899. This was the only money she received from the government; she was never paid for her efforts during the war.

On March 10, 1913, Harriet died of pneumonia at the age of ninety-three, after living two years in the home that she had helped to establish. The Auburn post of the Grand Army of the Republic gave her a military funeral, at which Booker T. Washington spoke. Harriet was truly the Moses of her people; she was also an abolitionist, a humanitarian, a nurse, and a spy. Principally, she is remembered for her Underground Railroad activities, about which she said: "I never ran my train off the track, and I never lost a passenger."

Charles Williamson

Sir William Pulteney, leader of an English syndicate that bought the Central New York lands of the Phelps-Gorham Purchase in the 1790s, commissioned Charles Williamson as his agent. Williamson, who had been a captain in the British Army, was captured by an American privateer while on his way to the Colonies during the Revolutionary War. He returned to England, where he received his commission as agent for Lord Pulteney. Williamson returned to the United States and became a citizen. He located in Bath because of its accessibility to the Susquehanna River, via the Conhocton and Chemung Rivers, and the markets of Philadelphia and Baltimore.

Williamson's men, Benjamin Patterson and Charles Cameron, cleared Pulteney Square in Bath and built the agency house, log cabins, and a tavern. Williamson continued to operate the land office that Oliver Phelps had established in Canandaigua. It was the base from which he offered promotions to prospective buyers for his parcels of land, thus stimulating the movement of settlers into the region.

Williamson served as Ontario County's representative in the

State Assembly from 1796-98, was appointed a judge of Ontario County in 1795, and became the first judge of Steuben County in 1796. He served as a lieutenant-colonel of militia and was instrumental in the construction of roads in the region. He established the first newspaper in the area, the *Bath Gazette.* Colonel Williamson also built the first theatre in the region in Bath; it offered plays by the French playwright, Moliere.

Williamson's home in Bath was on Lake Salubria; he also had homes in Geneva and on the bluff of Keuka Lake. Williamson built an inn at Geneva that was the finest stopping point between the Hudson River and Niagara Falls. In 1795, he laid out a race track at Bath and announced a fair, with horse races, wrestling matches, and a barbecue. Two thousand people gathered at Bath. They came from as far away as New England, New Jersey, and Virginia. The featured horse race was Williamson's mare, Virginia Nell, vs. Sheriff Dunn's New Jersey Silk Stocking; Williamson's horse lost. This was the first in a unbroken string of fairs that allows Bath to claim its Steuben County Fair as the oldest continuous county fair in the country.

Williamson chose to name his town Bath for Lord Pulteney's seat in England. The Town of Pulteney on the west side of Keuka Lake was named for Lord Pulteney, as was Pulteneyville on Lake Ontario. Not only does Bath have a Pulteney Square, but so do Geneva, Hammondsport, and Prattsburg. The Rochester suburb of Henrietta was named for Lord Pulteney's daughter, Henrietta Laura Pulteney, Countess of Bath, England.

The colonel made a significant contribution to the early growth of the Finger Lakes Region; he helped prepare the region for the industrial growth that came with the building of the Erie Canal and the railroads. Samuel McCormack, in a "memoir" about Charles Williamson, called him "the Father of the Western Part of the State of New York."

Eugene Zimmerman

Eugene Zimmerman, "Zim," the son of Joseph and Amelie Zimmerman, was born on May 26, 1862, in Basil, Switzerland. Zim, a world-class cartoonist, spent the most productive years of his life in Horseheads, New York. Amelie Zimmerman died shortly after the birth of their third child, also named Amelie, in 1864. Joseph Zimmerman was unable to care for the children and placed them with relatives. Zim was cared for by an aunt and uncle in Thann, Alsace, France. Joseph immigrated to America to avoid the impending Franco-Prussian War and found a job in a bakery in Paterson, New Jersey. In 1869, Zim's aunt and uncle, who were concerned about Alsace's annexation by Prussia, sent him to America for his safety.

Zim was given small tasks at the bakery where his father worked, including making designs with frosting as his artistic ability emerged. His education consisted of attendance at a German private school, the Paterson public schools, and tutoring. He painted signs for the bakery and made his first attempts at cartooning at the age of eight. He worked on a farm for two years and then as an office boy for an insurance and real estate agent, where his tasks included the painting of signs. William Brassington, a successful signpainter, noticed Zim's signs and offered him a three-year apprenticeship.

In 1878, Brassington moved to Elmira, taking the young signpainter with him. Zim said of his apprenticeship with Brassington: "He was very kind to me, allowing me to do all the work while he attended to collecting the bills and spending our earnings." Zim saw Mark Twain on the streets of Elmira frequently, and painted a sign for the law office of David B. Hill, future Governor, U.S. Senator, and Presidential candidate.

A rival signpainter, J. C. Pope of the Empire Sign Company of Horseheads, was attracted by Zim's work, particularly his illustrations. Zim accepted a position with the Empire Sign Company and moved to Horseheads. He began to sketch in his spare time as a hobby. Unfortunately, the Empire Sign Company failed, and Zim returned to Elmira.

116

On a vacation trip to New York City, Zim's uncle suggested that he show his sketchbook to Joseph Keppler, publisher of *Puck,* the comic weekly. Keppler, the successor to the great cartoonist, Thomas Nast, was impressed with Zim's sketchbook and offered him a job. Zim was a prolific artist, and many of his drawings were purchased by advertisers. Zim said of his time with *Puck:* "Besides learning newspaper art, I also learned how to live without eating until my salary would again permit me to indulge in three squares a day. My salary was increased, of course, as time wore on and my clothes wore out."

Another cartoonist, Bernard Gillam, suggested to Zim that he leave *Puck* and join the staff of *Judge. Judge,* edited by a former editor of the Elmira *Gazette* and partially financed by Senator Chauncey Depew, was a larger and ultimately more successful weekly than *Puck.* He matured professionally at *Judge* and over the next twenty-eight years became well-known across the country as "Zim."

On September 29, 1886, Zim married his girlfriend, Mabel Alice Beard of Horseheads, who moved to Brooklyn so that her husband could be near the offices of the *Judge.* However, they both preferred the fresh air and small town atmosphere of Horseheads so they returned to Mabel's hometown. Zim commuted to the New York offices of *Judge* every other week on the Delaware, Lackawanna, and Western's *Phoebe Snow.*

In 1890, Zim and his father-in-law, Alvah Peter Beard, built the Queen Anne-style "Zim House" at 601 Pine Street in Elmira. Zim decorated the interior of the house with a gun collection, Indian artifacts, and illustrations of his own and other artists, including a caricature of him done by his friend, Enrico Caruso. His work room was described as "A drawing board steadied on a roll-top desk, north light streaming in and his chair in a position from which, when he wanted to, he could look out on Mill Street and wave to friends. He could also study passing dogs, horses, and cats that he would use later in drawings."

Zim loved music. He organized two bands, one in the late 1880s and another from 1909 until 1916, when most of its members joined the military in World War I. In 1910, he designed a bandstand which he and his father-in-law built in Teal Park to give his band a place to play.

In 1894, *Muncey's Magazine* published an evaluation of Zim's work:

> Eugene Zimmerman ... stands alone in point of originality of conception and treatment. He is what artists denominate an "acrobat," but a careful scrutiny of his work will reveal a world of truth behind his grotesque exaggerations ... he views nature through a magnifying lens ... and we cannot but feel that it is a merry lens, untempered with malice or spleen, and one that compels us to laugh with him.

In 1896, Zim visited Thomas Edison in his laboratory in Orange, New Jersey. Edison admired his work and invited him to sketch one of his early movie cameras. Zim began to draw political cartoons, including cartoons of William Jennings Bryan and David B. Hill. In 1926, his political cartoon containing a caricature of President Theodore Roosevelt, "It's a Pretty Good Year for Big Fish," was on the cover of *Judge.*

In 1910, wrote *This and That about Caricature,* his first book about caricature. In the following year, he wrote *Zim's Foolish History of Horseheads,* which he said contained "Barefaced facts, fibs, and contradictions, written in the hope of reducing our tax rate and for the uplift of the village in general." The book contains humorous stories of the people of Horseheads. In 1912, he published *Zim's Foolish History of Elmira,* which contained material about General Sullivan's campaign through the area during the Revolutionary War as well as many sketches of the Elmirans of the day.

Many of his stories of "Homespun Phoolosophy" were published in the *Cartoons Magazine* from 1916-18. He established the Correspondence School of Cartooning, Comic Art, and Caricature, and he began to reach a worldwide audience. In 1926, Zim was elected president of the American Association of Cartoonists and Caricaturists. He was also a member of the

American Press Humorists. In 1927, Zim completed his second book about Horseheads, *The Foolish History of Horseheads.*

Zim wrote and illustrated twenty books on cartooning and caricature for his correspondence courses. He illustrated a series of works by James Whitcomb Riley and Bill Nye in the *Collier's Magazine* as well as Ring Lardner's *Regular Fellows I Have Met.* He wrote a column for the *Chemung Valley Reporter* and contributed a weekly cartoon for the Elmira *Sunday Telegram.*

In late January, 1935, Zim fell outside of his home and never fully recovered. On March 26th, he died of a heart attack. He was buried in Maple Grove Cemetery in Horseheads. A memorial committee erected a seven-foot granite shaft with a plaque of his profile as a memorial in Teal Park.

The Reverend Harry Malick summed up Zim's life in his eulogy:

> Zim might well be characterized as a lover of
> God's great outdoors, friend to all mankind,
> tender hearted as a child; kind beyond expression,
> generous to a fault, liberal and tolerant in his
> religion, gentle in spirit, exponent of a simple and
> homely philosophy of life, a talented artist who
> gave freely of his time and service to whomever
> solicited it, famed the world over for his
> caricatures of humor, entertainment, and satire
> and yet this man ... loved modesty and obscurity
> better than renown and publicity, and thus he
> almost hid his genius and greatness. . . .

In 1980, Zim's daughter, Laura, deeded Zim House to the Horseheads Historical Society, including his cartoons, correspondence, papers, and sketches, with the provision that the property at 601 Pine Street be preserved and open to the public. The Horseheads Historical Museum, which contains considerable Zim memorabilia, is located in the Zim Center at Grand Central Avenue and Broad Street.

Statue of Andrew White, Cornell University

Chapter 4

"Justice is the only worship.
Love is the only priest.
Ignorance is the only slavery.
Happiness is the only good.
The time to be happy is now,
The place to be happy is here,
The way to be happy is to make others so."

Creed—Robert G. Ingersoll

Chester Arthur

Chester Alan Arthur, the twenty-first President of the United States, was born on October 5, 1824, in Fairfield, Vermont. He was the fifth child and first son of William Arthur, who was a Baptist minister, and Malvina Stone Arthur. The family moved frequently when William was transferred to new ministries within the church. They lived in Perry, near Letchworth State Park, from April, 1835, until September, 1837, and in York, Livingston County, from September, 1837, until late 1839. Arthur spent some of his formative years, from age ten to age fifteen, in the Finger Lakes Region. In late 1839, William Arthur began a series of assignments with the church in the area of Albany, Schenectady, and Troy.

One of Arthur's school principals remembered him as "frank and open in manners and genial in disposition." A boyhood friend thought that Arthur displayed traits that indicated his future career in politics. "When Chester was a boy, you might see him in the village street after a shower, watching the boys build a dam across the rivulet in the roadway. Pretty soon he would be ordering this one to bring stones, another sticks, and others sods and mud to finish the dam; and they would do his bidding without question. But he took care not to get any dirt on his hands."

In 1845, Arthur entered Union College as a sophomore. He took the liberal arts courses that made up the college curriculum at the time, joined the Dephian Institute debating society, was elected to Phi Beta Kappa, and graduated with honors in 1848. During his first five years after college, he taught school and studied law. In 1853, he was a law clerk in the office of Culver & Parker in New York; he was admitted to the bar and taken into the law office partnership in the following year. He became the Judge Advocate General of the Second Brigade of the New York Militia. In 1860, Governor Edwin Morgan, for whom Arthur had campaigned, appointed him Engineer-In-Chief of the militia.

In April, 1861, with the outbreak of the Civil War, Arthur was appointed to the additional assignment of Assistant Quartermaster General of New York. He was assigned the responsibility of providing equipment, food, and housing to the thousands of troops moving through New York on their way south. He contracted out the feeding of the troops, insisted on formal requisitions for all material and services, kept accurate accounts, and insisted on specifications being met. In the following year, he was promoted to Quartermaster General.

New York's harbor defenses were in poor shape; the forts had been allowed to fall into disrepair. As Engineer-In-Chief, Arthur was responsible for improving the harbor defenses. He summoned a board of engineers who recommended stringing a boom of stone cribs connected by chain cables across the channel to prevent ships from entering the harbor. Large quantities of lumber were required to construct the defenses. Arthur, on his own authority, purchased thousands of board feet of lumber quietly to prevent the price from being driven up. He subsequently sold the unused lumber at a profit to the State.

The reconstruction years were prosperous years for Arthur. During General Grant's 1868 presidential campaign, Arthur was on the executive committee of the Republican Party in New York City. He also served as chairman of the executive committee of the Republican State Committee and became a leading member of the "Conkling Machine," named for Roscoe Conkling, U.S. Senator from New York.

On February 19, 1872, Arthur was named to the position of Collector of the Port of New York. He was responsible for collecting the tariff duties on imports through the port of New York, which were most of the imports to the United States at the time. He was responsible for an organization of 1,000 men and was well paid for his efforts. The position was a U.S. Government position and was the largest and most important job outside of Washington. Arthur dispensed patronage for the party to other parts of the country in addition to New York. He was the principal Republican organization leader in New York City.

Thomas L. James, a deputy in the Collector's office and later the Postmaster of New York, observed of Arthur: "His knowledge of the revenue laws was perfect, and he possessed a judicial mind, well balanced in every respect, which caused his decisions to be almost always invariably right. His power of dispatching business was remarkable. Work did not wear on him as it does on many. He easily threw it off and he did it well."

Rutherford B. Hayes, a believer in civil service reform, was elected President in 1876. He attempted to prevent all federal office holders from active participation in party organizations by issuing an Executive Order. The President's advisors recommended the replacement of the individuals in the three most responsible jobs in the Port of New York Collector's Office: Collector, Deputy Collector, and Naval Officer. Arthur had made fewer political appointments in the Collector's office than his predecessors, but the administration in Washington thought that it was time to make sweeping changes. On July 19, 1878, Arthur was replaced as Collector of the Port of New York. He was not charged with any wrongdoing, but his removal did not enhance his reputation.

In June, 1880, Arthur attended the Republican National Convention in Chicago, where he expected to see General Grant receive the nomination. However, the deadlock between Grant and James G. Blaine went on for twenty-eight ballots. Finally, the delegates to the convention nominated James Garfield, who had given a masterly nominating speech for his fellow Ohioan, John Sherman. Garfield was considered a conciliatory candidate who represented all of the non-Grant delegations.

The delegates first choice for a Vice-Presidential candidate was Levi P. Morton, a wealthy New York banker and importer, who was an advocate of "sound money." When the candidacy was offered to Morton, he looked for Senator Conkling to obtain his approval. The Garfield supporters became restless and decided not to wait for an answer from Morton. The Garfield backers then offered the Vice-Presidential nomination to Arthur, who accepted without consulting Conkling. Conkling was angry with Arthur for accepting without his approval, but it was a case of a man of decision obtaining the nomination and a cautious banker missing the opportunity.

Early in the Garfield administration, relations were strained between the President and the Vice-President. Arthur continued to support the Stalwarts, the Conkling faction of the party, in putting forward candidates for office. Garfield rejected most of the Stalwart's candidates, including the recommendation of Levi P. Morton for Secretary of the Treasury. As presiding officer of the Senate, Arthur attempted to use his influence in opposing the Garfield appointments that required Senate approval.

On July 2, 1881, Charles Giteau, a disappointed office seeker, shot President Garfield and cried out, "I am a Stalwart of the Stalwarts ... Arthur is President now." Garfield was conscious, but he wasn't strong enough to transact the duties of his office. The government languished during the summer months; the Constitution wasn't sufficiently clear to allow Arthur to perform the duties of the President in these circumstances. Arthur resided in his home in New York City until word of Garfield's death reached him on September 19, 1881.

Arthur took the oath of office at his home on the evening of September 19th. On September 22nd, Chief Justice Waite of the Supreme Court administered the oath again in a formal ceremony in the Vice-President's room in the Capitol in Washington. President Arthur gave a brief inaugural address, which was well-received by the press:

Men may die, but the fabrics of our free
institutions remain unshaken. No higher or more
reassuring proof could exist of the strength and
permanence of popular government that the fact
that, though the chosen of the people be struck
down, his constitutional successor is peacefully
installed without shock or strain except the sorrow
which mourns the bereavement. All the noble
aspirations of my lamented predecessor which
found expression in his life, the measures devised
and suggested during his brief administration to
correct abuses, to enforce economy, to advance
prosperity, and to promote the general welfare, to
insure domestic security and maintain friendly
and honorable relations with the nations of the
earth, will be garnered in the hearts of the people;
and it will be my earnest endeavor to profit, and
to see that the nation shall profit, by his example
and experience.... Summoned to these high duties
and responsibilities and profoundly conscious of
their magnitude and gravity, I assume the trust
imposed by the Constitution, relying for aid on
divine guidance and the virtue, patriotism, and
intelligence of the American people.

Initially, Arthur retained all the members of Garfield's
cabinet, but within seven months he had replaced all but the
Secretary of War, Robert Lincoln. None of his appointments was
influenced by political boss Conklin, and none was made to spite
his detractors. He operated more as a statesman than a politician,
and he did not provide positions in his administration for his
friends and his political cronies. Two of his early actions as
President were the vetoes of the Chinese Exclusion Bill, which
was advocated by the Pacific coast states contrary to the Treaty of
1880, and the River and Harbor Bill that required an excessive
appropriation.

He strongly advocated the passage of the Civil Service
Reform Act (the Pendleton Act), which became the underlying

law of Federal Civil Service. He disappointed some of his previous political allies by striking down the spoils system. Despite political pressure to the contrary, he backed the prosecution of the dishonest officeholders who had bilked the government via "Star Route" contracts with the U.S. Postal Service. Star routes were a class of mail service developed to provide postal service to areas of the rapidly expanding country that were not served by railroads or branch lines of railroads. The fast-growing service did not have adequate controls.

Arthur strongly supported national defense, and he secured appropriations to expand the U.S. Navy; he became the sponsor for the creation of a modern navy. Construction of the *Atlanta, Boston, Chicago,* and the *Dolphin* were begun during his administration, and Pearl Harbor was acquired for a naval base.

Arthur also addressed tariff reform in his term of office. The tariffs that had been established during the Civil War were still in effect and in need of change. The northern industrialists, particularly those in the iron and steel industries, were obtaining a duty of twenty-eight dollars a ton for steel rails and were making excessive profits during a time of rapid expansion of the railroads. The passage of the Tariff Act of 1883 was one of the important events of Arthur's administration.

In 1882, Arthur appointed a commission to relocate the boundary between Mexico and the United States. In the following year, a commercial treaty promoting trade with Mexico was signed. Arthur promoted the general remonetization of silver. He negotiated a treaty with Nicaragua that permitted the United States to build a canal, a railway, and a telegraph line across Nicaragua, but the treaty was not ratified by the U. S. Senate.

Three intercontinental railways were completed during Arthur's term as President: the Northern Pacific, the Southern Pacific, and the Atchison, Topeka and Santa Fe. On February 21, 1885, he dedicated the Washington Monument, which was completed during his term of office. One of the last acts of Arthur's administration was the appointment of Ulysses S. Grant as General of the Army, five-star general's rank.

In 1884, Arthur failed to obtain his party's nomination for the presidency; the nomination went to James G. Blaine, who lost the election to Grover Cleveland. Arthur returned to the practice of law, but his health began to fail. In February, 1886, he was diagnosed as having Bright's disease, and he subsequently developed serious heart trouble. He died of a cerebral hemorrhage on November 18, 1886.

Although Arthur was not elected to the office of the presidency, he measured up to the requirements of the job upon the death of President Garfield. Of his years in office, Woodrow Wilson observed:

> His message and state papers read like the productions of a man of unusual capacity, information and literary power. He seemed to make his appointments with a view to the efficiency of the public service, rather than with a view to political advantage. He dealt with bills sent to him by congress in a way that lacked neither courage or discrimination. Faction was quieted, and the course of affairs ran cool ... with an air in which men could think.

In 1899, at the dedication of a nearly eighteen-foot full-length statue of Arthur in Madison Square in Manhattan, Elihu Root, Secretary of War in President McKinley's cabinet and later Secretary of War and Secretary of State in Theodore Roosevelt's cabinet, said of Arthur:

> He was wise in statesmanship and firm and effective in administration. Honesty in national finance, purity and effectiveness in the civil service, the promotion of commerce, the re-creation of the American navy, reconciliation between the North and South and honorable friendship with foreign nations received his active support. Good causes found in him a friend and bad measures met in him an unyielding opponent.

Ezra Cornell

Ezra Cornell, the principal benefactor of Cornell University, was born on January 11, 1807, at Westchester Landing, New York. He was the oldest of eleven children of Elijah Cornell and Eunice Barnard Cornell. In 1818, the Cornell family, who were birthright Quakers, moved to an area called Quaker Basin in Deruyter, Onondaga County. Elijah was a potter, but hard economic times forced him to change his vocation to farming.

At the age of seventeen, Cornell built a shop for his father and a year later built a two-story house to replace the family's log cabin. In 1826, with nine dollars in his pocket, he walked thirty-three miles to Syracuse to find work as a carpenter. He built two sawmills and eventually moved to Homer, where he worked in a shop that made wool-carding machinery. He studied mechanics and technical drawing.

In April, 1828, he walked to Ithaca where he worked as a mechanic at a cotton mill. A year later, he worked as a mechanic at Colonel Jeremiah Beebe's plaster and flour mills on Fall Creek, at the foot of Ithaca Falls. Gypsum, also called land plaster, was brought to Ithaca on barges from Union Springs to be ground in mills. Gypsum, one of Ithaca's major products, was used as plaster, fertilizer, and as an ingredient of Portland cement. Cornell became the manager of Colonel Beebe's mills and was given the nickname "Plaster Cornell."

In March, 1831, Cornell married Mary Ann Wood, the daughter of a farmer from nearby Etna. Since Mary Ann was an Episcopalian, he had married "out of meeting" and was excommunicated from the Deruyter Society of Friends. He built a home near Fall Creek and a new flour mill for Colonel Beebe. During the 1830s, he speculated in real estate.

The Panic of 1837 forced Colonel Beebe to sell his mills and Cornell lost his job. He farmed on Colonel Beebe's farm, which he rented, and was a partner in a small grocery store at Ithaca Falls that failed. In 1842, he obtained the rights to sell the Barnaby and Mooers Double Mold-board plow that two of his neighbors had patented. During the summer of 1842, he was moderately successful at selling plows in Maine. However, he made an acquaintance that was to change his life: F. O. J. Smith— congressman, editor of the *Maine Farmer,* and entrepreneur.

Smith told Cornell that Congress has appropriated $30,000 for Professor Morse to test the practicality of laying telegraph line in a pipe between Washington and Baltimore. Smith had signed a contract to lay the pipe at $100 per mile and now he needed equipment that would allow him to make a profit on the job. Smith asked Cornell to design two machines for him, one to dig the trench for the pipe and a second machine to fill in the trench.

Cornell inspected a sample of the pipe to be laid and was confident that the job could be done with one machine, not two; the furrow would be so narrow that it would close itself. He sketched a machine that would feed wire in a flexible tube coiled on a reel into a furrow two and a half feet deep and a quarter of a inch wide. Smith agreed to pay for its construction. Cornell demonstrated the machine successfully to Professor Morse and was contracted to lay the line between Washington and Baltimore.

Cornell laid a half-mile of line a day; however, having doubts about the insulation on the wire, he built a machine to withdraw the wire from the pipe and reinsulate it. During the winter of 1843-44, he studied electricity and concluded that the line should be run above ground on glass-insulated poles. Early the next spring, he installed the line above ground in time for Morse to send his historic message from the chambers of the Supreme Court in Washington: "What hath God wrought." Cornell was at the receiving end of the message at the Pratt Street railroad station of the Baltimore & Ohio Railroad in Baltimore.

In the spring of 1844, Cornell installed the telegraph line between Philadelphia and New York for Morse and his business associates, the Magnetic Telegraph Company. In 1844, he invested $500 in the Magnetic Telegraph Company, which was half of his salary as construction chief. By July, 1849, he had installed one-third of the telegraph lines in the country. He began the transition from installer to owner of telegraph lines. In 1852, he was elected president of the New York and Erie Telegraph Company.

By the mid-1850s, there were too many competing telegraph

lines over parallel routes. Hiram Sibley proposed the combination of the short, unprofitable lines west of Buffalo into one network; then he purchased many of these lines. On April 4, 1856, the Western Union Telegraph Company was formed. Cornell, a director and the largest stockholder, proposed the name for the new company. However, he had become tired of the corporate infighting, and he played no active role in running the company. His investments continued to appreciate in value; the value of his stock in the Erie and Michigan Telegraph grew from $50,000 in 1857 to $2,000,000 in 1865.

In 1857, Cornell purchased the DeWitt farm, which contained the slope between the Cascadilla and Fall Creek gorges and the hilltop overlooking Ithaca and Cayuga Lake. It had special significance for him; his first view of Ithaca was from this farm. He raised purebred cattle, planted fruit trees, and experimented with various crops.

He built a public library for Ithaca and Tompkins County. He purchased the property, drew the plans for the building, and supervised the construction of the Cornell Free Library. He gave this gift to the community before philanthropy became popular.

In 1861, Cornell was elected to the State Assembly. In the following year, he was appointed president of the State Agricultural Society, which automatically made him a trustee of the Ovid Agricultural College. He and the other Ovid Agricultural College trustees petitioned for a land grant after the passage of the Morrill Act, which provided each state with public lands to be used for establishing a college. People's College in Montour Falls was also competing for a land grant, but its sponsor, State Senator Charles Cook, was unable to raise the matching funds.

In November, 1863, Cornell was elected to the State Senate, where he met fellow Senator Andrew Dickson White of Syracuse. White suggested to Cornell that he establish a new college with the land grant endowment and part of his fortune, instead of backing either the Montour Falls or Ovid sites. Cornell offered to donate his 300-acre hilltop farm, build the facilities, and endow the college with $300,000, if the land grant college were built at Ithaca. No one could match the $300,000 (later increased to $500,000), and Ithaca was chosen as the site of the land grant college for the State of New York.

Cornell and White shared the planning for Cornell University; Cornell concentrated on building and financial issues, and White was responsible for academic matters. One of White's early accomplishments was convincing Cornell to consider classics and humanities with the same importance as agriculture and mechanics, which were Cornell's principal interests. White was unanimously elected the first president of the university.

On October 8, 1868, the university opened with 412 students (332 freshmen and 80 upperclassmen). This began the fulfillment of the motto on Cornell University's Great Seal: "I would found an institution where any person can find instruction in any study." The early years were turbulent, but controlled. Discussion centered on the nonsecular nature of the college, the absence of religion courses, and the election of a layman as president. The nonsectarian aspect of university was important to the founders, who specified that: "the Board of Trustees shall be so constituted ... that at no time shall a majority thereof be of one religious sect, or of no religious sect."

Cornell was a very moral, strong-willed individual who was molded by his early Quaker upbringing. In 1865, he joined the First Unitarian Society of Ithaca when it was established and attended regularly until his death. He died in Ithaca on December 9, 1874.

Historian Carl Becker referred to him as a "tough-minded idealist." He was a man of principle, which he displayed in a letter to his son in September, 1840: " ... do right because it is right, for the sake of right and nothing else. Every act should be measured by that rule—'is it right?' Let a pure heart prompt an honest conscience to answer the question and all will be well." English historian James Anthony Froude, who met Cornell while visiting the United States, observed that "Mr. Cornell would be a sublime figure anywhere; he seems to me the most surprising and venerable object I have seen in America."

Millard Fillmore

Millard Fillmore, the thirteenth President of the United States, was born on January 7, 1800, in Summerhill, Cayuga County. He was the second child of Nathaniel Fillmore and Phoebe Millard Fillmore. The only President born in the Finger Lakes Region started life in a log cabin; his beginnings were as humble as those of Andrew Jackson and Abraham Lincoln. The Fillmores moved to New York from Vermont, but, instead of finding fertile farm soil, they found an unyielding clay soil that made life a constant struggle.

Nathaniel Fillmore didn't want his son to toil as a farmer, so he apprenticed him to the owners of a carding and cloth-dressing mill in New Hope. Fillmore's formal education was in reading, writing, and arithmetic. At home, he had access to a Bible, an almanac, and a hymn book. He bought a dictionary, subscribed to a circulating library, and studied in between setting up the carding machines and changing the rolls on the machine.

Fillmore attended an academy established in Montville by Abigail Powers. During the winter of 1819, Fillmore courted Abigail, and the six-foot-tall, blond farm youth and the blue-eyed redhead fell in love. However, they could not afford to marry for another eight years.

Fillmore taught school in Sempronius to earn money to buy out his apprenticeship at the mill. Then he clerked in the law office of County Judge Wood in Montville. However, Fillmore thought that Judge Wood was "more anxious to keep me in a state of dependence and use me as a drudge in his business than to make a lawyer out of me." In 1822, the Fillmore family moved to East Aurora, where the young student of law taught school and served a Justice of the Peace on Saturdays.

Fillmore moved to Buffalo, which was booming with Erie Canal construction activity, to continue his legal studies at the law office of Rice and Clary. After a year with Rice and Clary, Fillmore was admitted to practice by the Court of Common Pleas and became a partner in the firm. He was now in a position to support a family. On February 5, 1826, he and Abigail were married at St. Matthew's Episcopal Church in Moravia.

He was admitted to try Court of Appeals and Supreme Court cases. In 1832, he helped to write Buffalo's City Charter. In 1828, he was elected State Assemblyman from Erie County; he served three terms in Albany. He sponsored the law that abolished imprisonment for debt and legislation that eliminated religious tests for court witnesses.

In 1836, Fillmore was elected to Congress. His record in Congress indicates a strict interpretation of the Constitution. He became chairman of the powerful House Ways and Means Committee and was responsible for the Tariff Law of 1842. He pushed for the appropriation of $30,000 to Professor Morse for the installation of a telegraph line between Washington and Baltimore, which triggered the dynamic expansion of the telegraph industry.

In 1847, Fillmore was elected Controller of the State of New York. In 1848, He supported the candidacy of Henry Clay for President. However, Zachary Taylor, "Old Rough and Ready," won the nomination. Fillmore was nominated for Vice-President as a conciliatory gesture to the Clay supporters.

Taylor and Fillmore were elected and were inaugurated on March 4, 1849. Fillmore was effective in presiding over the Senate and in improving the use of rules of order in conducting the chamber's business. He reversed an earlier position taken by John C. Calhoun that the Senate was a States-General, or a deliberative body of the states. Fillmore asserted that the Senate served a sovereign nation, which was greater than the states themselves.

On July 9, 1850, President Taylor stood in the hot sun for an extended period of time during a dedication ceremony. He returned to the White House, ate a large quantity of sour cherries, and drank several glasses of cold milk. This may or may not have contributed to his contracting a fever and dying that evening. Fillmore, nominated in conciliation to the Clay forces, was now President Fillmore.

Taylor's cabinet resigned immediately; President Fillmore received recommendations from Daniel Webster on filling the cabinet positions, except for Secretary of State. The new Secretary of State was Webster, who became a driving force in the Fillmore Administration.

In 1852, President Fillmore proposed to Japan that they open their doors to the West. Admiral Oliver Hazard Perry was sent to the Far East with his great white fleet to negotiate with the Japanese government. President Fillmore instructed Admiral Perry to be firm but open about objectives of the visit, which were: providing a fueling station for U.S. ships, establishing commerce between the two countries, and opening a major Asian country to the West. Admiral Perry's expedition led to the signing of the Treaty of Kanagawa between Japan and the United States in 1854.

President Fillmore lost popular support when he signed the Fugitive Slave Law, which authorized the return of slaves captured in the North to their southern owners. The bill didn't have the necessary two-thirds approval of congress and required his signature for passage. The Governor of Virginia stated that: "any repeal of the Fugitive Slave Law, or any essential modification of it, is a mutual repeal of the Union." By signing it, President Fillmore thought he was preventing, or at least postponing, civil war. He realized that he would not be re-elected if he signed the bill. However, the Attorney General pronounced it to be constitutional, and the President thought that he acted for the people in signing the bill into law.

In 1852, General Winfield Scott won the Whig nomination for President, but lost the election to Franklin Pierce. Fillmore returned to Buffalo, where he became one of the founders of the University of Buffalo. He was Chancellor of the University for twenty-eight years. Fillmore was the first president of the Buffalo Historical Society and was a founder of the Buffalo Public Library. He was also a founder of the Fine Arts Academy and president of the General Hospital.

Fillmore is remembered in Buffalo by Fillmore Avenue, Millard Fillmore College of the University of Buffalo, and Millard Fillmore Hospital. Around the state, he is remembered by Fillmore Glen State Park in Moravia and the Village of Fillmore in Allegany County.

Robert G. Ingersoll

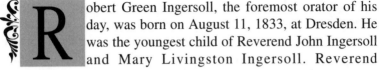obert Green Ingersoll, the foremost orator of his day, was born on August 11, 1833, at Dresden. He was the youngest child of Reverend John Ingersoll and Mary Livingston Ingersoll. Reverend Ingersoll, a Congregationalist minister, moved to a new assignment every two years. The Ingersolls lived in Dresden from 1833 until 1835, when Reverend Ingersoll was reassigned to Cazenovia.

Later in life, Ingersoll was a successful lawyer, politician, family man, and philanthropist, but he was principally known as the "Great Infidel." He didn't believe in organized religion or that there could be proof that God exists, but he didn't deny the existence of God. Ingersoll didn't understand the concept of hell. He irreverently paraphrased his perception of a typical minister's speech, "First: There is a God; Second: He has made known his will; Third: He has selected me to express this message; Fourth: We will now take up the collection; and Fifth: Those who fail to subscribe will certainly be damned."

In place of organized religion, he substituted his own versions of Christianity's beliefs:

> I believe in Liberty, Fraternity, and Equality—
> The Blessed Trinity of Humanity.

> I believe in Observation, Reason, and Experience—
> The Blessed Trinity of Science.

> I believe in Man, Woman, and Child—
> The Blessed Trinity of Life and Joy.

> ... It is far more important to build a home than to erect a church. The holiest temple beneath the stars is a home that love has built. And the holiest altar in all the wide world is the fireside around which gather father and mother and sweet babes.

Prior to the Civil War, Ingersoll and his brother, Ebon, practiced law in Peoria, Illinois. He married Eva Parker and had two daughters, Eva Robert and Maud Robert. Two of his personal strengths, speaking ability and a fantastic memory, contributed to his success as a lawyer. He was an optimist who radiated a joy for life, and he had the aura of a winner. He impressed people. On a trip to England, Ingersoll and his family visited St. Paul's Cathedral. The staff at St. Paul's told Chauncey Depew, the New York Central Railroad magnate, on a later visit, that Ingersoll was the most remarkable American to visit the cathedral.

In 1860, he joined the U.S. Army as Colonel of the 11th Regiment, Illinois Volunteer Cavalry. In December, 1862, Ingersoll, Chief of Cavalry of the Sixth Division, and 800 of his men were overwhelmed by 2,500 cavalry commanded by Confederate General Nathan Bedford "fustest with the mostest" Forrest. The Confederates testified that Ingersoll fought well: "Ingersoll made a good fight. It was enough to make a Christian out of him but it did not. His famous lectures years after show that while we did not convert him, he loved everybody the rest of his life, and if he really believed there is no hell we convinced him that there was something mighty like it."

On a winter evening after the Civil War, Frederick Douglass, the publisher and antislavery leader, traveled to Peoria. He told a friend that he dreaded going to Peoria because no hotel there would give him a room. On a previous trip, he walked the streets all night to keep from freezing. Douglass' friend told him to contact Ingersoll, who would take him in anytime, day or night. His reception at the Ingersoll home "would have been cordial to the most bruised heart of any proscribed and stormbeaten stranger." Douglass couldn't understand the negative feelings of many people toward the "Great Infidel."

In February, 1867, Ingersoll began a two-year term as Attorney General of Illinois. In 1868, he campaigned for Governor, but failed to obtain the nomination. His loss was blamed on his religious beliefs. Political analysts thought that if he had suppressed those beliefs, he would have won. The convention committee asked him to remain silent on religious issues, but he refused, commenting that "My position [on religion]

I would not, under any circumstances, not even for my life ... renounce. I would rather refuse to be President of the United States than to do so."

In 1876, his rousing nominating speech for presidential candidate James G. Blaine at the Republican National Convention in Cincinnati made Ingersoll a national figure. Many famous people were awed by Ingersoll's oratorical ability. Mark Twain said about an Ingersoll speech: "It was the supremest combination of English words that was ever put together since the world began." Reverend Henry Ward Beecher thought that Ingersoll was "the most brilliant speaker of the English tongue of all men on the globe." Elizabeth Cady Stanton listened to him speak for three hours to 3,000 people who called him back for a thirty-minute encore.

Ingersoll was a strong family man. He put women, in general, on a pedestal and idolized his wife and daughters; he was a strong believer in women's rights. Home life was important to him. A friend observed: "Whoever crossed the threshold of the home of Robert G. Ingersoll entered paradise." Mrs. James G. Blaine, after a stay with the Ingersolls, said: "Perhaps I never felt so welcome anywhere in my life." Parker Pillsbury, the abolitionist, observed: "It's a perfect atmosphere of love from the head of the family on down. Even the horse enters into it and seems to appreciate it."

Despite these viewpoints, many people were violently opposed to Ingersoll and spoke against him. He received death threats and many suggested that he should be deported. In 1895, Hoboken churchgoers attempted to jail him under the New Jersey blasphemy law. A minister argued that "Hoboken is bad enough without an advent of Ingersollian blasphemy." The Boston Public Library banned his articles, pamphlets, and papers.

However, those who knew him saw his positive side. A Rochester *Democrat* columnist wrote that "Robert G. Ingersoll is not orthodox in theory, but we should like to see a better Christian in practice ... It is really so nice an article of infidelity that a good deal of it might be passed around with entire safety."

Ingersoll died on July 21, 1899, while visiting his daughter and son-in-law at Dobb's Ferry, New York. At the funeral, Dr. John Livejoy Eliot read the tribute that Ingersoll gave at the funeral of his brother, Ebon, which included the lines:

> He loved the beautiful, and was with color, form, and music touched to tears. He sided with the weak, the poor, the wronged, and lovingly gave alms ... He believed that happiness is the only good ... and love is the only priest. He added to the sum of human joy; and were every one to whom he did some loving service to bring a blossom or flower, he would sleep tonight beneath a wilderness of flowers."

Both Robert G. Ingersoll and his wife, Eva Parker Ingersoll, were buried at Arlington National Cemetery. The tombstone overlooking Ingersoll's grave bears the inscription: "Nothing is grander than to break chains from the bodies of men—nothing nobler than to destroy the phantoms of the soul."

William Pryor Letchworth

William Pryor Letchworth, businessman, conservationist, and philanthropist, was born on May 26, 1823, near Watertown. He was the fourth child and second son of Josiah Letchworth and Ann Hance Letchworth. While he was growing up, the Letchworth family lived in the Cayuga County villages of Moravia and Sherwood. Young Letchworth's first job was an apprenticeship in Auburn at Hayden and Holmes, a retail and wholesale saddlery hardware business that was both a manufacturer and an importer. He became known for his intelligence, industriousness, and his financial insight.

In 1845, Hayden and Holmes sent him to New York City for further training. In 1848, upon his return to Auburn, he became a partner in an old, highly regarded Buffalo firm, Pratt and Company, which was renamed Pratt and Letchworth. The business served both retail and wholesale customers and was also a manufacturer and an importer. The firm employed between 500 and 800 men and owned an iron manufacturing company.

In 1854, after sixteen years of long work weeks, little social life, and no vacations, Letchworth's health declined. His brother, Josiah, joined the company and shouldered many of the detailed burdens of running the business. Letchworth took a well-deserved Florida vacation. In 1857, his interests broadened into art, literature, and social activities; he traveled to Europe for the first time. Upon his return from Europe, his brother, George, who had been with Hayden and Holmes, joined Pratt and Letchworth.

He wanted a restful place in the country; he looked for property in the Niagara Falls area. A friend suggested the Genesee River Valley to him. In the spring of 1858, Letchworth first saw the Genesee River gorge—from the Portage railroad bridge spanning the gorge. His view was of Upper Falls, 234 feet below him, and a rainbow rising from the mist above Middle falls. He was captivated by the scenic, peaceful forests and the mild roar of 107-foot Middle Falls. He wrote: "I perceived the valley's capabilities and determined that if I could get a foothold within its borders, my lot should be cast here." At the relatively young age of thirty-five, he was tired; he resolved to buy property in the area and establish a country home.

In February, 1859, Letchworth purchased 200 acres from nine landowners. The Seneca Indian name for the site of the homestead was An-de-ka-ga-kwa meaning "the place where the sun lingers." He remodeled the homestead and renamed it Glen Iris (Glen of the Rainbow). He hired an associate of Frederick Law Olmstead, who designed Central Park in New York City. Over the next fifty years, Letchworth spent $500,000 on landscaping.

Among Letchworth's first guests were the "Nameless," a literary group that included writers, a sculptor, and a drama critic. They roamed around the property and named the scenic overlooks and the distinctive features: *Devil's Oven, Inspiration Point, Sugar Loaf Rock,* and *Tea Table Rock.*

He purchased additional land, including 500 acres during the Civil War, to protect the gorge and all three waterfalls—Upper, Middle, and Lower—from development. In particular, he wanted to safeguard the valley from purchases of land by utility companies. He had the foresight to place his estate under the jurisdiction of the American Scenic and Historic Preservation Society; otherwise, the public might not have Letchworth State Park to enjoy today.

At the age of forty-seven, Letchworth retired from Pratt and Letchworth. In 1871, he sold his interest in the firm to his brother, Josiah. He declined a request to run for Congress, but he accepted an appointment as Commissioner of the State Board of Charities. He became active in social reform, including providing support to the Craig Colony for Epileptics at Sonyea, Letchworth Village (a home for retarded children in Rockland County), and Industry (a house of detention for boys).

In 1872, Letchworth had one of last remaining buildings of the Seneca Indian Nation, the Council House at Caneadea, disassembled and reassembled near Glen Iris. He also moved the cabin built by Mary Jemison, "the white woman of the Genesee," for her daughter, Nancy, in nearby Gardeau Flats to Glen Iris. On October 1, 1872, he held the "Last Council of the Genesee," which was attended by ex-President Millard Fillmore and Iroquois representatives. Letchworth was given the Indian name, Hai-wa-ye-is-ta, which means "the man who always does the right thing." In September, 1910, the bronze statue of Mary Jemison, "the White Woman of the Genesee," sculpted by Henry K. Bush-Brown was unveiled near Glen Iris.

In February, 1903, Letchworth suffered a stroke that paralyzed his left side. He died in December, 1910, and was buried in Forest Lawn Cemetery in Buffalo. On December 31, 1906, his 1,000-acre estate had been deeded to the State of New York and renamed Letchworth State Park. The efforts of William Pryor Letchworth preserved one of the most scenic areas in the eastern United States.

Elihu Root

 lihu Root, the third of four sons of Oren Root and Nancy Buttrick Root, was born on February 15, 1845, in Clinton, New York. Oren Root, professor of mathematics at Hamilton College, was known to his students as "Cube" Root. Elihu's maternal great-grandfather, John Buttrick, commanded the minutemen at Concord Bridge, where he gave the order to fire the "shot heard 'round the world" that began the Revolutionary War.

In the fall of 1845, the Root family moved to Seneca Falls, where Oren Root had accepted the position of principal of the academy. They lived in Seneca Falls during the time of the first Women's Rights Convention, called by Lucretia Mott and Elizabeth Cady Stanton in 1848. In November, 1849, Oren Root returned to Hamilton College as professor of mathematics. Root's parents lived in Clinton for the remainder of their lives.

Root attended the local academies in Clinton and was tutored by his father. He entered Hamilton College in the fall of 1860 and graduated with high distinction in the spring of 1864. He won the sophomore mathematics prize, was president of the College Baseball Club, and was elected to Phi Beta Kappa.

Root decided to study law; he was influenced by many members of his family who had chosen that vocation. His older brother, Oren, was a lawyer who later became a professor of mathematics (and was nicknamed "Square" Root). Both his father and mother had brothers who were attorneys, one of whom was a County Judge. Three members of the Hamilton College Board of Trustees were lawyers, including Horatio Seymour—who later was nominated as the Democratic candidate for President.

Root taught at the Rome Academy for a year to earn money to attend law school in New York City. On October 12, 1864, he was enrolled as a private in Company G, 101st Infantry Regiment of the New York State Militia in Rome. He was never called to active duty. He enrolled in the New York University Law School in the fall of 1865 and supported himself by teaching part-time at fashionable schools for young women. In mid-1867, he received his law degree and was admitted to the practice of law.

Root was a successful lawyer because he brought many strong personal attributes to the practice of his profession. He worked hard; he was known for his endurance and ability to focus on the subject at hand. His notable memory and mastery of detail led to victories in the courtroom, mainly due to his devastating cross-examinations.

During 1871-73, he served as a junior defense counsel during the trial of William M. ("Boss") Tweed, who was accused of bribery and fraud involving contracts with New York City. Root's reputation suffered by accepting a corrupt political boss as a client, but he maintained that a lawyer has a obligation to defend a client until the jury has returned a verdict of guilty. His practice involved banking issues, estate settlements, railroad suits, and municipal cases.

In 1877, Root met Clara Frances Wales, the daughter of philanthropist Salem H. Wales. They were engaged in October, 1877, and were married early in the following year. They had a daughter and two sons. Root was known as a devoted husband and family man. Some of his career decisions were made for family reasons.

In 1881, Root was granted permission to argue cases before the Supreme Court of the United States. He became a corporation lawyer. The Havemeyer refining companies were his clients; they were known as the Sugar Trust. He suggested how they might avoid litigation, and he handled cases in which they attempted to recover payment of excessive duties.

Root also worked for the Whitney-Ryan traction syndicate, which consolidated Manhattan's streetcar lines. He helped to reduce their taxes, to secure municipal franchises, to check rivals via injunction, and to reorganize their syndicate. He felt that it was his role to advise his clients what the law permitted, and what it didn't permit. Later, when he moved to Washington, D.C., his background as a corporation lawyer was viewed by some of his peers as a liability.

By the late 1890s, Root knew many men who were active in politics, including John Hay, Henry Cabot Lodge, Theodore Roosevelt, and William Howard Taft. In 1897, President McKinley asked Root to go to Spain as his minister to resolve a controversy with Cuba. Root declined because of his inability to speak Spanish and his lack of experience in diplomacy. In 1898, he resolved some legal complications in Theodore Roosevelt's campaign for Governor of New York. The Rough Rider admitted that without Root's help, he would not have been ruled eligible to seek the Governor's office.

On July 21, 1899, President McKinley asked Root to become his Secretary of War. The President assured Root that he needed his legal talents and ability to resolve problems, not his military knowledge or experience. Root followed a well-intentioned but weak Secretary of War. He was immediately confronted with a myriad of challenges, including restoring the reputation of the War Department, providing an army to put down an insurrection in the Philippine Islands, and providing a colonial policy for the United States, the victor of the Spanish-American War.

Root immediately took charge of the War Department. His logical, probing mind coupled with his industry and administrative ability produced early results. He granted a measure of self-government to Hawaii and began to deal with problems in Puerto Rico, Cuba, and the Philippines.

As a result of the Spanish-American War, Puerto Rico had lost her two major tariff-free markets, Cuba and Spain. Also, a hurricane on August 8, 1899, wiped out two-thirds of the island's coffee crop. Root allocated $400,000 out of contingency funds to provide immediate relief to the island and asked President McKinley to exempt Puerto Rico from the U.S. tariffs imposed by the Dingley Act.

In Cuba, Root acted to put down disorder and to make arrangements for the installation a civil government. He authorized the cleaning up of the island from the ravages of war and approved the construction of roads, sanitation facilities, and schools. He replaced the Military Governor with Brigadier General Leonard Wood, whose term became a model for other military governorships. In 1900, a convention was held to draft a new Cuban constitution, and, on May 20, 1902, the United States met its commitment to withdraw from an independent Cuba.

Root's biggest challenge was re-establishing peace in the Philippines and preparing the islands for self-rule. On February 4, 1899, Emilio Aguinaldo led a insurrection against the U.S. troops in the Philippines. Most of these 21,000 troops were due for discharge and had to be replaced with a new army with an authorized strength of 65,000. By early 1900, Aquinaldo was reduced to guerrilla activity by a successful military action planned by Major General Elwell Otis.

On March 16, 1900, President McKinley appointed William H. Taft as chairman of the Second Philippine Commission to organize a civil government. On July 1, 1900, Root's proposals received congressional approval, and Taft was appointed Civil Governor, later Governor General, of the Philippines.

One of Root's most important contributions as Secretary of War for both Presidents McKinley and Theodore Roosevelt was his reorganization of the army and his creation of a general staff. The army's education and training facilities had been severely reduced by previous Secretaries of War. Root created the Army War College and revitalized the special service schools: artillery, cavalry, engineers, and infantry. Also, he rehabilitated the moribund National Guard and allocated $2,000,000 to provide between 250,000 and 300,000 reservists.

Root abolished the position of Commanding General of the Army that had dated from the War of 1812, and, in its place, established a General Staff Corps. He believed in civilian supremacy and authority with responsibility. Authority flowed from the President as Commander-in-Chief of the armed forces to the Secretary of War to the Chief of Staff. The Chief of Staff, who would not necessarily be the officer with the most seniority, was responsible for preparing plans, maintaining military readiness, and coordinating mobilization, when required. All chiefs of bureaus would report to him and he advised the Secretary of War on military issues. The Chief of Staff was assisted by forty to fifty officers who rotated between line and staff jobs.

On February 1, 1904, Root resigned as Secretary of War, partly due to his wife's discomfort with Washington society. President Theodore Roosevelt tried to talk him out of resigning; he reluctantly accepted his resignation. Roosevelt wrote to Mrs. Root: "You know how much, how very much Elihu has been to me. I shall never have, and can never have, a more loyal friend, a more faithful advisor; nor will the government ever be served by any man with greater zeal, efficiency and success." William Howard Taft, his successor as Secretary of War confided to a friend: "Following Secretary Root ... leaves me no room for distinction as Secretary of War. All I can do is merely follow ... his footsteps."

Root returned to the practice of law in New York at a salary of more than $100,000 a year, compared with his annual government salary of $8,000. However, he maintained his close contacts with the President, including the reviewing of his public addresses. Just prior to Roosevelt's re-election in 1904, Root wrote to him: "I congratulate you on attaining the respectable age of forty-six. You have made a good start in life and your friends have great hopes for you when you grow up."

On July 1, 1905, Secretary of State John Hay died. Root had filled in for Hay as Secretary of State in one of Hay's illnesses— during the Boxer rebellion in 1900. Root was Hay's choice as his successor. Root had helped to formulate China policy in 1900, had contributed to the Platt Amendment on Cuba in 1901, and had been a member of the Alaskan Boundary Tribunal in 1903. He had spoken frequently on the subject of foreign affairs during the presidential campaign of 1904; he was not a novice on the subject.

In Root's opinion: "The main object of diplomacy is to keep the country out of trouble." He maintained close contact with the Senate's Foreign Relations Committee and always acted on the basis that, according to the Constitution, foreign relations is the joint responsibility of the executive and legislative branches of the government.

Root's carefully drafted documents coupled with his understanding of the art of the possible assured his success with his Senate colleagues. Also, his working relationship with President Roosevelt was complementary. They both contributed original ideas; Teddy was the more impulsive of the two. Root usually played the restraining role, but sometimes their roles were reversed.

Root made notable improvements to the consular service and established the Division of Far Eastern Affairs. He began the modernization of the State Department filing system, which had been in use since 1789. During the summer of 1906, he was elected as honorary president of the Pan-American Conference in Rio de Janeiro, and he improved the country's relationships with the Latin American countries. Also, he resolved all of the ongoing issues of contention with Canada. He signed treaties of arbitration with Austria-Hungary, Denmark, Great Britain, Holland, Norway,

Sweden, Switzerland, and other countries. Generally, he contributed significantly to international peace.

On January 27, 1909, Root resigned as Secretary of State to prepare for his term in the U.S. Senate, which began in March of that year. In 1910, he was the chief counsel for the United States at the Hague Tribunal convened to arbitrate the differences concerning fisheries between Great Britain and the United States. He was also appointed to the Permanent Court of Arbitration by President Taft. He played a leading role in the passage of the Federal Reserve Bill of 1913, which provided for a Federal Bank under the control of the U.S. Government.

Late in 1910, he was elected president of the Carnegie Endowment for International Peace. Senator Root was viewed as the leader of the peace movement in the United States. In 1912, he was awarded the Nobel Peace Prize.

On March 4, 1915, Root completed his term in the Senate and did not seek re-election. His Senate term was not as productive as his years in the cabinet were. He was a conservative serving during a period of progressivism. His efforts to maintain the status quo was considered by some of his peers to be negativism. At a minimum, he succeeded in preventing the progressives from effecting change faster than it could be absorbed by his constituents.

President Wilson sent private citizen Root to Moscow in 1917 to encourage Kerensky's Revolutionary Government to pursue their war effort from the east in support of the allies during World War I. Kerensky's overthrow by Lenin and the Bolsheviks frustrated his efforts. After the armistice, his advice was sought on the Covenant of the League of Nations. In 1920, he was a member of the League of Jurists of the League of Nations that met in the Hague to plan for a court of international justice. In November 1921, he was appointed to the International Conference on Armament Limitation by President Harding.

Root is considered by historians to be one of the most effective Secretaries of War and Secretaries of State during the first half of the twentieth century. He played a significant role in promoting the cause of international peace. On February 7, 1937, Elihu Root died of bronchial pneumonia, just over a week before his ninety-second birthday. Following a service in the Hamilton College Chapel, he was buried on a hillside overlooking his Alma Mater.

William H. Seward

William Henry Seward, Abraham Lincoln's Secretary of State, was born in the hamlet of Florida, Orange County, New York, on May 16, 1801. He was one of five children of Samuel Sweezy Seward and Mary Jennings Seward. Samuel was a doctor, land speculator, and merchant, as well as a county judge and postmaster.

In July, 1820, Seward graduated from Union College, where he was a member of the Adelphic Debating Society and Phi Beta Kappa. After graduation, he studied law in Goshen and in New York City. In October, 1822, he was admitted to the bar and, several months later, joined the law practice of Judge Elijah Miller in Auburn.

Judge Miller's daughter, Frances Adeline Miller, had been a classmate of Seward's sister, Cornelia, at Mrs. Willard's Female Seminary in Troy. Seward had met Frances when she visited Cornelia at their home in Orange County. Seward and Frances courted and became engaged during the summer of 1823. On October 20, 1824, they were married at St. Paul's Episcopal Church in Auburn.

On a trip to Niagara Falls, a wheel came off the young couple's wagon in Rochester. A young newspaper editor, Thurlow Weed, came to their assistance, and a lifelong friendship was formed between one who sought office and one who sought power. Seward joined the national Republican party, and, in September, 1828, he was elected chairman of the party's young men. From 1828 to 1830, Seward was active in the Anti-Masonic party. In 1830, he won the election as that party's candidate for State Senator. In 1832, he was re-elected to the State Senate.

In 1838, Seward was elected Governor of New York, with considerable help from his campaign manager, Thurlow Weed.

147

Weed was also instrumental in Seward's winning a second term as Governor. However, they were both pointing toward a national office for Seward. In 1848, their goal was reached when Seward was elected to the U.S. Senate. He was re-elected to the Senate in 1854 and positioned himself for his party's nomination for the Presidency in 1856.

In June, 1856, James Buchanan was nominated for President at the Democratic National Convention in Cincinnati. Buchanan had just returned home from his post as Minister to the Court of St. James and had the advantage over the other candidates of not being involved in the slave state / free state issues of the previous several years. In June, 1856, the Republican Party was only several months old when it held its national convention in Philadelphia. When Seward was called "the foremost statesman of America" at the convention, the delegates cheered more loudly than for any other candidate, including for successful nominee John C. Fremont.

Thurlow Weed and Seward's other advisors advised him not to run in 1856. They thought that Buchanan would beat the nominee of a newly established party; they advised Seward to aim for 1860. In hindsight, when Abraham Lincoln beat Seward for the Republican nomination for President in 1860, they realized that their friend's best opportunity had been in 1856.

In a campaign speech for his party's candidates in 1858, Seward referred to the country's two incompatible political systems, one based on slave labor and the other representing free labor. He predicted an "irrepressible conflict" as the country grew and the two systems were in frequent contact. He stated that the country must become either entirely a slaveholding nation or one of free labor. In his opinion, the Democratic Party should be turned out of office because it was a a tool of the slaveholders.

In 1860, successful Republican candidate Lincoln's first days in office were trouble-filled because most of his cabinet members thought they would make a better President than he would. His Secretary of State, William H. Seward, shared this opinion. However, Seward later said of Lincoln, "He is the best of us." Seward was a valuable asset to Lincoln during his transition into the Presidency, particularly in matters of protocol. Seward was loyal to his chief; he survived many delegations to President Lincoln requesting that he dump his Secretary of State.

On the black April day that President Lincoln was shot by John Wilkes Booth, the plot included plans to assassinate Vice-President Andrew Johnson and Secretary of State William Seward. Mr. Johnson escaped his fate, but Lewis Payne gained access to Seward's house on the pretext of delivering medicine. Payne insisted on instructing Seward about the medicine and climbed the stairs to Seward's bedroom.

Seward's son, Fred, blocked Payne's entrance to his father's bedroom. He was rewarded by being struck on the head with Payne's pistol, after it misfired. Payne entered Seward's bedroom and stabbed him repeatedly; he wounded him in the face and neck, broke his jaw, and slashed his right cheek. Seward's daughter, Fanny, screamed, alerting his son, Augustus, who wrestled Payne out of the bedroom and down the stairs. Payne fled but was captured later.

Both Seward and Fred were in serious condition for weeks after the attack. In mid-May, Seward returned to the State Department for brief visits, but could not return to his office full-time until July. President Johnson asked Seward to stay on as Secretary of State; he served until the end of President Johnson's term.

After the Civil War, Seward began to consider acquisitions for the United States. He considered purchasing the Danish West Indies, but the price was too high. In the 1840s and 1850s, Russia wanted to retain Russian America, as Alaska was called. However, Russia's plans for expansion became focused on the lower Amur River Valley, which they had just purchased from China. Russia thought that further expansion into Alaska from the United States and Canada was inevitable; furthermore, Alaska was indefensible in time of war. Also, the Russian treasury was in need of an infusion of gold.

During the winter of 1864-65, Hiram Sibley of Rochester, president of the Western Union Telegraph Company, visited St. Petersburg and was told that Russia was interested in selling Alaska. Sibley conveyed this message to the U.S. Minister to Russia, Henry Clay, who passed it on to Seward. Seward immediately began negotiations with the Russian Minister to the U.S., Edward Stoeckl.

Seward was so anxious to prepare the treaty for the Senate that he kept the State Department open all evening on March 29, 1867. By early the next morning, he and Stoeckl had the treaty drawn up, signed, and ready for submission to the Senate. The U.S. purchased Alaska for $7,000,000, and Seward was showered with criticism for buying "Seward's folly." However, Minister Clay appraised the value of Alaska at $50,000,000.

In 1868, when Ulysses S. Grant was elected President, Seward retired from public office. He made several world tours during the first few years of his retirement. On October 10, 1872, he died at his home at Auburn, while appealing to his family to love one another. He may not have attained his goal of the highest office in the land, but he certainly had a life filled with accomplishments.

Mary Clark Thompson

Mary Lee Clark, the third of five children of farmer and lumberman Myron Holley Clark and Zilpha Clark, was born in Naples in 1835. Myron Clark moved his family to Canandaigua in 1837, after being elected sheriff of Ontario County. Mary attended Canandaigua schools and, in 1849, enrolled at the Ontario Female Academy.

In 1850-51, Myron Clark was president of the Village of Canandaigua. In 1852-54, he served in the State Senate, where he sponsored railroad legislation that resulted in the consolidation of several independent railroads into the New York Central Railroad. He was known for his diligence and his anti-slavery and pro-temperance views. In 1854, he was elected Governor of New York State.

While living in Albany, Mary met Frederick Ferris Thompson, a New York City banker. The Thompson family published the *Bank Note Reporter,* a weekly newsletter that contained articles on U.S. currency and the financial standing of the nation's banks. Later, Frederick, with his father and brother, established the successful First National Bank in New York City.

On June 17, 1857, Mary and Thompson were married in Canandaigua. Their primary residence was a New York townhouse, but they spent their summers in Canandaigua. In 1863, they purchased a large property from the Holberton family, who had named the house Sonnenberg (Sunny Hill) for a small town in Germany. In 1887, they replaced the house with a forty-room mansion, but retained the name, Sonnenberg. The rusticated gray stone mansion, which is trimmed in red Medina sandstone, is a blend of Elizabethan, Richardson Romanesque, and Tudor architectural styles.

Toward the end of his life, Thompson was less active at the First National Bank; he turned over the day-to-day management of the bank to a partner. He became a philanthropist, and he contributed to and became a trustee of Teachers College (the predecessor of Columbia University), Vassar College, and Williams College, which was his alma mater. He died in 1899.

Mary Clark Thompson, who was left with a substantial legacy in her husband's will, became "Canandaigua's Lady Bountiful." Reverend Livingston Taylor, pastor of the First Congregational Church, spoke of her giving as:

> ... that perfect cycle which, for this community, so richly covered the whole span of life, from the cradle to the grave: the lodge at the gate of our beautiful world for the honor and comfort of motherhood, and to welcome the newborn; the places where children play and youth grows strong and agile and right-minded; the great house of healing where the sick may go; the pleasant home in which for declining years there is comfort and security; and that lodge at the other gate, dedicated to the use and consolation of those who come to it with their dead.

Reverend Taylor referred to Thompson Memorial Hospital and its maternity wing, the Howell Street playground and swimming pool, Clark Manor House (a home for the aged), and the Woodlawn Cemetery Chapel.

Mary also contributed to the community in many other ways. She saved the largest hotel in Canandaigua, the Canandaigua Hotel on Main Street, which had become run down and was going to be converted into a corset factory. She bought the hotel, renovated it, and restored it to its former grandeur. She donated the plans and the property for the construction of the U.S. Post Office on Main Street, which served the city for many years.

She made significant contributions to the building funds of the First Methodist Church, St. Mary's Catholic Church, the Ontario County Historical Society, the Wood Public Library, and the YMCA. Her method of operation was to pledge a substantial sum and then challenge her fellow Canandaiguans to contribute the remainder. She also made numerous contributions on a personal level, such as college scholarships to the children of her employees.

In her later years, she traveled widely, including seven trips around the world. She became a collector of books, ceramics, furniture, manuscripts, paintings, samplers, statuary, and tapestries. Then she became a contributor of these items; for example, she donated French tapestries to the Vassar College Library.

On July 28, 1923, Mary Clark Thompson died after a short illness. In tribute to her, Canandaigua businesses, city offices, and county offices were closed and the flag was flown at half staff on City buildings. She was buried next to her husband in the Clark family plot in Woodlawn Cemetery. Inscribed on a tombstone above her and her husband's graves is a passage from Matthew 25:40: "Verily I say unto you, inasmuch as ye have done it unto the least of these my brethren, ye have done it unto me."

The Thompson estate was sold to the U.S. Government, which built a Veteran's Administration Hospital on the farmlands. In 1972, a nonprofit educational corporation, Sonnenberg Gardens, Inc., was chartered by an act of Congress to preserve the mansion and gardens for display to the public.

James W. Wadsworth, Jr.

J ames Wolcott Wadsworth, Jr., the only son of James W. "Boss" Wadsworth, was born on August 12, 1877, in Geneseo. At the age of six, he was given a pony and learned to ride. When he was nine, the "Boss" gave him a horse, along with the responsibilities of caring for it—combing, feeding, and grooming. The following year, he began working on the Home Farm, including cultivating, haying, and weeding. He learned farming in Geneseo and on the family's 2,000-acre Street Farm in Avon.

Wadsworth spent the winters in Washington, D.C., with his parents; his father was the Congressmen from the district. Young Wadsworth received good counseling from his father, particularly on the the subject of service to the community. The "Boss" advised him: "It doesn't suffice for you to be happy in your own home. You get out and be useful."

Wadsworth left home for the pre-preparatory Fay School in Southboro, Massachusetts, when he was ten years old. From the Fay School, he went to St. Mark's preparatory school and then to Yale University. He had played baseball for the Geneseo town team and continued with the sport at Yale. He made the varsity in his senior year and was named a Walter Camp All-American first baseman.

Wadsworth took required courses in his first two years at New Haven. In his last two years when he could take electives, his favorite courses were history, philosophy, and political economy. He made "gentlemanly Cs" in his courses, an approach to academics that was popular at the time. He graduated in 1898, just in time to join the volunteers for the Spanish-American War.

Wadsworth joined Battery A of the Pennsylvania Artillery-Volunteers, a well-drilled Philadelphia outfit staffed with many young aristocrats. He was appalled at the lack of practical field training for his unit. Battery A didn't fire a single round of live ammunition in six weeks at their staging area at Newport News, Virginia. It was obvious to him that the United States, which had enjoyed peace since 1865, did not know how to prepare for war. Fortunately, his unit was never tested. The war was over before

Battery A could be sent to Cuba. However, they were sent on a brief mission to Puerto Rico.

The "Boss," however, did get to Cuba as President McKinley's Inspector of the Army in Cuba. On July 3, 1898, the Spanish fleet was destroyed by the U.S. Navy off Santiago de Cuba, and, two weeks later, the Spanish Army surrendered at Santiago. The "Boss" participated in determining the terms of surrender for the Spanish General Toral with Admiral Sampson, Colonel Theodore Roosevelt, Generals Shafter, Wheeler, and Leonard Wood.

In the spring of 1899, Wadsworth returned to Geneseo from a round-the-world cruise on the Army Transport *SS Sherman,* which sailed from New York with the U.S. Third Infantry bound for garrison duty in the Philippines. The "Boss" gave him the 725-acre Kemp Farm and the adjoining, newly purchased Hampton Farm. A grateful son said, "Thanks to the Boss and the silver spoon, I was on my own." During the winter when farm work was slack, he worked in the Geneseo Valley National Bank to learn business methods.

Wadsworth met Alice Hay, daughter of Secretary of State John Hay, in Washington. He frequently visited the Hay family at their summer residence at Lake Sunapee in New Hampshire. What began as a childhood friendship grew into love and devotion that lasted through their lifetimes. On September 30, 1902, they were married in New Hampshire. They honeymooned in the Berkshires and moved into their home, Hampton, on Hampton Farms.

With encouragement from his father, Wadsworth's political career began with the presidential election of 1900. In Geneseo and in neighboring towns, he drummed up votes for the McKinley-Roosevelt ticket. In 1903, he made his first political speech to a gathering of farmers in nearby Brooks Grove. Halfway through his prepared speech, he lost his train of thought, retraced his steps, and recovered to finish the speech. From that point on, he usually spoke extemporaneously, instead of relying on a prepared text.

In 1904, he was nominated to the State Assembly by the county Republican leaders. He traveled around the district making speeches. He concluded one speech with: "I know I'm very young and have a lot to learn, but I'm going to follow the example of Mr. Root, Mr. Teddy Roosevelt and Mr. Depew, and I'm sure you'll never find that I've misrepresented you." His political naivete lasted until he arrived in Albany, which was in the final throes of control by the "interests"—big business and the railroads.

In his second term in office, he was nominated Speaker of the Assembly, the second most powerful office in the state. Until the end of his political career, he wondered why the Governor had chosen such an inexperienced assemblyman for the post. His first action was to abolish seniority in selecting a majority leader and committee chairmen. The old guard in the Assembly was surprisingly willing to go along with the new Speaker.

One of the Assemblymen that Wadsworth got to know well and to like was Al Smith of New York City. Robert Wagner was another of his contemporaries. On several occasions, Wadsworth was on the other side of an issue with ex-President Theodore Roosevelt, who still wielded immense power in the state. Wadsworth stood his ground. The New York *Sun* observed: "Today Mr. Wadsworth stands forth as the one Republican leader in the nation who has met the Hon. Theodore Roosevelt in a fair fight and neither fled nor lost."

From 1911 until 1914, Wadsworth stepped down from politics while Democrats controlled both the Assembly and the State Senate. At the request of an aunt, he took over as manager of the 525,000-acre J. A. Ranch in the Texas Panhandle, which was the source of many of the cattle sent east to the Wadsworth farms in the Genesee Valley. It was not being run efficiently; he reorganized its operations and steered it in new directions. He found the work very satisfying.

Wadsworth stayed in touch with politics; in 1912, he was the chairman of the New York delegation at the Republican National Convention in Chicago. In the summer of 1914, he received a telegram informing him of Senator Elihu Root's retirement and requesting him to become a candidate for the U.S. Senate. He won the election over his Democratic opponent, James W. Gerard of Geneseo, the United States Ambassador to Germany.

As he was about to be sworn as U.S. Senator, Elihu Root advised Wadsworth "not to fill his shoes, but to succeed him."

Root and John Hay were the two individuals who influenced Wadsworth's political outlook the most. He also respected Henry Cabot Lodge and valued his advice.

Wadsworth was appointed to the Committee on Agriculture and the Military Affairs Committee, an important assignment with the coming war in Europe. He supported every effort to strengthen the U.S. military. Wadsworth was an active member of the Military Affairs Committee in improving the efficiency of industry in producing material for the war effort. On November 6, 1918, he sailed for Europe to observe conditions at the front, but arrived after the armistice had been signed.

Wadsworth was the principal author of the National Defense Act of 1920. In drafting the act, his sub-committee sought the advice of Generals John J. Pershing and Leonard Wood. A smaller regular army, a substantial federally assisted National Guard, and Universal Military Training were major components of the Bill. The Bill was weakened before it passed, and one of its major elements, Universal Military Training, was eliminated.

In 1950, speaking of Wadsworth's efforts of thirty years previously, General George C. Marshall said: "If Congress had passed the original Wadsworth bill I do not believe even a Hitler would have dared to provoke a second World War.... [But even though] the teeth and backbone of the Act had been emasculated ... The Act was a tremendous advance for the security of our national defense."

In 1920, during the Harding administration, Wadsworth asked to be reassigned to the Senate Foreign Relations Committee and the Senate Finance Committee. In 1926, he was up for re-election. He joined with his friend, Democrat Al Smith, in fighting prohibition. Wadsworth was one of the most visible Wets in the state, and he became a target of the Drys. Many of his upstate constituents were proponents of prohibition, and he knew that this stand put his re-election at risk. Furthermore, he had a worthy Democratic opponent, Robert F. Wagner of New York City.

Wadsworth's advisors counseled him, when speaking in dry counties, not to mention prohibition. He responded: "That's hypocritical. I don't believe in prohibition, and I'm going to say so right out in open meeting. I'm tired of people who talk dry and drink wet." He lost to Wagner by 116,000 votes; a Wet splinter group of the Republican Party received 230,000 votes, enough to prevent Wadsworth from being re-elected. In 1927, he organized the Association Opposed to Prohibition, whose members included Pierre and Irenee du Pont, J. J. Raskob, and Al Smith.

In 1932, he was asked by the Republican Party in the district to run for congress. His wife supported him in his decision to run. She reminded him that John Quincy Adams had served as a congressmen after he was President of the United States. He was assigned to the Committee of Elections and the Committee on Banking and Currency. Within a few months, he was transferred to the Committee on Interstate and Foreign Commerce, a more important assignment. Sam Rayburn, the Speaker of the House, was the committee chairman. Rayburn and Wadsworth formed a close working relationship.

In 1936, the Republicans sounded out Wadsworth's interest in becoming a candidate for the Presidency. He told them that he valued his intellectual independence, and that he was currently holding down two big jobs: running the Wadsworth estates in the Genesee Valley and serving as Congressman. He again served as chairman of the New York delegation at the Republican National Convention. He supported Alfred M. Landon of Kansas, who was trounced by President Roosevelt in the election.

Several years later there was a strong movement to make Wadsworth Minority Leader of the House. However, he couldn't bring himself to do the political maneuvering required to obtain the job. In 1937, he was elected chairman of the Republican Policy Committee. He had previously served a chairman of the Republican Caucus. On most issues, Wadsworth was on the opposite side from President Roosevelt. The issue that brought the two men together was their common perceived need to prepare the country's military for the coming war.

Wadsworth was co-author of the Burke-Wadsworth Selective Service Act, but the country was not ready for it. He was called a "warmonger" and received considerable abuse from isolationists, pacifists, and radicals. He responded: "To those who say to me, 'If you have an army you're going to use it; if you don't have an army perhaps you will remain a peaceful nation,' I say,

'Nonsense!' The American people can't be persuaded to go to war just for the fun of it."

Again in 1940, Wadsworth's name was put forth as a possible candidate for the Presidency. Again, he demurred. He felt that the many scars from his legislative battles over more than twenty years would work against him as a candidate. He supported Wendell Willkie, the Republican nominee, who was soundly defeated by Roosevelt.

On August 12, 1941, Wadsworth spoke in Congress in support of the Selective Service Act. Arthur Krock of the New York *Times* described it as one of the few speeches that had really influenced a congressional outcome in modern times. While he spoke, there was complete silence and no interruptions. When he finished, there was silence. Then, spontaneously, every member of the House rose and gave him a standing ovation.

The bill passed by one vote, 203 to 202. Thus, four months later when the Japanese attacked Pearl Harbor and the United States became involved in another world war, we were still unprepared—but not as woefully unprepared as we would have been had not Wadsworth persevered. He was active in serving on his congressional committees during the war, and, in 1944, he was given the additional assignment of vice-chairman of the Select Committee on Postwar Military Policies.

After the war, Wadsworth worked hard as a sponsor of combining the Department of the Army, the Department of Navy, and an independent Air Force into one organization—the Defense Department. It was called the Unification Act; it was received on the floor of Congress on February 26, 1947. It became Wadsworth's principal legislative interest, and he virtually rewrote the bill while it was before Congress.

In 1950, Wadsworth retired from Congress. Arthur Krock of the New York *Times,* the dean of Washington columnists observed:

> "A great public figure is passing.... [Wadsworth's retirement] calls to mind many a notable parliamentary struggle in which his wisdom, courage, and integrity were devoted to a high

> patriotic concept which rose above any partisan
> consideration. So often did Mr. Wadsworth
> occupy the uncrowned height in Congress that he
> came to be known as the conscience of the House,
> which though it might disregard, it admired and
> respected."

His retirement was brief. In 1951, during the Korean Conflict, Wadsworth was appointed chairman of the National Security Training Commission by President Harry Truman. Wadsworth had been experiencing stomach pains, but he accepted the responsibility. He directed the effort until he was forced to go to the hospital for treatment. The Commission's recommendations were documented, and the next step was to present their proposals to Congress. This task was left to others. On June 21, 1952, Wadsworth died. His son-in-law, Senator Stuart Symington, said of him: "He did not have integrity; he was integrity."

Andrew White

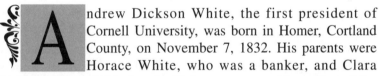

ndrew Dickson White, the first president of Cornell University, was born in Homer, Cortland County, on November 7, 1832. His parents were Horace White, who was a banker, and Clara Dickson White. White's grandfather was a wealthy pillar of the Homer community and a member of the state legislature. In 1839, the White family moved to Syracuse, where White attended the Syracuse academy and later the advanced Syracuse Classical High School. He was the editor of the high school magazine, *The Bee*.

Horace White insisted that his son attend Geneva College, the predecessor of Hobart College, because of its Congregationalist affiliation. White was not academically challenged by the school and left after one year. He was admitted to Yale University as a sophomore. In his senior year, he was editor of the *Yale Literary Magazine* and won the DeForest Prize for his oration, "The Diplomatic History of Modern Times," an early indication of his interest in diplomacy.

Upon his graduation, he accompanied Connecticut Governor Thomas Seymour, the newly appointed Minister to Russia, to St. Petersburg as his attache. White visited Oxford and Paris enroute to Russia; he lingered in France for several months to improve his fluency in French, which was the diplomatic language of Russia.

In the summer of 1855, he left Russia and enrolled at the University of Berlin in the fall. He was impressed with German scholarship, observing that: "In America, the course of studies is incomplete ... the school is more splendid in England and the scholarship is more splendid in Germany." He traveled through France, Italy, and Switzerland and added 700 books to his personal library.

In 1856, White returned to Yale to study for his Master of Arts degree. Upon receiving his degree, he accepted a position as professor of history and rhetoric at the University of Michigan. He was revered by his students, who weren't much younger than he was. White agreed with the concepts of Henry Tappan, the president of the University of Michigan: the importance of non-sectarianism, the education of women, and that the classics and the humanities should be on a par with agriculture, law, mechanics, and medicine. Also, White liked Tappan's practice of inviting guest lecturers to the campus, including George William Curtis, Ralph Waldo Emerson, Wendell Phillips, and Carl Shurz.

White told George William Curtis, while on a visit to Ann Arbor as a guest lecturer, of his ambition to establish a great university in Central New York, the greatest state. White envisioned a university serving a broad scope of interests. It should begin with agriculture and grow until it fulfilled the highest ideals of a university. The best teachers should be assembled from all over the world to serve it. The young scholar continued his outpouring to Curtis until the hour was late, concluding with the observation that we live in a country open to ideas and that some day his dream might be realized.

In 1860, Horace White died, leaving White $300,000 as his portion of the estate. In the summer of 1862, he obtained a leave of absence from the University of Michigan due to ill health and the need to settle his father's estate. He tried to enlist in the Union Army but was rejected for health reasons. He returned to Syracuse and busied himself with war work.

In the fall of 1862, White went to Europe to take health cures for his severe indigestion problems. Upon his return, he was elected to the State Senate from his Syracuse district and was appointed chairman of the Committee on Literature, which dealt with education issues. He met Ezra Cornell, the chairman of the Committee on Agriculture, in the Senate. One winter day, Cornell and White met on the Capitol steps and walked down Albany's State Street together. Cornell asked White: "I have about a half million dollars more than my family will need; what is the best thing I can do with it for the state?" White told Cornell of his dream of founding a great university:

> The choice, White said, was between charity and education. Charities should be left to the charitable instincts of the population at large. And since the state took care of the lower grades of education, it was the field of higher education that needed support. What was wanted was a larger and better endowed institution than now existed—one fully equipped for technical and scientific education; one which would stress history and modern literature as well as classical studies. Agriculture and the mechanic arts, as stipulated by the Land Grant Act, would benefit by sharing the same campus with the liberal arts and scientific schools, and by receiving equal rank.

Cornell took the young State Senator's advice. On February 7, 1865, White introduced a bill to the State Senate "to establish Cornell University, and to appropriate to it the income from the sale of public land granted to this state." Initially, Cornell was hesitant to give his name to the University, but White convinced him by citing Harvard University, Yale University, and Merton College of Oxford University as precedents. On April 27, 1865, Governor Reuben E. Fenton signed the bill and the fledgling university was born.

White wrote the university bylaws and, on October 21, 1866, submitted a Plan of Organization to the University Board of Trustees. The Honorable Andrew D. White of Syracuse was unanimously elected president of Cornell University. He observed, in a moment of self-deception, that "Nothing was further from my expectations or wishes." On October 8, 1868, the first class of students was admitted to Cornell University.

In the early years, the University's endowment had three components: Mr. Cornell's gift of $500,000, called the Founder's Fund; New York State's College Land Scrip Fund, money from the sale of land scrip by New York State to Mr. Cornell; and the Cornell Endowment Fund, which was money from the sale of land such as Wisconsin timberland.

White alternated between an academic and a diplomatic career. He served as Commissioner to Santo Domingo, Minister and Ambassador to Germany, Minister to Russia, and as head of the U.S. delegation to the Hague Peace Conference in 1899. Between 1872 and 1900, his name was frequently proposed as a candidate for Governor of New York. However, he had no aspirations to deal with the State's politics. In 1885, he retired as president of Cornell University.

He was frequently mentioned as a candidate for Secretary of State, but he was never appointed. In 1884, he was a dark horse candidate for the Republican nomination for President, but James G. Blaine was nominated. In 1900, he was proposed as the Republican candidate for Vice-President, but he was sixty-eight years old and bothered by health problems, so he demurred. Theodore Roosevelt was nominated and elected Vice-President. In 1901, President McKinley was assassinated at the Buffalo Exposition, and the Rough Rider became President.

White died on November 4, 1918. Cornell University was fortunate to have a person with White's vision as its first president. Andrew Dickson White was one of those rare individuals who had a dream, created a plan to accomplish that dream, implemented the plan, and watched his accomplishment grow throughout his lifetime.

Chapter 5

"The miracle, or the power, that elevates the few is to be found in their industry, application, and perseverance under the promptings of a brave, determined spirit."

—Mark Twain

L. Frank Baum

Frank Baum, the author of *The Wonderful Wizard of Oz*, was born in Chittenango, which is located fifteen miles east of Syracuse. Baum was the seventh child of Cynthia Stanton Baum and Benjamin Baum, a cooper who made his fortune in the oil fields of Pennsylvania in Titusville and Bradford. He was christened Lyman Frank Baum shortly after his birth on May 15, 1856, but he preferred to be called Frank.

The Baum family moved to Rose Lawn Farm, which was north of Syracuse in present-day Mattydale, when Frank was five years old. The fifteen-acre Rose Lawn Farm was adjacent to Spring Farm, the Baum's dairy farm. Young Frank developed a love for animals while living on the farm, and some of his farm memories stayed with him. He saw his first scarecrow on the farm and had a recurring dream of being chased by one.

Baum's first choice of a vocation was acting. He began his acting career in Syracuse and moved to New York City. He dabbled in writing plays in between his stage engagements. Upon his return home for the Christmas holidays in 1881, he met his cousin Josephine's Cornell University roommate, Maud Gage. Maud was the youngest daughter of Matilda Joslyn Gage, the women's rights activist. Frank and Maud fell in love, and he proposed to her during the summer of her sophomore year. Matilda Gage told Maud that she didn't want her to marry an actor. When Maud threatened to leave home, Matilda gave in and consented to the marriage. Frank and Maud were married on November 9, 1882, in the Gage home in Fayetteville.

After the birth of their first child, Frank Joslyn Baum, on December 4, 1883, Baum became more active in his father's oil business, which allowed him to spend more time with his family. Baum's father, Benjamin, was injured in a horse and buggy accident, suffered a lengthy illness, and died on February 14, 1887. The death of the financial mainstay of the family, coupled with the company's losses due to embezzlement by the accountant, left the family in reduced circumstances. They were forced to sell their farm.

Maud had two sisters and a brother living in Dakota Territory. They convinced the Baums to move to Aberdeen, a town of 3,000 residents in the Territory. Maud's older sister, Helen, and her husband rented a store to them. The Baums went into the dry goods business. However, the population of the town wasn't sufficient to support the enterprise. Baum closed the store and bought the local newspaper, the *Dakota Pioneer*, from a fellow Syracusan, John Drake. Lack of rain caused many crop failures in the Dakota Territory, and the circulation of the paper dwindled. Finally, Baum concluded that the sheriff wanted the paper more than he did, so he let him have the property.

The Baums moved to Chicago. He accepted a position as a reporter for the *Evening Post,* after being rejected by the *Tribune* and seven other newspapers. He supplemented his income with a second job as a salesman, since he now had a wife and four children to support. In October, 1897, Baum had his first book, *Mother Goose in Prose,* published by the Chicago publishing firm of Way and Williams. After being an actor, merchant, newspaperman, and salesman, Baum had finally found his niche—making children happy. *Mother Goose in Prose* was followed by *Father Goose, His Book* in September, 1899, and *The Songs of Father Goose* in the summer of 1900.

The story of *The Wonderful Wizard of Oz* evolved in Baum's mind long before he wrote it down. It grew out of storytelling that he did regularly with the neighborhood children. His first title for the book was *Emerald City*; his second choice for a title was *The Fairyland of Oz,* followed by *The Land of Oz.* Finally, after discussing the title with his illustrator, William Denslow, and with Maud, he chose *The Wonderful Wizard of Oz.* The story had everything: travel to a strange land, friendly companions, suspense, a predicament that had to be overcome, and obstacles— the deadly poppy field, the fighting trees, the kalidahs, the winged monkeys, and wicked witches. Above all, it was an American fairy tale.

Hollywood had made four versions of *The Wonderful Wizard of Oz* prior to the immensely successful MGM Technicolor version that premiered at Grauman's Chinese Theater on August 15, 1939. The cast included:

- Judy Garland as Dorothy
- Ray Bolger as the Scarecrow
- Jack Haley as the Tin Woodman
- Bert Lahr as the Cowardly Lion
- Frank Morgan as the Wizard
- Billie Burke as Glinda, the Good Sorceress

With an outstanding cast and songs by Harold Arlen and E. Y. Harburg, the movie became a classic. The producer, Mervyn LeRoy, knew that the movie would have to appeal to adults as well as children and realized that he would have to make this fairy tale a believable fantasy.

The Baums moved to Hollywood and built a home, Ozcot, which was located one block north of Hollywood Boulevard. Baum wrote more Oz books while they lived in Ozcot, including *Tik-Tok of Oz, The Scarecrow of Oz, The Lost Princess of Oz, The Tin Woodman of Oz,* and *The Magic of Oz.* L. Frank Baum died on May 6, 1919, at the age of sixty-two, after suffering from gall bladder problems that aggravated his heart condition. His life was occupied with doing what he wanted to do. He once said, "To please a child is a sweet and lovely thing that warms one's heart and brings its own reward."

Stephen Douglas

S tephen Arnold Douglas, the second oldest child of Dr. Stephen Douglas and Sally Fisk Douglas, was born in 1813 in Brandon, Vermont. His father, the town doctor, died of a stroke several weeks after Douglas was born. Stephen, his sister Sarah, and his mother moved in with his uncle Edward Fisk, who jointly owned a farm with Douglas' mother.

The future Senator from Illinois worked on the farm and attended school three months a year. When Douglas was fifteen, his uncle could not afford to send him to the Brandon Academy and suggested that he continue working on the farm. Instead, Douglas arranged to be apprenticed to a cabinetmaker in nearby Middlebury and subsequently in Brandon.

In 1830, Douglas' mother married Gehazi Granger, a wealthy farmer from Clifton Springs, New York. Granger enrolled his stepson in the Canandaigua Academy, where he studied the classical languages. The school was very progressive, and its student body included young men from all of the New England States and from Canada. The academy's superintendent, Henry Howe, was a noted scholar. Douglas was known for his analytical mind and his excellent memory. He developed an interest in politics and was remembered for a pro-Jackson speech before the debating society in 1832, the year of General Jackson's re-election.

In January, 1833, Douglas quit the academy to begin the study of law with a Canandaigua law firm. He left Canandaigua the following June to migrate westward. New York required seven years of study to become licensed to practice law. In Cleveland, only one year of study in a law office qualified a clerk for a license. The requirements in Illinois were even less demanding; a license could be had practically for the asking. He initially went to Cleveland, where he contracted malaria and decided that he needed a change of climate.

Douglas traveled to Cincinnati, Louisville, and St. Louis looking for a clerk's position in a law office without success. In Illinois, he initially tried Jacksonville and then Pekin before he ran out of money. He taught in Winchester to earn expense money. He returned to Jacksonville where he was granted a law license by a justice of the State Supreme Court who counseled that "he must apply himself closer to the study of the law." He rented an office in the Morgan County Courthouse and advertised his services in the local newspaper.

Central Illinois was just moving out of the frontier environment at this time. Douglas said of the times in his part of the state: "Equality and equal rights prevail and no man acknowledges another his superior." He became a midwesterner in dress, speech, and outlook. He was intelligent and ambitious, and he had few peers in debate. Within his first ten years in Illinois, he held a series of appointive and elective offices and organized the state Democratic Party.

Douglas was so effective in defending the President's actions in one debate that upon concluding his side of the argument, he was carried around on the audience's shoulders. The young man with the large head who was five feet, one inch tall and weighed 100 pounds when he moved west was given the nickname "The Little Giant." He developed the reputation as the best lawyer in Illinois for a bad case. His first important elected office was as the state attorney for the local district.

In 1836, Douglas was elected to the state legislature that met in the capital of Vandalia. A legislator from neighboring Sangamon County, Abraham Lincoln, led the delegation to move the capital to Springfield. President Van Buren appointed Douglas as Register of the Land Office in Springfield, and, suddenly, he was earning from $100 to $200 a day. He became an expert on public land policy. In Springfield, as in Jacksonville, he cultivated the editors of the newspaper and remained on good terms with them.

In 1838, the district Democratic party nominated Douglas as their candidate for Congress. He lost by thirty-five votes out of 36,000 to Lincoln's law partner, John T. Stuart, and returned to the practice of law. Within a year, he was selected as Chairman of the State Central Committee for the Democrats and debated across the state against Lincoln and other Whigs. In one debate, Lincoln destroyed Douglas due to the Little Giant's factual inaccuracies;

Douglas never repeated that mistake. In the election of 1840, Illinois voted with the Democrat Van Buren, and the Governor appointed Douglas as the Secretary of State for Illinois. Within several months, he was selected for the newly organized State Supreme Court.

In 1842, Douglas sought a U.S. Senate seat but failed by five votes in the legislature. In the following year, he campaigned strenuously and was elected to Congress, beating his Whig opponent handily. He was a natural politician with a large supply of personal magnetism. In his words: "I live with my constituents, eat with my constituents, drink with them, lodge with them, pray with them, laugh, hunt, dance, and work with them; I eat their corn dodgers and fried bacon and sleep two in a bed with them."

A Massachusetts editor with Douglas on a campaign tour observed:

> He can talk religion with the priests as well as politics with the statesmen.... He knows everybody; can tell the question that affects the locality; calls the name of every farm-owner along the way.... Now such a man as that, in contact with everybody, knowing everybody, and at the bottom wrapped up with the one idea of preferment, power and dominion over men, is not easily to be put down....

Douglas was reelected to Congress twice with large majorities. In his second term, he became one of President Polk's personal advisors and was appointed chairman of the Committee on Territories. In late 1846, he was elected to the U.S. Senate by the state legislature. In the Senate, he continued to display his expansionist tendencies. His goal was an American empire from coast to coast. While in the House of Representatives, he had introduced bills to annex Texas, to organize the Territory of Nebraska, and to establish military posts in the Oregon Territory.

Douglas and his Senate colleague Henry Clay were similar in many ways. They were both moderates, excellent debaters, proponents of compromise, and supporters of union on the North vs. South differences. They were on the same side on many issues. The Little Giant had his detractors, but Alexander Stephens of Georgia called him the "foremost patriot and statesman of his time."

Douglas sought the Democratic nomination for President in 1852. His principal competitors were Lewis Cass, who had run for President in 1848, and James Buchanan of Pennsylvania. Because the party leaders thought that the three candidates would split the vote and block each other out of the nomination, they kept Franklin Pierce of New Hampshire in the background as a dark horse to break a potential deadlock. Buchanan's supporters offered Douglas the Vice Presidential nomination if he would drop his candidacy and support the Pennsylvanian. Douglas refused. Buchanan's allies then tried some maneuvering for their candidate that backfired and assured Pierce the nomination on the forty-ninth ballot.

Douglas again allowed his name to be put forward for the Democratic nomination for President in 1856. The nomination went to Buchanan, who had been serving as Pierce's Ambassador to the Court of St. James. Because he had been out of the country for the past four years, he was the only leading Democrat whose name had not been besmirched by the violent battles in Congress over the passage of the Kansas-Nebraska Act. Because of his conservatism and his southern sympathies, Buchanan was probably the only Democrat who could defeat the new Republican Party's candidate. The Pennsylvanian was nominated and elected.

In 1856, Lincoln stated his opinion of Douglas:

> Twenty-two years ago, Judge Douglas and I became acquainted. We were both young then.... Even then we were both ambitious—I perhaps, quite as much as he. With me the race has been ... a flat failure; with him it has been a splendid success. His name fills the nation.... I would rather stand on that eminence than wear the richest crown that ever pressed a monarch's brow.

Douglas is perhaps best known for the Lincoln-Douglas

debates in campaigning for the the U.S. Senate in 1858. Their rivalry is probably as well known, or better known, than that between Jefferson and Hamilton or between Jackson and Calhoun. Lincoln and Douglas had much in common: both were self-made men, neither was born in Illinois, and both were "born" politicians. They respected each other; Douglas said of his opponent: "I shall have my hands full. He is the strong man of his party—full of wit, facts, dates—and the best stump speaker, with his droll ways and dry jokes, in the West. He is as honest as he is shrewd, and if I beat him, my victory will be hardly won."

In accepting Lincoln's challenge to debate, Douglas realized that he had everything to lose and his lesser known rival everything to gain. As the underdog, who was less well-dressed than the incumbent, Lincoln had the public sympathy with him. Lincoln also had the advantage of concentrating on the election at hand, whereas Douglas was campaigning both for the Senate and for the Presidential nomination two years hence.

Douglas tried to brand his opponent as an abolitionist in the debates. Lincoln hedged. The issue of slavery was the largest issue that separated them. Lincoln asserted that slavery was morally wrong, and that laws should be passed to prohibit it in the territories as a first step toward its ultimate extinction. The Republican candidate assured his listeners repeatedly that this action would not result in civil war. Douglas concentrated on his belief in the principle of self-government, and in the people's right to rule and to vote according to their convictions.

Lincoln proposed limiting slavery to its present locations as a first step to eradicating it. Douglas was against restricting it because he thought that civil war would result. He hoped that if it were left alone, ultimately it would disappear for economic reasons. Douglas won the debates with Lincoln and maintained his seat in the Senate. This victory over "Honest Abe" was a high point of Douglas' political career.

In April, 1860, the Democratic National Convention was held in Charleston. Fifty of the original 303 delegates bolted from the convention. At one point, Douglas received 152 votes, but he was required to have two-thirds of the original delegates instead of the remaining 253 delegates. The Charleston Convention recessed and reconvened in June in Baltimore. The fifty delegates who left the convention in Charleston nominated John C. Breckinridge as their candidate at a separate convention. Douglas received the nomination on the second ballot in Baltimore with 182 1/2 votes.

Lincoln received his party's nomination for President at the Republican National Convention in Chicago. Douglas had hopes of defeating the railsplitter during the first two months of the campaign. State elections in September indicated that Lincoln would win the northern states and therefore the Presidency. On March 4, 1861, Lincoln was inaugurated President of the United States. During the inauguration ceremony, Douglas held Lincoln's top hat when the nervous President didn't seem to know what to do with it. Within five weeks, the country was embroiled in a Civil War.

During the early months of the war, Douglas supported his friend from Illinois, who had undertaken such heavy responsibilities. Lincoln sent him on a mission to the midwestern states to ensure their loyalty. On May 1st, after delivering a speech in Chicago, Douglas suffered a severe attack of rheumatism and developed a high fever. The strain of the previous campaign and the sadness of losing the election had weakened him. On June 3, 1861, Stephen Arnold Douglas died. When told of his friend's death, President Lincoln wept openly.

Frederick Douglass

Frederick was born in February, 1818, in Talbot County, on the Eastern Shore of Maryland; he wasn't sure of the actual date of his birth. His mother, Harriet Bailey, was a slave and his father, whom he never met, was a white man. His master was Captain Aaron Anthony. In March, 1826, Frederick was sent to live with a member of Anthony's family, Hugh Auld, in Baltimore. Initially, Hugh's wife, Sophia, was kind to Frederick. He asked her to help him learn to read and write; she did so willingly until her husband heard what she was doing. Then the lessons stopped, and Sophia was no longer friendly to him. However, living in Baltimore was a good experience for him, and he had many opportunities to learn. Thomas Auld, Frederick's legal owner, brought him back to rural slavery in 1833. Frederick did not like Auld or his new wife, Rowena. He was not completely obedient, so Auld hired him out to Edward Covey, who had a reputation as a "slave breaker." Frederick endured six months of flogging and mistreatment, and then turned on Covey in a two-hour fight that Frederick won. After that, Covey did not bother him, but Frederick was even more committed to obtaining his freedom. He began to help his fellow slaves with reading lessons.

In April, 1836, Frederick and five other slaves made plans to escape. However, one of the five told authorities of their plans, and they were jailed in Easton. Instead of selling Frederick, Thomas Auld sent him back to Hugh and Sophia in Baltimore. Frederick became an experienced caulker in a boatyard, where there was considerable competition for jobs between poor white immigrants and slaves. He was badly beaten because he was perceived to have taken a job from a white immigrant.

Frederick continued his self-education with a membership in the East Baltimore Mental Improvement Society, a debating club. He met Anna Murray, a freed slave who was barely literate, at one of their meetings. They became engaged in 1838. They both saved money and made plans for an escape to the North. An argument with Hugh Auld motivated Douglass to board a northbound train and escape. The conductor asked to see his free slave papers, which he didn't have; Frederick showed him his seaman's papers instead. Despite some tense moments when he saw two local men who could identify him as a slave, he arrived in Philadelphia safely and then proceeded on to New York City.

Douglass stayed with David Ruggles, publisher of the anti-slavery quarterly, *The Mirror of Slavery.* He sent for Anna Murray, and they were married on September 15, 1838. Ruggles, who was active in the underground railroad, suggested to Frederick and Anna that they move farther north. They moved to New Bedford, Massachusetts, where Frederick hoped to find work as a caulker. They lived with Nathan Johnson and his wife. Johnson suggested that since Frederick was an escaped slave he should change his name. Johnson had just finished reading Sir

Walter Scott's *Lady of the Lake;* he suggested the surname of "Douglass," the name of the Scottish lord and hero. Frederick Bailey became Frederick Douglass.

When Douglass looked for work as a caulker, he found that prejudice existed in the North as well as the South. The white caulkers didn't want to work with blacks. He was forced to take odd jobs as a common laborer. Anna helped by doing domestic work. One day he found a copy of William Lloyd Garrison's anti-slavery newspaper, the *Liberator,* and it changed his life. Garrison was a strong-willed abolitionist. In addition to being an editor, Garrison helped to found the New England Anti-Slavery Society. Douglass subscribed to Garrison's paper and was moved by it.

Douglass attended the annual meeting of the New England Anti-Slavery Society in New Bedford on August 9, 1841, and a meeting on the next day on the island of Nantucket. Douglass was called upon to speak. He was nervous, but he spoke about his life as a slave and was well received. Douglass was asked to become a full-time lecturer for the organization. He reluctantly accepted a three-month assignment and stayed for four years. He improved his speech delivery techniques and became one of the most popular lecturers.

Douglass had to learn to overcome hecklers; the life of an abolitionist was not easy. On September 15, 1843, he was severely beaten in Pendleton, Indiana. He escaped with a broken wrist and bruises. Abolitionist newspaper editor Elijah Lovejoy was killed in Alton, Illinois, while defending his press from an incensed mob. Garrison was dragged through the streets of Boston with a rope around his neck and almost lost his life.

During the winter and early spring of 1844-45, Douglass took time out from the lecture circuit and wrote an autobiography, *The Narrative of the Life of Frederick Douglass, An American Slave.* In August of 1845, he traveled to England and went on a successful lecture tour of England, Ireland, and Scotland.

One month after his return to America, Anna and Ellen Richardson of Newcastle raised money and negotiated to buy Douglass' freedom. They went through American agents to buy his freedom from the Aulds for $711.66. The deed of manumission was filed at the Baltimore Chattel Records Office on

December 13, 1846, and Douglass was a free man.

He returned to England for another lecture tour in 1847. Upon his return to America, he proceeded with plans to publish an anti-slavery newspaper. His British friends raised $2,000 to help him get started. He was surprised when Garrison advised against it. Garrison, who did not want competition for his *Liberator*, said that there were already too many newspapers of that type.

Douglass started his newspaper in spite of Garrison's counsel against it. He knew that he would have to choose a base far from Garrison's in New England. Douglass chose Rochester, a booming city of 30,000 on the Erie Canal, where he had been well received in 1842 and 1847. The leading abolitionist of Central New York, Gerrit Smith, supported him and gave him the deed to forty acres of land near Rochester. Douglass moved his family there on November 1, 1847.

On December 3, 1847, the first edition of his newspaper, *North Star*, was published. He named the paper *North Star* because the north star was the guide that the slaves used when escaping from the South to freedom. In 1851, the *North Star* merged with the *Liberty Party Paper,* which was financed by Gerrit Smith; the resulting paper was called *Frederick Douglass' Paper.* In 1858, he began publishing *Douglass' Monthly* for British readers. The weekly ran until 1860, and he stopped the monthly in 1863. He had had a sixteen-year publishing career.

Douglass also supported the Women's Rights Movement. On July 14, 1848, his *North Star* carried this announcement: "A convention to discuss the Social, Civil, and Religious Condition and Rights of Women will be held in the Wesleyan Chapel at Seneca Falls, New York, the 19th and 20th of July instant." The masthead that Douglas used for the *North Star* was "RIGHT IS OF NO SEX—TRUTH IS OF NO COLOR."

In January, 1871, President Grant appointed Douglass to a commission to Santo Domingo (Dominican Republic). He moved to Washington, D.C., because he thought that more federal appointments would be forthcoming. In 1877, President Rutherford Hayes appointed him United States Marshal for the District of Columbia. He served in that position until 1881, when President James Garfield appointed him Recorder of Deeds for the

District of Columbia. He held that position until 1886.

Douglass' wife, Anna, died in August, 1882. In January 1884, He married Helen Pitts, his secretary in the Office of the Recorder of Deeds. The mixed marriage caused controversy, but Helen said, "love came to me and I was not afraid to marry the man I loved because of his color." Douglass' response to critics was that his first wife "was the color of my mother, and the second, the color of my father."

In September, 1889, President Benjamin Harrison appointed Douglass Minister-Resident and Consul-General to the Republic of Haiti. He resigned the office in July 1891. Douglass, one of the strongest anti-slavery voices of his time, died of a heart attack in Washington, D.C., on February 20, 1895.

Hiawatha

There were two Hiawathas: the Hiawatha described by Henry Wadsworth Longfellow in *The Song of Hiawatha* and the Onondaga chief who lived near Syracuse during the fifteenth century. Longfellow's Hiawatha was based on the Indian hero who, as described by Henry Rowe Schoolcraft in *The Myth of Hiawatha,* could take mile-long steps and turn into a wolf. The Hiawatha described by Longfellow could talk with the animals and could outrun an arrow shot through the air. He was an Ojibway who lived on the shores of Lake Gitche Gumee near Lake Superior, married Minnehaha, met white people, and became a Christian.

The real Hiawatha lived on the south shore of Cross Lake west of Syracuse during the mid-1400s. He was an excellent speaker who became a leader of the Onondaga Nation, married, and had seven daughters. His wife's name is lost to history, but it wasn't Minnehaha. Hiawatha's ideas were different from those of his peers; he spoke of peace, not war. The Iroquois Confederation, which initially included the Senecas, Cayugas, Onondagas, Oneidas, and Mohawks, was continually at war—sometimes among themselves but usually with other nations, such as the Hurons from Canada.

Hiawatha counseled for friendship among the nations at a time when retribution was a way of life. If an Iroquois were killed, the victim's male relatives would kill the murderer. If the murderer couldn't be located, one of his relatives would be killed in his place. Revenge was a way of life; it didn't matter if an innocent person lost his life.

An evil character named Ododarhoh lived south of the principal Onondaga village. He lived alone in a dark ravine near a marsh and slept on a bed of bullrushes. According to legend, the locks of his long, intertwined hair were living snakes. He was a cannibal who ate men, women, and children raw. He was a wizard feared by the nearby Onondagas. Ododarhoh committed the unspeakable crime of killing Hiawatha's wife and seven daughters (three daughters in some versions of the story).

Hiawatha threw himself to the ground and thrashed around in self-torture. His grief was so deep that people hesitated to approach him and offer their consolation. He left the village, built a lodge of hemlock branches, and became a hermit and an aimless wanderer. Hiawatha was expected to kill Ododarhoh, but it wasn't his nature to commit an act of revenge that wouldn't bring back his wife and daughters.

When Hiawatha was in depths of his despair, he was visited at his lodge by Degandawida the Peacemaker. Degandawida was a Huron evangelist who was attempting to convince the Iroquois Confederation to stop fighting among themselves and to live in peace. He wasn't having much success because he was an outsider and because he stuttered; he was not a good speechmaker. He sought the help of Hiawatha, who was respected within the confederation and was an outstanding speaker.

Hiawatha immediately became a follower of Degandawida; it was too late for preserving his own family, but perhaps he could work with the Peacemaker to save the lives of others. The concepts preached by Degandawida brought Hiawatha out of his grief. The Peacemaker had a scheme to convince the Onondagas and the other nations of the confederacy to implement the plans for peace that he and Hiawatha were proposing from village to village. His scheme was to convert Ododarhoh from his evil ways and to use Hiawatha as the instrument of this conversion. If the

Onondagas saw that Hiawatha, upon whom Ododarhoh had inflicted such a terrible injustice, could forgive his tormenter and convince him to follow the path of peace, then the rest of the Nation would follow.

Degandawida and Hiawatha visited the evil wizard at his lodge in the dark ravine, where Hiawatha placated Ododarhoh by singing to him and speaking the message of peace and of Iroquois unity. Ododarhoh's two visitors expected him to react violently, because they knew of the evil one's opposition to peace and unity. They expected to be attacked, but Ododarhoh raised his head and said that he would mend his ways and abide by these proposals of peace and unity. Hiawatha then combed the snakes, which symbolically represented evil and insane thoughts, out of the wizard's hair. Thus Hiawatha (Ayonwartha) was given his name, which meant "He Who Combs."

The Onondaga Nation followed Ododarhoh into the Iroquois Confederation and the Great Peace. An Onondaga village near Syracuse became the capital of the confederation and the location of the council fire. Ododarhoh was named "firekeeper," a position comparable to president of the senate. He became one of the most powerful of the sachems (chiefs).

Degandawida and Hiawatha continued to travel from village to village enlisting support for the confederation of the five original Iroquois nations. One day Hiawatha spoke to a gathering of the Cayuga, Mohawk, Oneida, Onondaga, and Seneca Nations near present-day Liverpool, on Onondaga Lake. He held a single arrow in his outstretched hand and, facing the chiefs, broke the arrow over his knee. Then he took from his quiver five arrows that were bound together with deerskin thongs. The five arrows represented the five nations of the Iroquois Confederacy, and when he tried to break them over his knee, he couldn't.

Hiawatha's demonstration of strength in unity was the underlying principle of the Iroquois Confederation. The Iroquois maintained a strong confederacy for over three hundred years. Hostile tribes, such as the Hurons, provided a lesser threat than before the Confederation was formed.

Hiawatha instituted wampum as Indian money for use in place of revenge. Murderers paid for their crimes in wampum, which was usually made of purple and white shells. Hiawatha was aware that a price couldn't be set for the value of human life, but it was better for a murder to pay the victim's family in wampum than continue a progression of killings. The wampum was made to carry a message as well as to have intrinsic value.

When Degandawida saw that his objectives had been accomplished, he said, "Now I shall be seen no more and I go whither none can follow me." Five years after he had arrived among the Onondagas, the master climbed into a white birch-bark canoe on the eastern shore of Onondaga Lake and paddled westward into the sunset. Hiawatha, who watched from the shore, remained to continue the work of the Peacemaker. Historians know little about Hiawatha's later life. The Mohawks claim that he lived among them as an elder statesman who cleared rocks and brush from rivers to make them more navigable and to facilitate improved communications among the villages.

According to Iroquois legend, Hiawatha left the Iroquois in the same manner that his mentor, Degandawida, did—paddling a birchbark canoe westward across a lake, which was thought to be Lake Champlain. The Iroquois associated white with sacredness. Their canoes were made of gray elm bark. The two men were thought to have found happiness in the Sky World, where strawberries grow as large as apples and flowers of white light always bloom. Hiawatha and the Peacemaker had a lasting influence on the Iroquois Confederation, who for centuries had the most powerful culture in the western hemisphere north of Mexico.

Red Jacket

Red Jacket was born at Canoga, south of Seneca Falls, in 1750. His father, Thadahwahnyeh, a Cayuga from the nearby village of Skoiyase, visited the Seneca village of Kanadesaga (Seneca Castle) frequently. In fact, he had helped to build some of the longhouses at Kanadesaga. He met and fell in love with Blue Flower of the Wolf clan during his visits to the Seneca village.

Thadahwahnyeh was not a Seneca, but he was a member of the Turtle clan, which was the clan of the ruler of Kanadesaga.

The marriage was arranged by Thadahwahnyeh's and Blue Flower's mothers. The marriage proposal was announced in the council house, and the prospective bride and groom were reminded of the duties of marriage by the chief matron. After the ceremony and the wedding feast, the bride and groom moved into a lodge in Cayuga territory in the valley of Canoga Creek. The lodge was near a deep spring with an ample flow of water. Many bubbles came to the surface of the water and the Cayugas believed that the spring had magical qualities. The spring is still there.

Within a year, Red Jacket was born at Canoga. The wife of Cayuga Chief Fish Carrier assisted at his birth. The proud parents traveled to Kanadesaga to show her haksaah (baby boy) to her relatives. He was not called Red Jacket until later in life. At the age of ten, he was welcomed into the Seneca Nation at the council house at Kanadesaga and given the name Otetiani, which meant "Always Ready." Red Jacket hunted and fished with the other Indian boys and began to travel widely around the region.

Red Jacket was a fast runner and was frequently used by the Senecas as a messenger. He was also employed as a messenger by the British during the Revolutionary War. For his services to them, the British gave him a scarlet jacket with fancy embroidery. It was a prized possession, and he wore it frequently. When a jacket wore out, the British would provide him with a replacement.

Red Jacket was not a warrior. In fact, he didn't take up arms until he was twenty-nine when his territory was invaded; every Iroquois man had to defend his home and village. He was against war with the American colonists. He viewed them as neighbors and counseled neutrality and peace. Red Jacket said: "This quarrel does not belong to us—and it is best for us to take no part in it; we need not waste our blood to have it settled. If they fight us, we will fight them, but if they let us alone, we had better keep still." After the war, Chief Little Beard expressed his views: "Red Jacket was opposed to the war, he was always in favor of peace, and how much better it had been, had we listened to his advice."

Red Jacket was called a coward for his views. Pro-war advocates, such as Chief Joseph Brant of the Mohawks, considered him to be weak because he advocated peace. Brant told Red Jacket's wife, "Leave that man; leave him, lest your children have a coward for a father."

Red Jacket heard Chief Logan, the son of chief Shikellemus of the Cayuga Nation, speak and was moved by his style and the method of delivery of his speeches. Red Jacket would return from wandering in the woods and be asked what he had been doing. He would reply that "He had been playing Logan." Red Jacket developed his skills as an orator in council meetings. When his shortcomings as a warrior were raised, he responded, "I am an orator. I was born an orator." When he became a chief, the Seneca bestowed him with the name Sagoyewatha, or "He keeps them awake."

In 1784, Red Jacket attended the treaty council at Fort Stanwix at present-day Rome. General Lafayette was present at this council, and he was impressed with the eloquence of Red Jacket. Red Jacket was opposed to the Iroquois giving up the land that the commissioners requested, but he was overruled. Chief Cornplanter, the warrior, was the principal voice of the Six Nations of the Iroquois at the council.

In 1792, President Washington invited the leading Iroquois chiefs to Philadelphia to promote better understanding between the Indians and the new government. Red Jacket and Farmer's Brother were among the fifty chiefs who met with Washington, Secretary of War Knox, and Colonel Pickering, the commissioner who negotiated with the Native Americans. Red Jacket spoke to the gathering:

> All is in a measure now quieted. Peace is now budding. But still there is some shaking among the original Americans toward the setting sun; and you of the thirteen fires and the King of England know what our situation is and the causes of this disturbance.... When you and the king made peace, he did not mention us and showed us no compassion, notwithstanding all he said to us and all we suffered. This has been the occasion of great sorrow and pain and great loss

180

to us.... When you and he settled the peace between you, the great nations never asked us for a delegation to attend to our interests. Had he done this, a settlement of peace among the western nations might have been affected. But neglect of this has brought upon us great pain and trouble.... Our chain of peace has been broken.

Washington gave Red Jacket a large, oval silver medal as a token of his esteem and friendship. Engraved on the medal are the likenesses of Red Jacket and President Washington sharing a peace pipe; a farmer with his oxen are in the background. The medal is now located at the Buffalo Historical Society.

In 1794, a council between the thirteen states and the Iroquois Confederacy was held in Canandaigua to discuss the Indians' concern with the loss of their lands. The United States was represented by Colonel Pickering, and Thomas Morris, the son of Robert Morris, financier of the Revolutionary War, attended. The Iroquois were represented by fifty-nine chiefs, including Cornplanter, Fish Carrier, and Red Jacket. Thomas Morris observed:

> Red Jacket was ... of middle height, well-formed, with an intelligent countenance, and a fine eye; and was in all respects a fine looking man. He was the most graceful public speaker I have ever known; his manner was most dignified and easy. He was fluent, and at times witty and sarcastic. He was quick and ready at reply. He pitted himself against Colonel Pickering, whom he sometimes foiled in argument. The colonel would sometimes become irritated and lose his temper; then Red Jacket would be delighted and show his dexterity in taking advantage of any unguarded assertion of the colonel's. He felt a conscious pride in the conviction that nature had done more for him, than for his antagonist.

Red Jacket disagreed with the treaty at Canandaigua, but eventually signed it so that the vote among the Iroquois would appear to be unanimous. A year or two later, when Morris told Red Jacket of Colonel Pickering's promotion from Postmaster General to Secretary of War, Red Jacket said: "Ah! We began our public career about the same time; he knew how to read and write; I did not, and he has got ahead of me.—If I had known how to read and write I should have got ahead of him."

In August, 1797, Thomas Morris convened a council with the leading chiefs of the Iroquois Confederacy at Big Tree (Geneseo) concerning the sale of Indian lands in Western New York. In the spring of 1791, Robert Morris had purchased the pre-emptive right to the lands in Western New York other than those lands involved in the Phelps-Gorham Purchase. He promised to survey the entire tract and to satisfy the Indian title. Robert Morris commissioned his son to represent him in obtaining the consent of the Indians to sell their land. Cornplanter, Farmer's Brother, Little Beard, Little Billy, and Red Jacket conducted most of the discussions for the Iroquois. Red Jacket, as the principal spokesman, told Morris the Indians' view of selling their lands: "We are not convinced that it is best to dispose of them at any price." Morris asked, "But what value can they be to you as they now are, any further than the consciousness that you own them?" Red Jacket responded:

> Yes, but this knowledge is everything to us. It raises us in our own estimation. It creates in our bosoms a proud feeling which elevates us as a nation. Observe the difference between the estimation in which a Seneca and an Oneida are held. We are courted, while the Oneidas are considered a degraded people, fit only to make brooms and baskets. Why this difference? It is because the Senecas are known to be the proprietors of a broad domain, while the Oneidas are cooped up in a narrow space.

While Red Jacket was still standing, one of the Senecas said, "He's a coward." Red Jacket replied: "Yes, I am a coward." Then he waved his hand around in a semi-circle pointing to the beautiful country that surrounded them. He added: "Assure me that you can create lands like these, which the Great Spirit has made for his red children, so that you can give us lands like them in return, and I will be brave: Until then I am a coward—I dare not sell these lands." Again, Red Jacket objected to the selling of the Iroquois lands, but eventually he signed the agreement with the other chiefs.

Strain had existed between Cornplanter and Red Jacket from the time of their youth. At a time when Cornplanter was losing influence in the confederacy, he tried to soften his loss of influence by cutting down one of his rivals, Red Jacket. Cornplanter convinced his brother, Handsome Lake the prophet, to accuse Red Jacket of witchcraft. A board of judges met, heard the charges against Red Jacket, and charged him with sorcery. If found guilty, he could be punished by death. The tribal court met at Buffalo Creek; the judges listened to the slanderous charges.

Red Jacket conducted his own defense. He began by looking each accuser in the eye and saying, "So that is the best you can do with lies!" He analyzed the character of his accusers, citing instance after instance that clearly showed their prejudice. He noted deed after deed in which his accusers had been dishonest, deceitful, and had acted contrary to the best interests of the Senecas. He concluded by saying, "Cornplanter, you're a cheat! You've heard me; and the prophet is an impostor." The judges returned with a verdict of not guilty. Cornplanter retired to his lodge and concerned himself with improving the living conditions of his people; he was no longer a force as a leader.

On January 20, 1830, Red Jacket died at the Buffalo Creek reservation as he approached eighty years of age. On his death bed, he said to his wife:

> I am going to die. I shall never leave this house alive. I wish to thank you for your kindness to me. You have loved me. You have always prepared my food, and taken care of my clothes, and been patient with me.... I should like to live longer for your sake. I meant to build you a new

house, and make you comfortable in it, but it is now too late.

He had at his side a bottle of the water from the spring at Canoga that he thought would assure him a safe passage to the next world.

Red Jacket always spoke in the Indian tongue and insisted that an interpreter translate his speeches into English. He did not believe in the Christian faith. In fact, he left his wife when she converted to Christianity. However he recognized the error of his ways and returned to her. On his deathbed, he told her: "I am sorry I left you because of your new religion. I am convinced it is a good religion, and has made you a better woman, and wish you to persevere in it." He was against all of the agreements that gave up the Indian lands, but he signed them anyway.

Colonel William Jones of Geneseo, the son of pioneer Horatio Jones, observed of Red Jacket: "For the great men of our own and of other times, have become so by education; but Red Jacket was as nature made him. Had he enjoyed their advantages, he would have surpassed them, since it can hardly be supposed that they, without these, would have equalled him." Jones maintained that Red Jacket's talents "were among the noblest that nature ever conferred upon man."

Nathaniel Rochester

Nathaniel Rochester, the second oldest son of John Rochester and Hester Thrift Rochester, was born on February 21, 1752, in Westmoreland County, Virginia. At the age of sixteen, he was employed by James Monroe, a Scottish merchant, at Hillsborough, North Carolina. In 1773, Rochester joined a partnership with his employer and Col. John Hamilton that was dissolved two years later at the beginning of the Revolutionary War.

In 1775, he was appointed a member of the Committee of Safety of Orange County, who collected money for the coming conflict, prevented the sale and consumption of British tea from East India, and procured arms and ammunition. Later that year, he attended the first Provincial Convention in North Carolina, which ordered the enlistment of four regiments of Continental troops and organized the minutemen and militia systems. He was appointed a Justice of the Peace, Major of Militia, and Paymaster for the minutemen.

In February 1776, Rochester commanded two companies of infantry and one company of cavalry in a successful effort to prevent the British General Alexander McDonald, who had raised a regiment of 1,000 Scottish settlers in North Carolina, from reaching the port of Wilmington and transporting the men to New York. In May, 1776, at the second Provincial Convention, Rochester was appointed Commissary General of Stores and Clothing for the North Carolina line of ten regiments, with the rank of Colonel. However, he became ill at Wilmington and was forced to retire from the army.

In 1777, Rochester was elected a member of the North Carolina Assembly, who appointed him Lieutenant Colonel of Militia and Clerk of the Court of Orange County. Later that year, he was selected to establish and manage an arms factory at Hillsborough. He resigned from the clerk's office and was appointed an Auditor of Public Accounts for the State and a Colonel of Militia.

In 1778, Rochester went into business with Col. Thomas Hart, who was Henry Clay's father-in-law. Hart purchased a large landed estate in Hagerstown, Maryland, and Rochester moved there to manage the estate. In 1784, Hart and Rochester purchased wheat, operated a large merchant flour mill, and sold flour. They also owned and ran nail and rope factories. In 1792, the partnership was dissolved, and Hart and Rochester ran separate businesses.

Rochester married in 1788 and became a member of the Maryland legislature two years later. From 1791 until 1797, he was Postmaster of Hagerstown, a position that he resigned to become a judge of the Washington County court. He was a judge for one year and subsequently was re-appointed Postmaster and later County Sheriff for three years. In 1807, he became the first president of the Hagerstown bank and in the following year was appointed an Elector of the President and the Vice-President of the

United States when James Madison was elected President.

In September, 1800, with his friends Major Charles Carroll and Colonel William Fitzhugh, Rochester visited the Genesee Country of Western New York for the first time. Carroll and Fitzhugh purchased 12,000 acres of land; Rochester bought an adjoining 400 acres in addition to 155 acres at Dansville. In 1802, Carroll, Fitzhugh, and Rochester revisited Genesee country and purchased for $17.50 an acre a 100-acre plot that later became part of the Village of Rochester. Rochester also purchased an additional 200 acres next to his original 400 acres.

On the second trip, the three Marylanders visited the abandoned mills of Ebenezer "Indian" Allen at the falls on the Genesee River. Allen had constructed the grist mill as part of an agreement with the region's original purchasers, Oliver Phelps and Nathaniel Gorham of the Phelps-Gorham Purchase. Phelps and Gorham had promised to build a grist mill for the use of the Indians if they would sell them a twelve by twenty-four-mile parcel of land along the Genesee River. Allen was given 100 acres for building the mill, but he wasn't the type of individual to stay with an endeavor for long.

Rochester saw the potential of the site immediately. His flour milling experience in Maryland provided the fuel for his vision. He viewed the site as the nucleus for a commercial center. During the nineteenth century, the Genesee region was the wheat-growing capital of the country, and Rochester became known as the "flour" city.

In May, 1810, Rochester settled his manufacturing, mercantile, and sheriff's business in Maryland and moved to Dansville, New York. He constructed a large paper mill and increased his property holdings to more that 700 acres. In 1814, he purchased a 445-acre farm in Bloomfield, Ontario County, and moved there. In 1816, he was appointed an Elector of the President and the Vice-President of the United States when James Monroe was elected President. While residing in Bloomfield, he was appointed a director of the Utica Bank branch at Canandaigua.

During the winter of 1817, Rochester went to Albany as an agent for the petitioners for a new county to be split off from Ontario County. He was unsuccessful in this first attempt. In April,

1818, he rented out his farm and moved to Rochester. In 1821, he was successful in his second attempt at getting a law passed to create the County of Monroe. He was appointed Clerk of the County and was elected a member of the Assembly from Monroe County. In 1824, he was appointed a commissioner of the Bank of Rochester and was elected president of the bank later that year.

The construction of the Erie Canal from the Hudson River to Lake Erie put the Village of Rochester on the map. Nathaniel Rochester worked with the Canal Commission and the state legislature to ensure that the canal passed through Rochester. He had to deal with the appeals of the citizens of Canandaigua to have the canal routed through the "Grande Dame" of the Finger Lakes Region. When construction of the canal started in 1817 at Rome, Rochester was a newly incorporated village with 800 inhabitants. The canal reached Rochester in 1823 and was completed in 1825.

In 1825, Rochester was a boomtown with a population of 5,000. Nathaniel Hawthorne captured the boomtown atmosphere when he wrote: "It is possible to look at [Rochester's] worn pavements and conceive how recently the forest leaves have been swept away.... The whole street, sidewalks and centre, was crowded with pedestrians, horsemen, stagecoaches, gigs, light wagons and heavy ox-teams, all hurrying, trotting, rattling, and rumbling, in a throng that passed continually, but never passed away...."

The aqueduct over the Genesee River, the longest stone bridge in the country, was considered to be an engineering marvel. It was 440 feet long and was supported by nine fifty-foot Roman arches. (Today it is the support for Rochester's Broad Street bridge.) In 1825, Nathaniel Rochester was one of the dignitaries that gathered to commemorate the joining of Lake Erie and the Atlantic Ocean. On October 27, 1825, the festivities began in Buffalo and continued with Governor Clinton and his entourage traveling the entire 363-mile length of his "ditch" to Albany and then on to New York. On November 4th, two casks of Lake Erie water were poured into the Atlantic Ocean in a "Wedding of the Waters" ceremony.

Nathaniel Rochester died in 1831, which was three years before the Village of Rochester, with a population of 12,000, was incorporated as a city. He lived to see his city experience explosive growth and to realize that his vision in selecting Rochester as a flour milling site was justified. Ultimately, twenty-one flour mills along the Genesee River ground 500,000 barrels of flour each year. Rochester was the country's flour milling center from the mid- to the late-1800s, when the wheat-growing and milling shifted to the Midwest with its large flat, open areas.

In 1834, Mt. Hope Nurseries, the first Rochester nursery and seed farm, was established by Patrick Barry and George Ellwanger. By the 1870s and 1880s, the area provided almost half of the country's commercially produced trees. Eventually, Nathaniel Rochester's city became known as the "flower" city instead of the "flour" city.

Joseph Smith

Joseph Smith, founder of the Mormon church, was born in Sharon, Vermont, on December 23, 1805, the fourth child and third son of Joseph Smith, Sr., and Lucy Mack Smith. Smith, Sr., had difficulty making ends meet by farming the rocky soil of Vermont. He tried farming in several New England locations without success.

During the winter of 1812-13, young Smith contracted typhoid fever and developed an abscess on his leg. The doctors decided to amputate the leg, but he was strong-willed even at the age of nine. He refused to let the doctors amputate it, and he subjected himself to an operation in which the diseased bone was removed without the benefit of anesthesia. The leg was saved, but he walked with a limp for the rest of his life.

In 1816, the family moved to Palmyra, New York. They were penniless upon their arrival in the small frontier village, but they were willing to work hard. Joseph, Sr., and his two oldest sons, Alvin and Hyrum, did odd jobs such as harvesting, well-digging, and making maple syrup. In 1820, Smith thought that he should join a church, but he could not find a denomination that was aligned with his understanding of the gospel of Jesus Christ as set forth in the new testament.

188

Smith went into the woods by himself in response to the Epistle of James, Chapter 1, verse 5: "If any of you lack wisdom, let him ask God," and said that a pillar of light fell upon him:

> ... immediately I was seized by some power which entirely overcame me, and had such astonishing influence over me as to bind my tongue so that I could not speak. Thick darkness gathered around me, and it seemed to me for a time that I were doomed to sudden destruction ... just at this moment of great alarm, I saw a pillar of light exactly over my head, above the brightness of the sun, which gradually descended until it fell upon me.
>
> It no sooner appeared than I found myself delivered from the enemy which held me bound. When the light rested upon me I saw two personages, whose brightness and glory defy all description, standing above me in the air. One of them spake unto me calling me by name and said—pointing to the other—"This is my beloved Son, hear him."
>
> My object in going to inquire of the Lord was to know which of all the sects was right ... I was answered that I must join none of them, for they were all wrong, and the personage who addressed me said that all their creed were an abomination in His sight; that those professors were all corrupt, that "they draw near to me with their lips but their hearts are far from me; they teach for doctrines the commandments of men: having a form of godliness but they deny the power thereof."

A second visitation occurred to Smith on September 21, 1823, in his room at home late on a Sunday evening:

... a personage appeared at my bedside, standing in the air, for his feet did not touch the floor. He had on a loose robe of most exquisite whiteness ... his whole person was glorious beyond description ...

I was afraid; but the fear soon left me. He called me by name, and said that his name was Moroni; that God had work for me to do; and that my name should be had for good and evil among all nations, kindreds, and tongues ... He said there was a book deposited, written upon gold plates, giving an account of the former inhabitants on this continent, and the sources from whence they sprang. He also said that the fullness of the everlasting Gospel was contained in it, as delivered by the Saviour to the ancient inhabitants; also that there were two stones in silver bows—and these stones, fastened to a breastplate, constituted what is called the Urim and Thummin—deposited with the plates; and the possession and use of these stones were what constituted "seers" in ancient and former times; and that God had prepared them for the purpose of translating the book.

Smith went to the hill described in the vision, several miles south of Palmyra and east of the Palmyra-Canandaigua mail road. He found the plates and the breastplate with the Urim and Thummin under a large stone near the top of the hill on the west side. They were in a box made of stones cemented together. However, the messenger would not allow him to take the objects with him; he was not to have them for four more years. He was asked to meet the messenger at Hill Cumorah each year at the same time.

In October, 1825, Smith was hired to search for a silver mine in the Susquehanna Valley by Josiah Stowell of South Bainbridge, New York. Treasure hunting or "money-digging" was a fad at the time. He roomed with the Hale family in Harmony, Pennsylvania, near the perceived site of the mine. Smith became attracted to Emma Hale, a twenty-one-year-old schoolteacher. When the search for the mine was concluded, unsuccessfully, Smith worked for Stowell at South Bainbridge. He frequently visited Emma at Harmony. Smith and Emma were married on January 18, 1827; they moved in with his parents in Palmyra.

On September 21, 1827, Smith went to Hill Cumorah, where the messenger Moroni gave him the plates, the Urim and Thummin, and the breastplate. He began the laborious task of translating the plates with one of the "seer" stones. Smith entrusted a loyal neighbor, Martin Harris, to take the transcript of the translation to New York City for evaluation; Charles Anthon of Columbia College said they were "Egyptian, Chaldaic, Assyric, and Arabic."

In 1829, Smith chose Egbert B. Grandin of Palmyra, publisher of the *Wayne Sentinel,* to publish the *Book of Mormon.* Martin Harris mortgaged his farm for $3,000 to pay Grandin for 5,000 leather-bound copies of the 590-page book. On April 6, 1830, Smith and six witnesses formally signed the papers to organize the Church of Jesus Christ at Peter Whitmer's farm in Fayette. Now known as the Church of Jesus Christ of Latter-Day Saints, they were called "Mormons" because the messenger Moroni's father, Mormon, was the major compiler of the ancient records.

On January 2, 1831, Smith had a revelation to move the church, which consisted of sixty members, from Palmyra to Kirtland, Ohio. The church in Kirtland, which had been founded by missionaries, had grown to 100 members. There was resistance to the new church in Ohio, and on March 24, 1832, Smith was dragged from his home and tarred and feathered. Another Mormon, Sidney Rigdon, was beaten severely. Some of the church members moved to Missouri, but there was more antagonism towards them in Missouri than in Ohio.

In May, 1839, many of the Kirtland members of the church moved to Commerce, Illinois, which they renamed Nauvoo. The City of Nauvoo received a charter from the State of Illinois that gave it considerable autonomy. Between 1841 and 1844, Nauvoo grew so rapidly that it became the largest city in Illinois, even larger than Chicago. The practice of plural marriage, polygamy, was inaugurated by the church in 1842, a practice that caused dissension within the church and outrage outside of it.

One June 7, 1844, the *Nauvoo Expositor* published its first issue openly criticizing Smith's leadership of the church. Smith and the city council authorized the destruction of the *Nauvoo Expositor's* press. Smith and his brother, Hyrum, were jailed in Carthage, Illinois, for the suppression of the *Nauvoo Expositor*. A mob stormed the jail and Smith and Hyrum were murdered on June 27, 1844. The Council of Twelve announced in 1845 that the church in Nauvoo would leave Illinois. A site was selected for a temple in Salt Lake City in July, 1847. On December 27, 1847, Brigham Young was sustained as the President of the Church of Jesus Christ of Latter-Day Saints to carry on the work of Joseph Smith.

William Tolley

D
r. William Pearson Tolley, Chancellor of Syracuse University from 1942 to 1969, was born in Honesdale, Pennsylvania, on September 13, 1900. He was the third of five children of Adolphus Tolley and Emma Sumner Tolley. His early years were spent in Honesdale and Carbondale, Pennsylvania, where his father owned shoe stores. In 1903, Adolphus Tolley moved his family to Binghamton, where he opened another shoe store.

Upon his graduation from Binghamton Central High School, Tolley enrolled at Syracuse University. His parents' goal was for the university to prepare their son for the ministry, the vocation of both his maternal and paternal grandfathers; his goal was to prepare himself to study law. However, upon his graduation from Syracuse University in 1922, he enrolled in Drew Theological Seminary in Madison, New Jersey. Tolley received his M.A. from Syracuse University in 1924 and his bachelor of divinity degree from Drew in 1925. He continued his academic work at Columbia University; he earned an M.A. in 1927 and a Ph.D. in 1930.

Upon his graduation from Drew in 1925, Tolley stayed there as alumni secretary and assistant to the president while he studied at Columbia University. Now that he was earning a salary, he could make long-term plans. He married his high school sweetheart, Ruth Canfield, after he graduated from Drew. In 1930, he intended to stay at Drew to implement plans that he had helped to formulate.

The acting president of Allegheny College of Meadville, Pennsylvania, Dr. Clarence Ross, asked to speak with Tolley about becoming the next president of the college. Dr. Tolley met with one of the members of the board of trustees and then with the entire board. He was very direct in his answers to the board's questions; he thought that his responses had ruined his chances for the presidency of Allegheny College. However, they were impressed with his forthrightness; he was offered the position and he accepted it.

His first unpopular decision as president was to de-emphasize football. Allegheny played nationally ranked teams such as the University of Pittsburgh. In order to remain competitive, Allegheny had to provide more football scholarships than they could afford. Many alumni reacted negatively to de-emphasizing football, but, in the long run, it was viewed as the correct decision.

The experience that he gained at Allegheny College matured him as a leader in academia. He developed a reputation as an efficient administrator. In 1942, when William Pratt Graham retired as Chancellor of Syracuse University, Dr. Tolley was invited to become the seventh chancellor of the university. He accepted and began his new duties on September 19, 1942.

Dr. Tolley responded to government requests to accommodate large numbers of G. I. Bill students after World War II. Student enrollment doubled in the fall of 1946 to 11,937, and increased to 15,000 in 1948. Graduate school enrollment grew from 400 in 1942 to 1,250 in 1946, and to 8,000 by 1964. Some university presidents refused to respond to the academic needs of the veterans, but Syracuse University supported the G. I. Bill students beyond reasonable expectations.

Dr. Tolley could ignore protocol if he thought it was for the good of the university. Dr. Tolley and his wife, Ruth, spent a week as houseguests at the home of Thomas Watson, Sr., Chief

Executive Officer of the IBM Corporation, and his wife, Jeanette, where they were shown a sculpture by a friend of the Watsons, Malvina Hoffman. The Tolleys visited Malvina, who told them that she was upset by the circumstances of one of her teachers, the Yugoslavian sculptor, Ivan Mestrovic.

During World War II, Mestrovic was imprisoned by the Germans. Through the Pope's intervention, he was released and permitted to travel to Italy. However, he was ill, unable to sell any of his work, and therefore was in financial trouble. Columbia University had just turned down Malvina's request to hire him. Dr. Tolley instructed Malvina to send Mestrovic the following cable: "You have appointment as professor of sculpture at Syracuse University, effective September this year. Will pay expenses for you and your family to come to States. Don't worry. Love. Malvina."

Dr. Tolley returned to Syracuse and asked the director of the School of Art if he was familiar with Mestrovic's work. The director spoke highly of him. Then Dr. Tolley mentioned to the Dean of the College of Fine Arts that he had heard that Mestrovic could be brought to this country. He suggested to the Dean that he check with the director of the School of Art to get his opinion on adding Mestrovic to the faculty. The director was very enthusiastic about the Yugoslav sculptor. Dr. Tolley then asked the Dean if he wanted to bring Mestrovic to Syracuse. The Dean was incredulous, "Do you know how to do it?" Dr. Tolley said: "I think I do." He didn't tell the Dean that he had broken the rules, but it worked.

In the first twenty years of Dr. Tolley's administration, total enrollment grew from 5,000 to 20,000, including 5,200 at off-campus centers. Graduate school enrollment grew from 500 to 5,500, and 600 evening school students expanded to 5,500 evening and part-time students. Also, from 1942 to 1962, the size of the faculty tripled, while increasing in quality. In 1942, the assets of the university were valued at $15,000,000. Thirty new buildings were built on the campus from 1946 to 1962, with a total capital outlay of over $42,000,000.

In 1942, the operating budget was $3,700,000; in 1962, it was $38,500,000. The book value of the endowment increased from

194

$4,500,000 to $23,000,000 over the twenty-year period. Syracuse university retained its passion for excellence during a time of considerable expansion. The university continued to grow, in all ways, during the last five years of Dr. Tolley's administration.

In a sense, Dr. Tolley put Syracuse University on the map. Today, it is truly a national university. The University was fortunate to have had an individual like Dr. Tolley at the helm during its critical growth years. He began his career as an educator, never wavered from his path, and finished his career as an educator. Dr. Tolley was clearly a man who liked doing what he did. It is reflected in a quotation in his 1988 book, *At the Fountain of Youth: Memories of a College President:* "Ponce de Leon came to America looking for the fountain of youth. He did not find it. He should have looked for it on the campuses of our schools and colleges. It is on the campuses of our colleges that our outlook is full of promise and hope."

Mark Twain

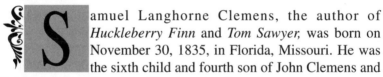 amuel Langhorne Clemens, the author of *Huckleberry Finn* and *Tom Sawyer,* was born on November 30, 1835, in Florida, Missouri. He was the sixth child and fourth son of John Clemens and Jane Lampton Clemens. Clemens was born in a two-room rented clapboard house in a frontier village with a population of 100. In his later life, he said that many important people in history couldn't claim to have increased the population of their community by one percent when they were born.

Clemens was born two months prematurely. His mother admitted: "When I first saw him, I could see no promise in him. But I felt it was my duty to do the best I could. He was a poor looking object to raise." When she was in her eighties, he asked her if she was concerned about him when he was a baby. She said, "Yes, the whole time." He asked, "Afraid I wouldn't live?" She paused, and said, "No, afraid you would."

When Clemens was four years old, the family moved to Hannibal, Missouri, where his father opened a general store on

Main Street. Hannibal, which he called that "half-forgotten paradise," was his home for fourteen years. It provided much of the backdrop for his novels. Clemens and his friends all had a goal of working on a Mississippi River steamboat—as a clerk, engineer, firemen, or pilot—preferably as a pilot.

John Clemens died of pneumonia when Clemens was eleven years old. He contributed to the family finances by delivering papers after school. In 1848, Clemens worked as a "printer's devil" for the local newspaper, the *Courier.* In 1850, he worked for his brother, Orion, when he moved back to Hannibal from St. Louis and started a weekly newspaper.

Clemens left home in 1853 and worked for a St. Louis newspaper to earn money to go to America's first World's Fair in New York, where he enjoyed the libraries and the theater. From New York, he moved on to Philadelphia, where he worked as a typesetter on the *Inquirer.* He visited Washington, D.C., and returned to the Midwest by way of New York.

He read an article about the Amazon River and decided to go there, harvest the coca plant, and make his fortune. In Cincinnati, he met Horace Bixby, pilot of the riverboat *Paul Jones.* His early ambitions returned, and he persuaded Bixby to train him as a river pilot. Clemens changed his mind about going to South America. His experiences with Bixby formed the basis for his book, *Life on the Mississippi,* which he wrote twenty-five years later. Clemens earned his license as a Mississippi River pilot in September, 1859, and at the age of twenty-three was earning as much as the Vice-President of the United States. However, the outbreak of the Civil War ended both navigation on the river and his job as a river pilot.

Clemens traveled to Carson City, Nevada, with his brother, Orion, who had just been appointed Secretary of the Nevada Territory. While in Nevada, Clemens tried prospecting, without any luck, both in the Humboldt region and the Esmeralda Hills. Next, he hiked 130 miles to Virginia City to write for the *Enterprise,* where he first began to use the name Mark Twain. Artemus Ward, the best-known humorist of the time, visited Virginia City and encouraged Twain to submit a piece to the New York *Sunday Mercury.* It was published in early 1864.

The restless Twain moved to San Francisco in May, 1864, to

work for the *Daily Morning Call.* While in San Francisco, the Sacramento *Union* paid him to do a series on the Hawaiian Islands. Upon his return from Hawaii, he went on the lecture circuit. He lectured at Cooper Union in New York City. While in New York, he published his first book, *The Celebrated Jumping Frog of Calaveras County and Other Sketches.*

The San Francisco *Alta California* financed a trip around the world in return for periodic reports. Clemens sailed from New York to Europe on the steamship *Quaker City.* Twain met Charles Langdon of Elmira, New York, on the ship, and they became friends. Charles showed his new friend a miniature portrait of his sister, Olivia Langdon, and forty years later, Twain said: "From that day to this, she has never been out of my mind." He met Olivia and her family in New York over the Christmas holidays of 1867.

Twain worked on his book, *The Innocents Abroad,* in early 1868 and didn't get to Elmira to visit Olivia until August. Olivia's father, a wealthy coal dealer, didn't know what to make of this humorist of the West and Midwest, but he was very comfortable with him. Twain proposed to Olivia and was rejected; Olivia thought that they should maintain a brother-sister relationship. She was ten years younger than he and wasn't sure of herself. Twain made two more visits to Elmira. When Mr. Langdon was assured of Twain's character and his ability to support his daughter, Olivia accepted his proposal. They were engaged in February 1869 and married in 1870.

Twain bought a one-third interest in the *Buffalo Express,* and he and his new wife moved to Buffalo. In the spring of 1871, Twain and Olivia stayed at Quarry Farm on East Hill overlooking Elmira and the Chemung River Valley. This began a practice that lasted for over twenty years; Twain wrote many of his books while summering at Quarry Farm. He wrote *Roughing It* during the first summer.

The Twains moved to Hartford, Connecticut, from Buffalo. It was to be their "permanent home." They built a large, unusual home in the Nook Farm literary colony, a 100-acre tract on the western edge of Hartford. Other Nook Farm authors included Harriet Beecher Stowe, who wrote *Uncle Tom's Cabin*, and

Charles Dudley Warner, editor of the *Hartford Courant* and of *Harper's* magazine. Twain's house had nineteen large rooms, a pilothouse balcony, Gothic turrets, and a porch like a riverboat deck. They lived in the house from 1874 until 1891; it is now a Mark Twain Museum.

Twain began writing *The Adventures of Tom Sawyer* in 1870, but the bulk of it was written during the summer of 1874 at Quarry Farm. He finished writing *The Adventures of Huckleberry Finn* in his octagonal study at Quarry Farm in 1875.

By 1884, Twain owned his own publishing company. He published the *Memoirs* of Ulysses S. Grant, which the ex-President wrote to pay off the debts of Grant and Ward, his unsuccessful Wall Street firm. Grant finished this *Memoirs* several days before dying of throat cancer. Within a year of his death, Julia Grant received royalties of $350,000, the largest sum earned by an author up to that time.

In 1889, Twain published *A Connecticut Yankee in King Arthur's Court*. In 1896, he undertook an around-the-world lecture tour to replenish his finances. In August, while sailing from South Africa to England, he and Olivia learned that their daughter, Suzy, who had stayed with an aunt in Elmira, had died of meningitis. Both Twain and Olivia were staggered by this blow. She had been their favorite.

Twain was lionized upon his return to New York. He was awarded honorary doctorates by Oxford University, Yale University, and the University of Missouri. He said, "If I am not called at least 'Doc' from now on, there will be a decided coolness." Olivia died on June 5, 1904, in Florence, Italy, where they had gone for her health.

Twain moved to Stormfield, Connecticut, near Redding, in 1908. His daughter, Jean, who lived with him, died on December 23, 1909. Upon her death, he said, "I shall never write any more." He died on April 21, 1910, and was buried in Elmira, New York. Twain's life spanned almost seventy-five years and was bracketed by two Halley's comets. Halley's comet crossed the skies two weeks before he was born in 1835 and again near the time that he died in 1910.

Brigham Young

Brigham Young, the sixth child and third son of John Young and Abigail (Nabby) Howe Young, was born on June 1, 1801, in Whitingham, Vermont. John Young was a farmer who moved frequently because of increasingly worn-out soil. Nabby Young was a relative of Elias Howe, one of the inventors of the sewing machine, and Samuel Gridley Howe, an eminent nineteenth century reformer. She suffered from tuberculosis and had difficulty caring for the children and doing the chores around the house.

In 1802, John Young moved the family to Smyrna, Chenango County, New York. John cleared land for farming and built a log dwelling in an area known as Dark Hollow. The family's next move was to Genoa in Cayuga County, east of Cayuga Lake. At an early age, Brigham was introduced to hard work, including logging and driving a team of horses. The family was poor and hired Brigham out to neighbors to earn additional income. Brigham attended the Drake School House and was tutored by his mother.

The Youngs were Methodists who initially had been New England Congregationalists. In Brigham's opinion, his parents were "the most strict religionists that lived upon the earth." The children were not allowed to use words such as "devil" and "I vow." Brigham held back from joining the Methodist church or any other church. He said a prayer to himself: "Lord, preserve me until I am old enough to have sound judgment, and a discreet mind ripened on a good, solid foundation of common sense."

Nabby Young died on June 11, 1815, just after Brigham's fourteenth birthday. He had been close to his mother; in his words: "Of my mother—she that bore me—I can say no better woman lived in the world." His older sister Fanny, who had helped care for him as a child, returned home and became the stabilizing influence in the family. Brigham developed into an independent individual with a deliberate manner.

In 1815, the family moved again—to the Sugar Hill district of Schuyler County near Tyrone. Their farm had many maple trees, and they went into maple sugar making to supplement their income. Maple sugar could be bartered for flour and other necessities. In 1817, John Young married Hannah Dennis Brown, a widow with several children of her own. He broke up his household and moved in with his new wife. Sixteen-year-old Brigham's father told him: "You now have your time; go and provide for yourself."

Young moved to Auburn, where he became an apprentice to learn the trades of carpentry, glazing, and painting. One of his early projects was the finish carpentry and painting of the new home of Judge Elijah Miller, the father-in-law of William H. Seward, a future Governor, U.S. Senator, and Secretary of State. The Seward Mansion, which Seward inherited from Judge Miller, has an ornate fireplace mantel crafted by Young. Young also worked on the construction of the Auburn Theological Seminary, where he slid off the roof and was saved by hanging onto the gutter in the eaves until help came.

In 1823, Young moved to Port Byron, a fast-growing town on the new Erie Canal. He worked in a furniture repair shop, a wool carding mill, a pail factory, and a boatyard. One of his employers observed that he "would do more work in a given time and secure more and better work from his help without trouble than any man they have ever employed." In 1824, Young joined the Methodist church. He insisted on being baptized by immersion, although that wasn't the usual Methodist practice at the time.

On October 5, 1824, Young married Miriam Works, a beautiful blonde whom he had met while working at the pail factory. Their daughter, Elizabeth, was born in Port Byron. In 1828, the family moved to Oswego, where he worked on the construction of a large tannery. When the tannery was finished in the following year, he moved his family to Mendon, where his father and several of his sisters had settled. Young built a house at the corner of Cheese Factory and Mendon-Ionia Roads. He also constructed a large undershot water wheel on Trout Creek, which flowed through his property. It provided power for grindstones, lathes, and saws.

In June, 1830, their second daughter, Vilate, was born. The childbirth temporarily incapacitated Miriam, who suffered with tuberculosis—the same ailment that had afflicted her mother-in-law. Young took part-time jobs so he could do more of the household chores while Miriam was bedridden. The family remained poor and contracted small debts.

While living in Port Byron, Young heard "rumors of a new revelation, to the effect of a new Bible written upon golden plates ... at Palmyra. I was somewhat acquainted with the coming forth of the *Book of Mormon* ... through ... the newspapers [and] many stories and reports ... circulated ... as the *Book of Mormon* was printed and ... scattered abroad." In June, 1830, Young saw a copy of the *Book of Mormon* when Samuel Smith, the brother of Joseph Smith who found the golden plates on Hill Cumorah, visited Mendon to preach about Mormonism and to sell copies of the "golden Bible."

In January, 1830, Young, his brother Phineas, and his good friend and neighbor Heber Kimball traveled to Columbia, Pennsylvania, the location of the nearest Mormon church, to observe the Mormons interpreting their religion, prophesying, and speaking in tongues. Young returned to Mendon and then visited his brother, Joseph, a Methodist minister in Canada, to ask his opinion of the new religion. In early April, John, Sr., Joseph, and Phineas were baptized into the Mormon religion.

On April 14th, Young was baptized by Elder Eleazer Miller in the stream behind his home. He said that before his clothes "were dry on my back [Elder Miller] laid his hands on me and ordained me an Elder, at which I marveled. According to the words of the Savior, I felt a humble, child-like spirit, witnessing unto me that my sins were forgiven." Ordination as an Elder gave Young the authority to preach the gospel. The rest of the family followed him in joining the new religion.

Four of the things that Young liked about Mormonism were its similarities to Puritanism, with its emphasis on common sense; its espousal of "Christian Primitivism," the restoration of Christianity as it existed at the time of Jesus Christ; its authoritarianism, which required unquestioning loyalty to the Mormon prophet Joseph Smith; and its lay priesthood, which provided a path to status and influence.

On September 8, 1832, Miriam Young died of tuberculosis. Young and his two daughters moved in with his friend, Heber Kimball. That fall, Young and Kimball traveled to the main Mormon settlement in Kirtland, Ohio, just east of Cleveland, to meet Joseph Smith—the founder of the Church of Jesus Christ of Latter Day Saints. Upon meeting the charismatic Mormon prophet, Young spoke in tongues and asked the Latter Day Saints leader's opinion of his gift of tongues. Smith "told them that it was of the pure Adamic language.... It is of God, and the time will come when Brother Brigham Young will preside over this church."

Young returned to Mendon to preach Mormonism. He traveled around upstate New York and Canada baptizing converts. In September, 1833, he moved to Kirtland to be near Joseph Smith and the center of Mormon activity. He courted Mary Ann Angell, a former Baptist from Seneca, New York. In February, 1834, Young and Mary Ann were married by Sidney Rigdon, an influential Mormon leader. Early in the following year, Smith appointed Young one of the the Council of Twelve Apostles, which was modeled on the apostles of the New Testament. They were responsible for overseeing the Mormon churches and missionary activity.

From 1835 through 1837, Young traveled around upstate New York, New England, and Canada spreading the word of Mormonism. On a return visit to Kirtland during this time, he supervised the completion of the Kirtland Temple. Smith began to encounter difficulties in Kirtland when he attempted to establish his own bank. Because of his indebtedness and his plan to print his own money, Smith was denied a state banking charter. He proceeded to establish the bank anyway; however, it was affected adversely by the Panic of 1837.

In 1838, Young was drawn into the conflict between the Mormons and non-Mormons in Missouri. The non-Mormons were concerned about the Mormon's economic and political control of the region. A series of armed clashes began in Gallatin, Missouri, when non-Mormons attempted to prevent Mormons from voting. Three Mormons were killed at Crooked River, Caldwell County, and seventeen Mormons were killed and fifteen wounded seriously at Haun's Mill, Caldwell County, by an unruly mob of over 200 men.

The Governor of Missouri, Lilburn Boggs, called out the Missouri militia and issued the order that the Mormons "must be exterminated or driven from Missouri, if necessary, for the public good." Joseph Smith turned himself in to the authorities and his brother, Hyrum, and Sidney Rigdon were arrested. Young was the senior member of the Council of the Twelve Apostles who was not in captivity. He appealed to the Missouri Legislature for compensation for Mormon property that had been seized. The Mormons received a token payment, and, due to threats to their lives, left Missouri for Illinois.

In 1839, Young made his last visit to upstate New York while enroute to a successful mission for the church in England that more than doubled the membership there. He promoted the increase in the number of English Elders and the immigration of English Mormons to the United States. Over the next six years, over 4,000 Mormons immigrated to the United States from Great Britain. He also established a Mormon periodical, the *Millennial Star,* in England. Young clearly established a reputation as an efficient administrator and organizer.

Smith escaped from his six-month captivity and established the center of the Mormon faith in Nauvoo, Illinois. In July, 1841, when Young returned to Nauvoo, he found that it had become a rapidly growing city of 3,000, that would expand to 10,000 by the end of 1841. The Nauvoo Charter gave the Mormons comprehensive powers of self-government, although they could not pass any laws contrary to the Illinois and U.S. Constitutions. The mayor and city council formed their own municipal court, and the city controlled its own militia, the Nauvoo Legion.

Young was elected to the Nauvoo city council and was appointed editor of the Nauvoo newspaper, *The Times and Seasons.* His commitment to Mormonism was severely tested in 1841, when Joseph Smith endorsed the practice of polygamy for the Latter Day Saints. Smith may have been influenced by the practices of the Oneida Community in New York State when he supported the concept of plural marriage. Initially, Young was appalled by the practice. He said that it "was the first time in his life that I had desired the grave." When he expressed his views to Smith, he was told, "Brother Brigham, the Lord will reveal it to you."

Young was faced with the dilemma of either practicing polygamy or defying the prophet Joseph Smith. Eventually, he accepted the concept of plural marriage. In June, 1842, he married 20-year-old Lucy Ann Decker Seeley. On November 2, 1843, he married Augusta Ann Adams and Harriet Cook. In May 1844, he married his fourth plural wife, Clarissa Decker, the sister of his first plural wife. All of these wives lived in their own houses.

The practice of polygamy was probably the greatest source of difficulty for the Mormons, both within and outside of the church. Nauvoo was envied as the most prosperous city in Illinois, and its self-government was not easily accepted by non-Mormons. Smith began to realize that he must look to the Far West as "a place of refuge" where "the devil cannot dig us out." In February 1844, Smith asked the Council of Twelve to send a delegation west toward California and Oregon to build a temple and to establish a government of their own.

The delegation to the West was delayed by Smith's decision to run for the Presidency in 1844 as an independent candidate. Young and other Mormon leaders did much of the campaigning for the candidate. Smith had problems of his own back in Nauvoo. A group of dissidents led by William Law split off from the Latter Day Saints due to disagreements with Smith's policies, particularly polygamy. Law and his associates established a competing newspaper, the Nauvoo *Expositor.* Smith asked the city council to destroy the press and all copies of the newspaper, a blatant violation of freedom of the press.

Anti-Mormonisn feeling intensified around Nauvoo, and Smith, his brother, Hyrum, and two other Mormon leaders gave themselves up to county authorities in Carthage. On June 27, 1844, a large, organized mob entered the jail at Carthage and killed Smith and his brother, and wounded another of the Mormon leaders. Young, who was campaigning for Smith in Massachusetts at the time, returned to Nauvoo by a round-about route to avoid assassination.

Young's only serious rival for the Mormon Presidency was

Sidney Rigdon. Young's forceful speech, his alignment with the Council of Twelve, and his confidence that the church would make the right decision made him the clear choice. Although Smith's brother, William, supported Youngs election to the presidency, later he attempted to replace him. Anti-Mormonism sentiment continued to run high, and Illinois Governor Thomas Ford repealed the Nauvoo charter, which disfranchised both the city police and the Nauvoo Legion. Earlier, he had ordered the return of their state-supplied weapons.

Illinois justice was unable to convict the killers of Joseph Smith and his brother and anti-Mormon mobs burned barns and crops on farms around Nauvoo. Young realized that they would have to abandon Nauvoo and settle in a frontier sanctuary. Texas was considered as a possible site, as were California, Oregon, and the island of Vancouver. Young ruled out both Oregon and Vancouver because they were involved in ongoing disputes between the United States and Great Britain. He favored the Great Basin because it was remote and virtually uninhabited by whites.

In February, 1846, the main body left Nauvoo. Young organized twenty-four companies of 100 each and personally selected the leader of each company. Mormons were unable to sell most of their property, and that which was sold went for a fraction of its value. Both Utopian Robert Owen and the Catholic Church looked at the property, particularly the Temple, but decided not to purchase it. Before leaving Nauvoo, Young was continually threatened with arrest. The Mormons' trek to the West was the largest and most well-organized of all of the migrations.

They spent the first winter on Potawatomi Indian lands just north of Omaha, Nebraska. Young supervised the building of 538 log houses and 83 sod houses for 3,483 people. In early 1847, he assumed the personal responsibility for the pilot company of 159 pioneers, seventy-two wagons, sixty-six oxen, and ninety-two horses. The company, whose goal was to chart the path to the Great Salt Lake Valley for others to follow, used artificial horizons, a circle of reflection, and sextants. They did not employ professional guides.

Initially, they traveled the Oregon Trail along the Platt River. They averaged ten miles a day. The fuel for their fires was dry buffalo dung, or "meadow muffins." Along the way, they encountered hostile Pawnees and friendly Sioux Indians. On July 7, 1847, they reached Fort Bridger on the Green River. John C. Fremont's description of the Great Salt Lake Region was favorable; however, Jim Bridger, the famous scout, told them that the Indians in the area were unfriendly, and that the area's cold nights would prevent the growth of crops. As they reached within fifty miles of the Great Salt Lake (near Ogden, Utah), another scout gave them a favorable report of their destination, including its agricultural potential.

On July 24, 1847, Young got his first view of the Great Salt Lake Valley from the the mouth of Emigration Canyon and said, "This is the Place." Compared with Nauvoo, the Salt Lake Valley was dry and remote. It was forty miles long from north to south and twenty-five miles wide and was bounded by majestic snow-capped mountains. Young laid out the city with streets eight rods wide in a perfect grid.

During the winter of 1847-48, Young reorganized the First Presidency of the Church and appointed Heber Kimball First Counselor and his own cousin, Willard Richards, Second Counselor. Also, he assumed the designation of prophet, seer, and revelator that had been held by Joseph Smith. By spring of 1848, the settlement had grown from 300 to over 5,000 people.

During 1849 and 1850, Young sought statehood for Utah and sent two representatives to Washington, D.C., to lobby for statehood. He preferred to skip territorial status because it would involve federal observers that could limit his control. President Taylor denied their request for statehood; however, upon Taylor's death, President Fillmore granted territorial status to Utah, which was named for the Ute Indians in the region. The Mormons had called it Deseret. Young was chosen as Utah's first territorial governor, and Mormons were appointed as Associate Justice of the territory's Supreme Court, U.S. Marshal, and U.S. Attorney.

Young counseled keeping on friendly terms with the Ute Indians in the area. He asked the Mormons to "feed them and clothe them ... never turn them away hungry" and "teach them the art of husbandry." In his opinion, "It was cheaper to feed the Indians than to fight them." From 1850 to 1855, the number of

Mormons in the Salt Lake Basin grew from 1,000 to 60,000, mainly from the East, but the numbers included 15,000 from Great Britain.

In May 1857, President Buchanan sent 2,500 federal troops to Utah to remove Young as Territorial Governor. As had occurred earlier, anti-Mormon sentiment was rampant, principally due to their belief in polygamy. The original commander of the federal troops was replaced by Colonel Albert Sidney Johnston, who later distinguished himself as a Confederate general during the Civil War. The winter weather caused hardship for Colonel Johnston's contingent. As a goodwill gesture, Young sent 800 pounds of salt to Johnston who responded that he would "accept no favors from traitors and rebels."

Young accepted President Buchanan's appointed governor, Alfred Cumming, but refused to let Colonel Johnston's men enter Salt Lake City. Young threatened to burn every structure built by the Mormons if the army entered the city. The Mormons vacated the city until July 1858, when peace was made with the federal government.

The settlement continued to expand. Young was a good businessman and by the late 1850s had an accumulated wealth between $200,000 and $250,000, earned from lumbering, lumber mills, real estate, and a tannery. He married more plural wives until, ultimately, he had fifty-five, with whom he had fifty-seven children.

On August 23, 1877, Young became very ill and was diagnosed with cholera. His condition worsened, and he died on August 27th, exclaiming "Joseph! Joseph! Joseph!" John Taylor, the senior member of the Council of Twelve, became president of the Church in 1880.

Brigham Young provided leadership for the Mormon Church at a critical period in its history, which enabled it to become the largest religion established in the United States. Also, he contributed heavily to the growth of the American frontier and is viewed as one of the great colonizers in the history of the United States.

Henry Robert House, Owego

Chapter 6

"Great and dramatic changes have taken place in the world. Old values, old ways of thinking have changed—to give way to new and pressing problems that tax all our opportunism and purpose, and that call for the best we can contribute to the work of the world. But one fact stands out clear and challenging: the sound, basic principles of personal progress and success have not changed. They have been modified and accelerated in their operation—given new directions perhaps—but still the greatest rewards go to those who can give the most."

—L. G. Elliott

Chester Carlson

Chester Carlson began experimenting with a dry copy process in 1935, and, on October 22, 1938, he produced the first crude copy using his electrophotography process. Carlson, a patent attorney, filed a comprehensive patent in 1939. He spent five years looking for a sponsor to finance the further development and commercialization of his new technology. Over a five year period, he was turned down by the National Inventor's Council, the U.S. Army Signal Corps, and thirty-two companies, including A. B. Dick, Eastman Kodak, IBM, General Electric, and Remington-Rand (Univac). Carlson said that they all displayed "an enthusiastic lack of interest."

In 1944, he found an interested sponsor, the Battelle Memorial Institute of Columbus, Ohio. Battelle was to receive sixty percent of future proceeds in return for helping to develop the technology. They suggested the use of selenium instead of sulphur in the process, as well as the use of a specific black toner powder. They, too, were unsuccessful in promoting of the product. An Ohio State University professor renamed the process "xerography," from the Greek words "xeros," meaning dry, and "graphos," meaning writing.

Finally, John Dessauer of the Haloid Corporation of Rochester, New York, saw an article about electrophotography in *Radio News*. Dessauer's boss, Joe Wilson, Jr., wanted to increase the $100,000 yearly earnings of the company and had asked him to read technical journals to look for new products and/or processes. Haloid Corporation purchased the patent and rights to Carlson's technology from Battelle. They produced a flat plate copier in 1949 that required 3-5 minutes per copy, spent more on research and development than they earned each year, and, by 1956, received forty percent of their sales from xerography. The name of the company was changed to Haloid-Xerox.

In 1959, IBM was asked to manufacture copiers for Haloid-Xerox. IBM commissioned Arthur D. Little, a consultant from Cambridge, Massachusetts, to do a study of the market potential. The study identified a total potential market of 5,000 units of sales for Haloid-Xerox's new 914 copier. IBM declined the offer to participate in Xerography a second time, and Haloid-Xerox began to manufacture the model 914 copier themselves. By 1968, they had produced 200,000 of them. The fallacy in the Arthur D. Little study was in basing their recommendations on the estimate of the number of copies made at the point of origin, using the original. Most copies are made at the point of receipt from copies made elsewhere.

Haloid-Xerox changed its name to the Xerox Corporation in 1961. By 1988, three billion copies were being made each day worldwide, and the business of making copies had become a $22 billion a year business. The technology that nobody wanted made millionaires out of many people and revolutionized the way in which we communicate with one another.

Glenn H. Curtiss

Glenn Hammond Curtiss, the son of Frank and Lua Curtiss, was born in Hammondsport on May 21, 1878. He was named for the scenic glen near the village and for the village itself. He was mechanically inclined and became interested in bicycles. Curtiss raced bicycles and, while still in his teens, opened bicycle shops in Hammondsport, Bath, and Corning. He received so many orders for his Curtiss-built "Hercules" bicycles that he contracted their manufacture.

In 1901, Curtiss borrowed several thousand dollars and began to manufacture motorcycles. He became known for his design innovation and his fearlessness as a motorcycle racer. In 1904, he designed a two-cylinder air-cooled engine to power Thomas Scott Baldwin's dirigible, "California Arrow," which won an air meet in Oakland, California. His business grew from three employees in 1901 to 100 in 1908. On January 23, 1907, Curtiss won a motorcycle race at Ormond Beach, Florida, and set a speed record of 137.47 miles an hour. He was considered to be "the fastest man on earth."

On September 30, 1907, Curtiss joined F. W. Baldwin, Dr. Alexander Graham Bell, J. A. D. McCurdy, and Lieutenant Thomas Selfridge of the U. S. Army in forming the Aerial Experiment Association. The Association, chartered to conduct experiments in manned, heavier-than-air flight, established its headquarters in Hammondsport. On March 12, 1908, Casey Baldwin flew the Association's first aircraft, "Red Wing," for twenty seconds over a distance of 318 feet, 11 inches. It was the first public flight; the Wright Brother's flights were not announced in advance and open to the public.

On May 22, 1908, Curtiss flew the "White Wing" a distance of 1,017 feet. The "White Wing" was the first aircraft in America to use ailerons to control roll. The Wright Brothers used a wing warping mechanism to control their aircraft on the roll axis. On July 4, 1908, Curtiss flew the "June Bug" 5,090 feet to win the first leg of the Scientific American Trophy. In 1908, their fourth and last aircraft, "Silver Dart," was designed and built; on March

31, 1909, the Association was disbanded. One of their members, Lieutenant Selfridge, became American aviation's first fatality when he was killed in a flight with Orville Wright, who was injured in the crash.

On June 16, 1909, Curtiss flew the "Gold Bug" 24.7 miles to establish a new distance record and to win the second leg of the Scientific American Trophy. In August, 1909, he competed against the best aviators of Europe as the only American aviator and won the Gordon Bennett Cup speed race at Rheims, France, with a speed of 46.5 miles per hour. In 1910, the New York *World* offered a $10,000 prize for the first flight along the Hudson River between Albany and New York, retracing the route of Henry Hudson and Robert Fulton. With the "Albany Flyer," Curtiss won the prize as well as the third leg of the Scientific American Trophy, which earned him its permanent possession. In 1911, he was awarded the first pilot's license issued in the United States.

Curtiss received considerable coverage in the newspapers and the development of aircraft was encouraged by editors rather than scoffed at as it had been in the past. He provided demonstrations to the U.S. armed forces to convince them of the potential military uses of aircraft. In June 1910, He gave the first demonstration of aerial bombing to the Army and Navy at Keuka Lake. On January 18, 1911, one of Curtiss' pilots, Eugene Ely, successfully landed and took off form the deck of the *USS Pennsylvania.* One month later, Curtiss landed a seaplane fitted with pontoons along side the *USS Pennsylvania*, was hoisted on board, lowered back into the water, and flew back to land.

In 1912, Curtiss flew the world's first flying boat, which was a boat hull fitted with wings and an engine. Earlier seaplanes had been aircraft designed to operate from land that were provided with pontoons instead of wheels or skids. The publicity that Curtiss received resulted in many orders being placed for his aircraft. In 1913, he developed the JN-4 "Jenny," which became the most popular trainer of World War I.

In 1914, Curtiss rebuilt and flew Dr. Samuel Langley's "Aerodrome," which had been in two unsuccessful flights on the Potomac River prior to the Wright Brother's success at Kitty Hawk, North Carolina. Also that year, Curtiss completed the

Wanamaker Trans-Atlantic Flying Boat "America." The outbreak of World War I prevented the planned flight across the Atlantic Ocean in August, 1914. The "America" was sold to England for use as a submarine patrol aircraft.

The Curtiss Aeroplane and Motor Company received many orders from Great Britain for the "Jenny" aircraft during World War I. Curtiss opened new plants in Buffalo to keep up with the demand. In 1917, when the United States entered the war, additional demands were placed on the company until it had ten plants employing 10,000 people. At the end of the war, Curtiss flying boats were being flight tested along the Atlantic in preparation to fly them to England instead of delivering them by ship, which placed them at risk from German submarines. In May 1919, the Curtiss NC-4 flying boat, piloted by Lieutenant Albert Read, took of from Newfoundland in company with two other flying boats and landed in Horta before proceeding to England. This was the first trans-Atlantic crossing by air.

After the war, Curtiss devoted his energies to developing, with a partner, Hialeah and Miami Springs, Florida. He also pioneered the development of the house trailer and the travel trailer. He continued to strive to break speed records during the 1920s. In 1930, he flew a Curtiss Condor transport plane, with many dignitaries aboard, from Albany to New York, retracing the route of his earlier flight.

In July, 1930, Curtiss was operated upon for appendicitis in a Buffalo hospital. On July 23, 1930, he developed a blood clot and died at the age of fifty-two. He was one of the most productive of the early aviation pioneers. He was responsible for many of the early developments in aviation and was called "the father of naval aviation."

Orson Fowler

rson Fowler, who was born in Cohocton in 1809, became interested in phrenology while attending Amherst College. He and his classmate, Henry Ward Beecher, subscribed to the phrenological theory of Johann Kaspar Spurzheim, an Austrian doctor who believed that people's character could be analyzed by examining their craniums. Fowler and his brother, Lorenzo, became practicing phrenologists, the nineteenth-century version of psychiatrists. They measured the heads of artists, criminals, philanthropists, statesmen, and writers.

Fowler published the *American Phrenological Journal and Miscellany,* in which he provided a series of health, phrenological, and sex manuals. He advocated a wide range of reforms, including anti-lacing, dress reform, vegetarianism, teetotalism, and water cure. He considered himself to be an expert in sex education; he based his advice as a marriage consultant and sex scientist on his own experiences in three marriages. Fowler became famous and wealthy from his practice of phrenology and the publication of phrenological journals. By the late 1840s, he had the luxury of spending his energy on other interests. Walt Whitman took over as the editor of his publications during the 1850s.

In 1853, Fowler published a book entitled *A Home for All, or the Gravel Wall and Octagon Mode of Building* in which he recommended building with gravel or grout and sang the praises of octagonal houses and buildings. On a visit to Wisconsin, he visited a builder who used a mixture of sand, gravel, and lime in his construction. Fowler advocated the use of this material because it was: "Better than brick or wood and not as expensive.... Nature's building material is abundant everywhere, cheap, durable, and complete throughout.... The superiority of this plan must certainly revolutionize building, and especially enable poor men to build their own homes."

Fowler enumerated the many advantages of an eight-sided house: conservation of heat, efficient use of space, more available sunlight than a four-sided house, and the saving of time for the busy housewife. The main rooms of an octagonal house were usually square or rectangular; the left-over triangular shapes were used for closets, cupboards, and hallways. He suggested many innovations in his house designs, including central heating, dumb waiters, indoor toilets, speaking tubes, running water, and ventilators in every room.

In 1853, he moved into his own octagonal home in Fishkill, New York. The three-story, sixty-room house with a glass-domed octagonal cupola was built on a knoll overlooking the Catskill Mountains and the Hudson River. The main floor had four large octagonal rooms all connected by folding doors. It had an author's study, dancing room, gymnastic room, library, playroom, and prophet's chamber, and it was surrounded by a veranda on all sides. Visitors to "Fowler's Folly" included the women's rights advocates Amelia Bloomer and Lucretia Mott, and journalists Charles A. Dana and Horace Greeley.

By 1857, over 1,000 octagonal houses had been built all around the country, as well as other octagonal structures such as barns, blacksmith shops, pigpens, schools, and warehouses. Many eight-sided homes were built in the Finger Lakes Region. Most of the octagonal houses in the Finger Lakes Region were built in the last half of the nineteenth century.

The Panic of 1857 reduced Fowler's finances considerably. He rented his octagon house and 130-acre property that year to a New York realtor for $2,500 annually. During the Civil War, it became the Cuban Institute and Military Academy and later was a boarding house. By 1880, it was vacant and became the target of vandals.

The house was razed in 1897. It outlasted its architect by ten years. Fowler died in 1887. In 1925, Gertrude Knevel published *Octagon House,* which generated interest in Fowler's earlier book on the subject. In June, 1946, Walter Creese wrote of Fowler in *The Art Bulletin:* "It does not seem permissible to call Fowler a significant architect. His extraordinary importance for his own age was the result of his faculty for accurately estimating and capitalizing upon the bubbling intellectual currents that surrounded him." However, interest in octagonal houses has been long-lived; Dover Publications reprinted Fowler's book in 1973.

Konstantin Frank

Dr. Konstantin Frank showed that the Vitis Vinifera species of grapes, the European varieties, could be grown in the northeastern United States. Previous attempts at growing the less winter-hardy European varieties in the Northeast had failed for over 200 years.

Other viticulturalists recommended French-American hybrid varieties for the region, a compromise on quality but a species of grapes more likely to survive the severe winters. Dr. Frank, a strong-willed man, became controversial because of his public condemnation of French-American varieties. He asked why area vineyardists were not growing the world's premium varieties, such as Chardonnay and Riesling, and then he proved that they could be grown in the Finger Lakes Region.

Dr. Frank was born on July 4, 1899, in the Ukraine, the fourth of ten children born to German parents. His father was a farmer and vineyardist. As a young man, Dr. Frank fought in the White Russian army. He studied agriculture at the Polytechnic Institute of Odessa and organized collective farms in the southern Ukraine for the Communists. When he completed his studies, including enology and viticulture, he taught and did grape research at the local agricultural institute.

One story he liked to tell occurred while he was working at the Institute of Viticulture and Enology in the Ukraine. He was responsible for the first three Ford tractors received in the Ukraine from the United States. He decided to determine how heavy a load the tractors could pull. Instead of lining the tractors up side by side, allowing each tractor to pull one third of the load, he lined the tractors up in tandem, with tractor two hitched to tractor one, and tractor three between the load and tractor two. When all three tractors strained to pull the considerable load, they were not up to it structurally. Tractor three, attached to the load, was literally pulled to pieces and destroyed. Some of the metal parts were stretched, some were broken, and the tractor was not repairable; it had been demolished.

This occurred in the 1930s during the reign of Josef Stalin, and Dr. Frank was concerned about the repercussions of destroying one third of the USSR's Ford tractors. He wasn't sure how far up the chain of command the information was passed, but nothing happened and no one ever reprimanded him for destroying thirty-three and a third percent of the Ford tractors in the Soviet Union.

During the German occupation in World War II, he was the director of the institute in the Ukraine. When the war ended, he went to Austria and Bavaria and managed farm properties for the United States occupation forces.

Dr. Frank emigrated to the United States with his wife and three children in 1951, at fifty-two years of age; he didn't speak English, and he had forty dollars in his pocket. He washed dishes at an Automat restaurant in New York City to earn the fare to the nearest grape research station, the New York Agricultural Experiment Station in Geneva.

He described his experience to them and told them he hoped to be able to utilize his background. He said, "they let me hoe blueberries," and for two years he was given only menial chores to do. This experience provided him with some very definite opinions of the Experiment Station at Geneva.

He watched the Finger Lakes grapegrowers plant increasing acreage of French-American hybrid grapes, and asked why Vinifera wasn't being planted. He was told that the winters were too cold and that the European varieties couldn't survive here. Dr. Frank had grown Vinifera varieties in the Ukraine, along the Dneiper River, "where the temperature goes to forty below, where we had to bury the entire vine in winter, where when we spit, it froze before it hit the ground." He pointed out that the Vinifera vines didn't die from the cold, but from disease, such as mildew and fungus, and vine pests. Furthermore, modern technology knew how to control these problems.

Charles Fournier, president of Gold Seal Winery, heard Dr. Frank's comments and realized that he might be right. Fournier had seen Chardonnay and Pinot Noir varieties survive at Epernay and Rheims, which are seven degrees of latitude father north than Hammondsport. He had also seen temperatures drop below zero in the Champagne district of France. Fournier hired Dr. Frank as a consultant to Gold Seal in 1953.

Dr. Frank convinced Fournier of the importance of winter-hardy rootstock. He told Fournier that his research in the Ukraine had shown that, to survive the winter, Vinifera vines should be grafted onto roots that would allow the ripening of the wood of the vine, the canes, before the first freeze of the winter. Dr. Frank and Fournier traveled the Northeast in search of this type of rootstock, including trips to Ontario and Quebec.

They grafted Vinifera vines, such as Cabernet Sauvignon, Chardonnay, Gewurtztraminer, and Riesling, obtained from vineyards of the University of California at Davis, onto Canadian roots. Over a four-year period, thousands of grafted vines were planted. The winter of 1957 provided a severe test when temperatures dropped to twenty-five degrees below zero.

Gold Seal expanded their planting of Vinifera vines and had seventy acres planted by 1966. Dr. Frank bought property for a vineyard on Middle Road in Pulteney and planted his own vines. The first commercial New York State Vinifera wines were introduced by Gold Seal in 1961, and Dr. Frank called it "the second discovery of America."

By 1973, Dr. Frank's Vinifera Wine Cellars, Ltd., had expanded to seventy-eight acres of vineyards and a winery capacity of 60,000 gallons. His Trockenbeerenauslese 1961 was served in the executive mansion in Albany and at the White House. Dr. Frank became a U.S. citizen and a vocal pro-American. He displayed an American flag in the front windows of his one-story red brick home on Middle Road.

He built his winery behind the house and maintained a small pilot vineyard next to his home. In this vineyard he planted at least two vines each of about fifty varieties / clones. Included were some little-known varieties, such as Fetjaska from Hungary, Kara Burni from Bulgaria, and Sereksia Tschornay from the Ukraine.

Dr. Frank died in 1985. The Frank tradition is being carried on and expanded upon by his son, Willy, and his grandson, Fred. Willy began bottling a premium champagne with the Chateau Frank label in 1985 made in the methode champenoise French style, in which the secondary fermentation providing the bubbles takes place in the bottle in which it is served. His champagne is made of the same four grape varieties used by French Champagne-makers: Chardonnay, Pinot Noir, Pinot Blanc, and Pinot Meunier. Only limited quantities of the last two varieties are grown in New York State. He views the premier champagne-makers, such as Bollinger, as his competition. Willy asks the same question that his father asked, "Why not the best?"

Paul Garrett

aptain Paul Garrett, the dean of American winemakers in the 1930s, became a multi-millionaire making and selling wine. The title of "Captain" was not of military origin but was what his employees called him when they didn't call him "the boss." He was born in North Carolina in 1863, and by the age of fourteen was working for Medoc Vineyard, North Carolina's first commercial winery. It was owned by his father, country doctor Francis Garrett, and his uncle, Charles Garrett, who ran the winery.

Paul Garrett promoted wine made from the southern Scuppernong grape. He was the father of the Virginia Dare label, the best-selling wine in the United States in the twenty years prior to Prohibition. The original Virginia Dare wine was a blend of Concord, Scuppernong (which hid the foxy taste of the Concord grape), and California wine. He chose the name Virginia Dare—the first child born of English parents in America—because Scuppernong was the first American wine.

Paul Garrett established his first winery, Garrett & Company, in North Carolina in 1900, and by 1903 he owned five wineries in that state. He expanded into Virginia, and by 1913 he owned vineyards and wineries in Canandaigua, Hammondsport, and Penn Yan, as well as the Mission Vineyard and Winery at Cucamonga, California. In 1919, he owned seventeen plants processing grape juice or wine with a capacity of ten million gallons in the states of California, Missouri, New York, North Carolina, Ohio, and Virginia.

He could have retired as a multi-millionaire, but he held on to his wine empire, not believing that Prohibition would last. He lost millions of dollars on dealcoholized wine, a cola-flavored grape drink, flavoring extracts, and grape concentrates. When Prohibition was repealed in 1933, he was the only vintner capable of marketing wine in every wet state. Also, he was the first winery executive to promote the blending of New York State and California wines.

Garrett attempted to sell the California winegrowers on the concept of blending the native Labrusca grape varieties from the East, such as Concord, Delaware, and Ives, with the European (Vinifera) grape varieties from the West. He was ahead of his time with this concept. By 1970, the large California wineries began to blend Labrusca concentrates and juice from other states with their juice.

One of Paul Garrett's main themes was "American wine for Americans." He was in New York City promoting that concept when he contracted pneumonia and died on March 18, 1940, at the age of seventy-six. He truly was a captain in his industry, and his idea of an American wine industry based on blends of east coast and west coast wines has survived. The Virginia Dare trademark is now owned by the Canandaigua Wine Company, Canandaigua, New York, and is used for a line of wines. By 1967, only the white Virginia Dare had the Scuppernong taste.

Jonathan Goble

J onathan Goble, from the town of Wayne on the east side of Keuka Lake, invented the jinrikisha, a small, two-wheeled vehicle drawn by one or more men that was originally used in Japan. The first jinrikisha used in Japan was constructed by a carpenter named Frank Pollay in the Village of Pulteney, on the west side of Keuka Lake, disassembled, and sent to Japan in 1870.

The oldest of six children, Goble was born in 1827 on a farm in Wayne. Young Jonathan was a smart youth with a temper. He once wrote a letter to a farmer, against whom he held a grudge, threatening to burn down his farm. When the farmer's barn burned, Goble was thrown into jail until he proved he was elsewhere that night. The jail stay changed him, and upon his release, he joined the Wayne Baptist Church, and considered becoming a Baptist minister.

In 1852, Goble joined the U.S. Navy and served as a Marine on the *USS Mississippi*, the flagship of Commodore Perry's great white fleet that visited Japan in 1853. In 1854, Perry opened up the islands for trade with the signing of the Treaty of Kanagawa. Frank Pollay was the ship's carpenter on the *USS Mississippi*.

Goble completed his naval service and enrolled at the Hamilton Theological Seminary at Hamilton, New York, which later became the Colgate Divinity School. He was ordained a Baptist minister in 1859, and returned to Japan as a Baptist missionary with his wife, Eliza Weeks, who was also from Wayne. When he arrived in Kanagawa in 1860, he was the first Baptist missionary in Japan and the third missionary of any denomination to enter the country. They lived in Yokohama, which was a small fishing village at the time.

In 1869, Eliza became ill and had to be carried in a sedan chair, or palanquin, when she went out. The palanquin was a covered litter with poles along the sides that rested on the shoulders of two men, one in front and one in the rear. Eliza became very uncomfortable with the jostling that accompanied travel in the palanquin.

Goble saw a picture of a baby carriage in the American magazine *Godey's Lady Book* and conceived of a cross between a baby carriage and a sulky, as used in harness racing. The vehicle would be pulled by a man between shafts and would eliminate the jostling that caused his wife so much discomfort when traveling. He remembered his friend from the *USS Mississippi*, Frank Pollay, whom he heard had opened a wagon shop in Pulteney.

Goble sent a description and sketch of the vehicle to Pollay, who made the box, the shaft, and the wheels. He subcontracted the iron work. Pollay sent the components to Goble in Yokohama, who assembled them into the first jinrikisha in Japan in 1870. Later, three Japanese gentlemen claimed to have invented the jinrikisha, but their contributions were improvements, such as the addition of springs, a hooded top, and wheel guards. Charles

Shepard, the U.S. Consul in Japan, supported Goble's claim to being the inventor of the jinrikisha.

Within two years, the jinrikisha replaced the palanquin in Japan; it was easier to be a puller than a bearer. Its usage spread to China, India, and other countries in the Pacific Rim where manpower was readily available.

Goble was also known for translating the Gospel of St. Matthew into Japanese. The original copy of the translation was presented to the Wayne Baptist Church in 1871 by Goble, when he spoke at the church about his missionary work in Japan on a visit to the United States. It came to the Colgate-Rochester Divinity School in 1929, when the Rochester Theological Seminary and the Colgate Theological Institution (formerly the Hamilton Seminary) were combined.

Goble also sold Bibles and religious tracts while he was in Japan. In addition, he was an aide and interpreter to a member of the Japanese nobility, Lord Yammononchi. Goble lived in Japan as a missionary until 1882, when Eliza died. He returned to the United States in 1892 and lived in a home for retired Baptist ministers near Philadelphia. He died in a similar home in St. Louis in 1898. Frank Pollay outlived Jonathan Goble by fourteen years. Pollay was buried in Pulteney cemetery in 1912.

Seth Green

The New York State Fish Hatchery in Caledonia, established in 1870, was the first fish hatchery in the United States. The hatchery started as a private enterprise in 1864 by Seth Green of Rochester on property that he purchased on Spring Creek. Green had observed female salmon depositing fertilized eggs in prepared nests in Canada. It is a wasteful operation since the male salmon eats as many of the deposited eggs as he can find.

Although Green had not heard of the artificial propagation of fish, he experimented with propagation techniques in the Genesee River. He knew that his methods were more efficient than nature's techniques. Although artificial propagation of fish had been done for centuries in China, and by two Frenchmen and a Prussian army officer, Green was the American pioneer. In 1864, he began to propagate hundreds of thousands of trout fry in his hatchery on Spring Creek.

Green was one of the first three commissioners of the New York State Fish Commission when it was created in 1866. The other two commissioners were Horatio Seymour of Utica, who had served two terms as governor of New York State, and Robert B. Roosevelt, an uncle of Theodore Roosevelt. Green and Roosevelt collaborated on a book, *Fish Hatching and Fish Catching*. Green sold his private hatchery on Spring Creek to the state and became the first New York State Superintendent of Fish Culture, a position that he held for the rest of his life.

Green began the state program with 80,000 eggs from thirteen lake trout from Lake Ontario and with whitefish eggs from the St. Clair River near Detroit. He also propagated salmon and shad. By 1974, the New York State Department of Environmental Conservation had stocked 7.4 million trout and salmon from sixteen state hatcheries. Trout were stocked along 4,400 miles of 1,100 streams and in 700 lakes and ponds.

Seth Green died in 1888. The Isaak Walton league placed a bronze plaque at the State Fish Hatchery at Caledonia commemorating him as the father of fish culture and as a "world famous pioneer in conservation."

Henry Robert

Henry Martyn Robert was born in Robertsville, North Carolina, in 1837. In 1857, he graduated from the U.S. Military Academy and served as an assistant professor of natural philosophy and astronomy upon his graduation. In 1858, he was placed in charge of engineering operations in Washington Territory in a campaign against the Indians.

During the Civil War, he was responsible for the construction of defenses around Washington, Philadelphia, and New Bedford, Massachusetts. He helped to plan and build the defenses for New

York Harbor, Long Island and Long Island Sound, Galveston, Pensacola, and other coastal areas in addition to planning and implementing improvements to the Delaware, Hudson, St. Lawrence, and Tennessee Rivers. In 1901, he was appointed Chief of Engineers of the U.S. Army and promoted to Brigadier General.

As a twenty-five-year-old lieutenant, Robert was asked to preside at a meeting. He knew nothing about parliamentary procedure so he looked for reference material on the subject. He was surprised to find how little material was available and began to collect it. In 1876, Robert wrote the book, *Robert's Rules of Order*, while living in a house on Front Street in Owego. His rules were based on parliamentary procedure used by the British Parliament. These procedures were also used by the colonists in town meetings in New England. Until 1876, Thomas Jefferson's book on parliamentary procedure, which was published in 1801, was used for town meetings. Jefferson's book was also used by the United States Congress until Cushing's Manual was published in 1844.

Robert adapted the earlier parliamentary rules to meet the needs of "ordinary societies." His *Robert's Rules of Order* became the guide for clubs, organizations, and schools in the United States. It established procedures to deal with meetings that started late or lasted too long and reduced the disruptiveness of autocratic chairmen and selfish cliques. It enlightened attendees of meetings and reduced the probability of minority resolutions being forced through the approval process.

Subsequently, Robert published three additional books: *Robert's Rules of Order Revised*, in 1915; *Parliamentary Practice, An Introduction to Parliamentary Law*, in 1921; and *Parliamentary Law*, in 1923. He was a member of the American Association for the Advancement of Science and the American Academy of Political and Social Science. He died on May 12, 1923, at the age of eighty-six, and was buried in Arlington National Cemetery.

Henry Wells / William Fargo

enry Wells, the son of Presbyterian clergyman Shipley Wells, was born on December 12, 1805, at Thetford, Vermont. The family moved to Central New York, where Wells attended school at Fayette and worked on a farm. In 1822, he was apprenticed to Jessup & Palmer, tanners and shoemakers, in Palmyra. In 1841, he became the Albany agent for Harden's express, which ran between New York and Albany.

Two years later, Wells formed Livingston, Wells & Pomeroy's, which conducted express business between Albany and Buffalo. He made a weekly trip as messenger, traveling on six railroads and two stage lines. The company was the first to discontinue the charging of two fares, one for the messenger and a separate charge for a trunk. Wells' express company pioneered the working relationship between express companies and railroads.

The company carried mail for six cents a letter or one dollar for twenty letters. The Post Office charged from twelve to twenty-four cents a letter. With James W. Hale as a partner, Wells offered a mail service from New York to Bangor, Maine, via Boston that was strongly opposed by the government. Popular support favored the expressmen, and, in order to remain competitive, the government was forced to pass the Postage Act of 1845 that provided five-cent postage.

William George Fargo, the oldest of twelve children of William C. Fargo and Tacy Strong Fargo, was born on May 20, 1818, at Pompey, near Syracuse. At the age of thirteen, he rode a thirty-mile mail route twice a week. From 1831 until 1842, He clerked in a grocery store, worked in an inn, failed at running his own grocery store, and was the first freight agent at Auburn for the Auburn and Syracuse Railroad. In 1842, Fargo became the messenger between Albany and Buffalo for Pomeroy and Company, and in the following year became their agent in Buffalo.

In 1844, he became the messenger and, with Henry Wells and another partner, part owner of Wells & Company, which ran between Buffalo and Detroit. It was the first express company that operated west of Buffalo. In 1846, the express business was expanded from Albany to New York, and London and Paris offices were opened. In 1850, Wells & Company, Butterfield Wasson & Company, and Livingston, Fargo, and Company merged to form the American Express Company. Wells was president, and Fargo was secretary. Express service was expanded to Cincinnati, Galena, Chicago, Milwaukee, St. Louis, and Dubuque.

In 1852, Wells, Fargo & Company was organized to meet the demand for transportation to and from California. Up to that time, the usual means of traveling between the East and California was by steamship via the Panama Canal. The discovery of gold at Sutter's Mill in 1849 spurred travel between the two coasts. Their main competitor in California, Adams & Company, failed in 1855, leaving the field to them. Wells, Fargo & Company expresses carried gold dust, mail, packages, and passengers. They also conducted banking business for many of the communities they served.

Wells, Fargo & Company operated the pony express over the 2,000 miles between St. Joseph, Missouri, and Sacramento, California. Despite blizzards, floods, hostile Indians, and other obstacles, the mail went through in nine days on a fixed schedule. The pony express provided a way of communicating between the east and west coasts before the advent of railroads and the telegraph. It played a vital role in keeping California in the union.

The pony express was a superb operation, but, unfortunately, it lost money for Wells, Fargo & Company. With the completion of the telegraph across the country in October, 1861, the pony express went out of business. It filled a critical need in its time and occupies a romantic spot in U.S. history.

The express business earned large profits during the Civil War, which initially led to the forming of competing companies and later to the consolidation of marginally profitable companies. In 1866, the California legislature forced the consolidation of express companies and mail stages from Missouri to the Pacific into Wells, Fargo & Company. The stage business was discontinued with the completion of the Union Pacific Railroad.

In 1868, the Pacific Union Express Company was granted an

exclusive ten-year contract with the railroad. Severe competition led to the merger of the Pacific Union Express Company and Wells, Fargo & Company in the following year. In 1868 in the East, the Merchants Union Express Company became so influential that the American Express Company was forced to merge with it on equal terms. It became the American Merchants Union Express Company. Wells retired as president of American Express and Fargo became president of the merged companies. In 1873, the name of the consolidated company reverted to the American Express Company.

Fargo lived in Buffalo during the latter part of his life. He was active in local politics and served two terms as the Democratic mayor of the city from 1862-66. He was an easy-going, popular manager who took an interest in his employees, and they were devoted to him. Fargo died in Buffalo on August 3, 1881.

Wells traveled widely during the last ten years of his life. He was president of the First National Bank of Aurora and the first president of the Cayuga Lake Railroad. Wells suffered from an impediment of speech and, to help his fellow sufferers, established schools for stammerers in several cities.

In 1868, he founded the Wells Seminary for the Education of Young Women at Aurora and donated 111 acres for the campus. In 1870, the name was changed to Wells College. He also donated his home, Glen Park, which became the first building of the college.

On December 10, 1878, Wells died in Glasgow, Scotland. He was buried near his home in Aurora, the beautiful village on the east shore of Cayuga Lake. The early success and subsequent expansion of the American Express Company was due largely to the vision of Henry Wells. He foresaw the westward movement of the population and expanded to provide services to keep up with it. His partner, Fargo, was also a strong businessman. He displayed his ability during the period of post-war deflation and retrenchment, when he dealt successfully with the potential stagnation of the business. Together, Wells and Fargo made a strong team who made their mark in U.S. history.

Jethro Wood

J ethro Wood, the inventor of the cast iron plow, was born on March 16, 1774, in Dartmouth, Massachusetts. He was the only son of John Wood, a man of influence in the region, and Dinah Hussey Wood, a niece of Ann Starbuck, the virtual governor of Nantucket. They were members of the Society of Friends.

Jethro Wood was well educated, for the time in which he lived, and had access to a substantial library and a well-equipped workshop. He was good at working with his hands, even when quite young. His relatives told a story about him: "When only a few years old, he moulded a little plow from metal, which he obtained by melting a pewter cup. Then, cutting the buckles from a set of braces, he made a miniature harness with which he fastened the family cat to his tiny plow, and then endeavored to drive her about the flower garden."

On January 1, 1793, Wood married Sylvia Howland at White Creek, New York, and moved to Scipio, near Owasco Lake, where he spent the rest of his life. He was an inventor most of his adult life and it was said that:

> His chief desire was to invent a new mould-board, which, from its form, should meet the least resistance from the soil, and which could be made with share [the point of the plow in touch with the earth] and standard [the vertical piece which joins the mould-board and the beam, the horizontal part of the plow connected to the team], entirely of cast iron. To hit upon the exact shape for the mould-board he whittled away, day after day, until his neighbors, who thought him mad on the subject, gave him the soubriquet of the "whittling Yankee."

Jethro Wood was granted two patents for plows. His first plow patent was awarded in 1814, but he realized the shortcomings of this plow and destroyed the patterns. The patent granted to him on

September 1, 1819 was a significant improvement and was the design for which he sought royalties. The improvements in this design were the use of cast iron, the use of three replaceable parts (eliminating the need for sharpening the share), and the means of adjusting the connection of the mould-board and the beam, causing a deeper or shallower furrow. Wood considered the main improvement of his plow to be the use of cast iron. His patent included this text:

> The said inventor and petitioner wishes it to be understood, that the principal metallic material of his Plough is cast iron. He has very little use for wrought iron, and by adapting the former to the extent that he has done, and by discontinuing the latter, he is enabled to make the Plough stronger and better, as well as more lasting and cheap.

Earlier plows were constructed of wood with a sheet of iron fastened to the mould-board for additional strength.

Upon obtaining his second patent, he immediately began to manufacture his plows and introduce them to farmers in his neighborhood. They called his plow "Jethro's folly" and had no confidence in a plow made of pot metal, so he arranged a demonstration of his plow to counter his neighbors' negative views:

> One day he induced one of the most skeptical neighbors to make a public trial of the plow. A large concourse gathered to see how it would work. The field selected for the test was thickly strewn with stones, many of them firmly imbedded in the soil, and jutting up from the surface. All predicted that the plow would break at the outset. To their astonishment and Wood's satisfaction, it went around the field, running easily and smoothly, and turning up the most perfect furrow which had ever been seen. The small stones against which the farmer maliciously

guided it, to test the "brittle" metal, moved out of the way as if they were grains of sand, and it slid around the immovable rocks as if they were icebergs.

Incensed at the non-fulfillment of his prophecy, the farmer finally drove the plow with all force upon a large boulder, and found to his amazement that it was uninjured by the collision. It proved a day of triumph for Jethro Wood, and from that time he heard few taunts about the pot-metal.

It soon became evident that Wood's plow had several advantages over previous designs: two horses could do work that previously required a yoke of oxen, replacement parts could be purchased for seven or eight dollars, and it made a better furrow. Thomas Jefferson, who had retired to Monticello and was working on his own plow design, wrote Wood a letter of congratulation complimenting him on the merits of his new plow, even though Jefferson's own mould-board design differed considerably from his.

Wood's patent expired in 1833 and he was granted an extension for fourteen years. He realized very few royalties on his patent, even though plows made to his design were in use all over the country. Wood died in 1834, and his son, Benjamin, took up the struggle to obtain royalties. Henry Clay, Daniel Webster, and Congressman John Quincy Adams attempted to aid Benjamin Wood, but their main accomplishment was to obtain improvement to the patent laws.

The Circuit Court at Albany ruled that the plow in widespread use was, in fact, a unique design invented by Jethro Wood, and that all manufacturers must pay the heirs of Jethro Wood for the use of the design. However, this ruling was made in 1845 when the patent had only one more year to run. Benjamin left immediately for Washington to request a second extension on the patent. The exertion was too much for him and he died of a heart attack.

Two of Jethro's four daughters, Phoebe and Sylvia Ann,

traveled to Washington to take up the family cause. Clay and Webster supported their suit, and they sought the support of John Quincy Adams. The last words written by Mr. Adams were, "Mr. J. Q. Adams presents his compliments to the Misses Wood, and will be happy to see them at his house, at their convenience, any morning between 10 and 11 o'clock."

The note was found on February 21, 1848, the day that Adams had a stroke and died at his desk in the House of Representatives after saying, "This is the last of earth; I am content." The legislation, containing the words, "A bill providing that in these four heirs should rest for seven years the exclusive right of making and vending the improvements in the construction of the cast iron plow; and that twenty-five cents on each plow might be extracted from all who manufactured it," passed in the Senate, but was defeated in the House of Representatives.

Competing plow manufacturers had convinced their Representatives in the House that the Wood family had gained considerable wealth from Jethro Wood's design in the previous twenty-eight years and merely wanted to maintain the monopoly. It was estimated that royalties totaling $550 had been received by the family by 1834, the year in which Jethro Wood died. This sum didn't even cover legal costs.

Knight's American Mechanical Dictionary contains the following comments on the Jethro Wood cast iron plow:

> He made the best plows up to date ... It consisted in the mode of securing the cast iron portions together by lugs and locking pieces, doing away with screw-bolts, and much weight, complexity and expense. It was the first plow in which the parts exposed to wear could be renewed in the field by the substitution of cast pieces ... He met with great opposition, and then with much injustice, losing competency in introducing his plow and fighting infringers.

There were no teeth in the patent legislation of the time, and other inventors suffered similar fates, notably Elias Howe, inventor of the sewing machine (Initially, Mr. Singer enjoyed most of the benefits of that invention); Charles Goodyear, inventor of the vulcanization process for rubber; and Eli Whitney, inventor of the cotton gin. Eli Whitney's experience in a Georgia court was typical: "I had great difficulty in proving that the machine had been used in Georgia, although at the same moment there were three separate sets of this machinery in motion within fifty yards of the building in which the court sat, and all so near that the rattling of wheels was distinctly heard on the steps of the Court House."

Scientific American ranks Jethro Wood as an inventor with Benjamin Franklin, Robert Fulton, Charles Goodyear, Elias Howe, Cyrus McCormick, Samuel B. Morse, and Eli Whitney. William H. Seward, a counselor for the Wood family in their suit for royalties, observed that "No citizen of the United States has conferred greater economical benefits on his country than Jethro Wood—none of her benefactors have been more inadequately rewarded."

Epilogue Poem

Of all the spots on God's green earth,
The one I'd choose for my own
Would be the wonderful finger lakes
With their beauty of great renown
Sparkling waters and verdant hills
Nestled beneath azure skies;
To one who'd make this spot home,
He would live in a paradise
Indians say that God's own Hand
Planted His finger prints here
To bless the land for his children
To show them his garden rare
And as I gaze at its beauty
I cannot help but feel awed
To think that this marvel of nature
Was blessed by the Hand of God.

—From *Inspiration* by A. Glenn Rogers

Joseph Smith Homestead, Palmyra

Bibliography

Ackerman, Carl W. *George Eastman.* Boston: Houghton Mifflin, 1930.

Adams, Leon. *The Wines of America.* Boston: Houghton Mifflin, 1973.

Alexander, Charles C. *John McGraw.* New York: Viking, 1988.

Allen, James E., Jr. *An Uncommon Man: The Story of Dr. William Pearson Tolley and Syracuse University.* New York: Newcomen Society, 1963.

Allen, Opal Sweazer. *Narcissa Whitman.* Portland, OR: Binfords and Mort, 1959.

Altschuler, Glenn C. *Andrew D. White—Educator, Historian, Diplomat.* Ithaca: Cornell UP, 1979.

Andrist, Ralph K. *The Erie Canal.* New York: American Heritage, 1964.

Arrington, Leonard J. *Brigham Young: American Moses.* New York: Alfred A. Knopf, 1985.

Baker, George, ed. *The Life of William H. Seward with Selections from his Works.* New York: Redfield, 1855.

Barre, W.L. *The Life and Public Services of Millard Fillmore.* New York: Burt Franklin, 1856.

Baum, Frank Joslyn, and Russell P. McFall. *To Please a Child: A Biography of L. Frank Baum, Royal Historian of Oz.* Chicago: Reilly & Lee, 1961.

Belden, Thomas Graham, and Marva Robbins Belden. *The Lengthening Shadow: The Life of Thomas J. Watson.* Boston: Little, Brown, 1962.

Bloomer, D.C. *Life and Writings of Amelia Bloomer.* Boston: Arena, 1895.

Bonvillain, Nancy. *Hiawatha: Founder of the Iroquois Confederacy.* New York: Chelsea House, 1992.

Bourne, Russell. *Floating West: The Erie and Other American Canals.* New York: Norton, 1992.

Brandon, Ruth. *A Capitalist Romance: Singer and the Sewing Machine.* Philadelphia: Lippincott, 1977.

Bringhurst, Newell G. *Brigham Young and the Expanding*

American Frontier. Boston: Little, Brown, 1986.

Brodie, Fawn M. *No Man Knows My History: The Life of Joseph Smith, the Mormon Prophet.* New York: Alfred A. Knopf, 1971.

Bronner, Frederick Lidell, George Frederick Howe, and Hiram C. Todd. *Chester Alan Arthur.* Schenectady: Union College, 1948.

Brown, Jordan. *Elizabeth Blackwell.* New York: Chelsea House, 1989.

Capers, Gerald M. *Stephen A. Douglas: Defender of the Union.* Boston: Little, Brown, 1959.

Carmer, Carl. *Listen for a Lonesome Drum: A New York State Chronicle.* New York: Farrar & Rinehart, 1936.

Cazden, Elizabeth. *Antoinette Brown Blackwell: A Biography.* Old Westbury, N.Y.: The Feminist Press, 1983.

Chambers, Peggy. *A Doctor Alone: A Biography of Elizabeth Blackwell, the First Woman Doctor 1821-1910.* London: Abelard-Schuman, 1958.

Clarke, Mary Statson. *Bloomers and Ballots: Elizabeth Cady Stanton and Women's Rights.* New York: Viking, 1972.

Collier, Peter, and David Horowitz. *The Rockefellers: An American Dynasty.* New York: Holt, Rinehart & Winston, 1976.

Cooper, Ilene. *Susan B. Anthony.* New York: Franklin Watts, 1984.

Cramer, C.H. *Royal Bob: The Life of Robert G. Ingersoll.* Indianapolis: Bobbs-Merrill, 1952.

Cross, Whitney R. *The Burned-over District: The Social and Intellectual History of Enthusiastic Religion in Western New York, 1800-1850.* New York: Harper, 1950.

D'Ambrosio, Mary. "Matilda Gage." *Syracuse Magazine.* Mar. 1981: 33.

Dayton, George Draper. *George Draper Dayton: An Autobiography.* N.p.: n.p., 1933.

Dessauer, John H. *My Years with Xerox: The Billions Nobody Wanted.* Garden City: Doubleday, 1971.

Dimitroff, Thomas P. and Lois S. Janes. *History of the Painted Post Area: 200 Years in Painted Post Country.* Corning, NY:

Bookmarks, 1991.

Dorf, Philip. *The Builder: A Biography of Ezra Cornell.* New York: Macmillan, 1952.

Everson, William K. *The Films of Hal Roach.* New York: Museum of Modern Art, 1971.

Fausold, Martin L. *James W. Wadsworth, Jr.: The Gentleman from New York.* Syracuse: Syracuse UP, 1975.

Fitzgerald, John R. *The New Erie Canal: A Recreational Guide.* N.p.: n.p., 1993.

Forbes, B.C., and O.D. Foster. *Automotive Giants of America: Men Who Are Making Our Motor Industry.* New York: Forbes, 1926.

Fowler, Orson S. *The Octagon House: A Home for All.* New York: Dover, 1973.

Fradin, Dennis Brindell. *Hiawatha: Messenger of Peace.* New York: Margaret K. McElderry Books, 1992.

Gilbert, Frank. *Jethro Wood: Inventor of the Modern Plow.* Chicago: Rhodes & McClure, 1882.

Griffin, Elizabeth. *In Her Own Right: The Life of Elizabeth Cady Stanton.* New York: Oxford UP, 1984.

Griffis, William Elliott. *Millard Fillmore: Constructive Statesman, Defender of the Constitution, President of the United States.* Ithaca: Andrus & Church, 1915.

Hatch, Alden. *The Wadsworths of the Genesee.* New York: Coward-McCann, 1959.

Hawke, David Freeman. *John D.: The Founding Father of the Rockefellers.* New York: Harper, 1980.

Henry, Thomas R. *Wilderness Messiah: The Story of Hiawatha and the Iroquois.* New York: William Sloane, 1955.

Hill, Donna. *Joseph Smith: The First Mormon.* Garden City: Doubleday, 1977.

Holthusen, Henry F. *James W. Wadsworth, Jr.: A Biographical Sketch.* New York: G.P. Putman's sons, 1926.

Hotra, Lynda McCurdy. *Mary Clark Thompson: Canandaigua's Magnificent Benefactress.* Canandaigua, NY: Ontario County Historical Society, 1984.

Howe, George Frederick. *Chester A. Arthur: A Quarter-Century of Machine Politics.* New York: Frederick Ungar, 1935.

Hubbard, J. Niles. *An Account of SA-GO-TE-WAT-HA or Red Jacket and His People.* New York: Burt Franklin, 1971.

Huggins, Nathan Irwin. *Slave and Citizen: The Life of Frederick Douglass.* Boston: Little, Brown. 1980.

Hughes, Thomas Parke. *Elmer Sperry: Inventor and Engineer.* Baltimore: Johns Hopkins UP, 1971.

Ingels, Margaret. *Willis Haviland Carrier. The Father of Air Conditioning.* Garden City: Country Life Press, 1952.

Jennings, Walter Wilson. *A Dozen Captains of Industry.* New York: Vantage, 1954.

Jessup, Phillip C. *Elihu Root.* New York: Dodd, Mead, 1938.

Kather, Jan Strausser. *Zim: The Life Story of Eugene Zimmerman.* Horseheads, NY: Horseheads Historical Society, 1978.

Kerr, Laura. *Lady in the Pulpit.* New York: Woman's Press, 1951.

Kneeland, Donald E. *Spirits of the Genesee / Finger Lakes Region.* N.p.: Lark, 1984.

Lader, Lawrence. *The Margaret Sanger Story and the Fight for Birth Control.* Garden City: Doubleday, 1955.

Lader, Lawrence, and Milton Meltzer. *Margaret Sanger: Pioneer of Birth Control.* New York: Crowell, 1969.

Larned, J.N. *The Life and Work of William Pryor Letchworth.* Boston: Houghton Mifflin, 1912.

Lauber, John. *The Making of Mark Twain: A Biography.* New York: American Heritage, 1985.

Leopold, Richard W. *Elihu Root and the Conservative Tradition.* Little, Brown, 1954.

Lewis, Eugene W. *Motor Memories: A Saga of Whirling Gears.* Detroit: Alved, 1947.

MacDonald, Ray W. *Strategy for Growth: The Story of the Burroughs Corporation.* New York: Newcomen Society, 1978.

MacManus, Theodore F., and Norman Beasley. *Men, Money, and Motors: The Drama of the Automobile.* New York: Harper, 1929.

Mau, Clayton. *The Development of Central and Western New York.* Dansville, NY: Owen, 1958.

May, George S., ed. "John North Willys." *The Automobile Industry, 1920-1980.* New York: Facts On File, 1989.

McClard, Magan. *Harriett Tubman: Slavery and the Underground Railroad.* Englewood Cliffs: Silver Burdett Press, 1991.

Melone, Henry R. *History of Central New York.* Indianapolis: Historical Publishing, 1932.

Meltzer, Milton. *Mark Twain: A Writer's Life.* New York: Franklin Watts, 1985.

Merrill, Arch. *Bloomers and Bugles.* New York. American Book-Stratford, 1958.

—. *Fame in our Time.* New York: American Book-Stratford, 1960.

—. *From Pumpkin Hook to Dumpling Hill.* New York· American Book-Stratford, 1969.

—. *Gaslights and Gingerbread.* New York: American Book-Stratford, 1959.

—. *Shadows on the Wall.* Interlaken, NY: Empire State Books, 1987.

—. *The White Woman and Her Valley.* New York: American Book-Stratford, n.d.

Miller, Douglas T. *Frederick Douglass and the Fight for Freedom.* New York: Facts On File, 1988.

Nevins, Allan. *John D. Rockefeller.* New York: Scribner's, 1959.

Nolan, Jeanette Covert. *The Little Giant: Stephen A. Douglas.* New York: Julian Messner, 1969.

Palmer, Richard F., and Karl D. Butler. *Brigham Young: The New York Years.* Provo: Charles Redd Center for Western Studies, 1982.

Parker, Arthur C. *Red Jacket: Last of the Seneca.* New York: McGraw-Hill, 1952.

Peer, Dick. "Amory Houghton, Jr.: Firm Believer in Area Community." Corning *Leader* 6 April, 1992: 2D.

Pryor, Elizabeth Brown. *Clara Barton: Professional Angel.* Philadelphia: U of Pennsylvania P, 1987.

Rabbitt, Mary C. "John Wesley Powell: His Life & Times." *Geotimes* May-Jun 1969: 10-18.

Rapp, Marvin A. *NEW YORK STATE: A Student's Guide to Localized History.* New York: Columbia UP, 1968.

Rayback, Robert J. *Millard Fillmore: Biography of a President.* Buffalo: Henry Stewart, 1959.

Reeves, Thomas C. *Gentleman Boss: The Life of Chester Alan Arthur.* New York: Alfred A. Knopf, 1975.

Robinson, Ray. *Baseball's Most Colorful Managers.* New York: G.P. Putnam's Sons, 1969.

Rochester, Nathaniel. *A Brief Sketch of the Life of Nathaniel Rochester.* Rochester, NY: n.p., n.d.

Rogers, Cameron. *Colonel Bob Ingersoll: A Biographical Narrative of the Great American Orator and Agnostic.* Garden City: Doubleday, 1927.

Rogers, Glenn. *Forgotten Stories of the Finger Lakes: Dramatic Tales of Fact and Legend.* Geneva, NY: n.p., 1953.

Rogers, Walter P. *Andrew White and the Modern University.* Ithaca: Cornell UP, 1942.

Rogers, William. *THINK: A Biography of the Watsons and IBM.* New York: Stein and Day, 1969.

Rosenberg, Jerry M. *The Computer Prophets.* New York: Macmillan, 1969.

Ross, Ishbell. *Child of Destiny: The Life Story of the First Woman Doctor.* New York: Harper, 1949.

Seeley, Lyman J. *Flying Pioneers at Hammondsport, New York 1900-1914.* N.p.: n.p., 1929.

Seelye, Elizabeth Eggleston. *Brant and Red Jacket.* Chicago: M.A. Donohue, 1907.

Shipps, Jan. *Mormonism: The Story of a New Religious Tradition.* Urbana: U of Illinois P, 1985.

Sifikis, Carl. "Publick Universal Friend." *American Eccentrics.* New York: Facts On File, 1984.

Sloate, Susan. *Clara Barton: Founder of the American Red Cross.* New York: Fawcett, 1990.

Stanton, Elizabeth Cady. *Eighty Years and More: Reminiscences 1815-1897.* New York: Schocken, 1971.

Stearns, Monroe. *Mark Twain.* New York: Franklin Watts, 1965.

Swanson, June. *I Pledge Allegiance.* Minneapolis: Carolrhoda, 1990.

Taves, Ernest H. *This Is the Place: Brigham Young and the New Zion.* Buffalo: Prometheus, 1991.

Taylor, M.W. *Harriet Tubman.* New York: Chelsea House, 1991.

Tolley, William Pearson. *At the Fountain of Youth: Memories of a*

College President. Syracuse: Syracuse UP, 1989.

Topalian, Elyse. *Margaret Sanger.* New York: Franklin Watts, 1984.

Turner, O. *History of the Pioneer Settlement of Phelps' and Gorham's Purchase and Morris' Preserve.* Rochester, NY: William Alling, 1851.

Van Duesen, Glyndon G. *William Henry Seward.* New York: Oxford UP, 1967.

Wampler, Cloud. *Dr. Willis Carrier: The Father of Air Conditioning.* New York: Newcomen Society, 1949.

Weisberg, Barbara. *Susan B. Anthony.* New York: Chelsea House, 1988.

Williamson, Samuel T. *Imprint of a Publisher: The Story of Frank Gannett and His Independent Newspapers.* Toronto: Robert M. McBride, 1948.

Wisbey, Herbert A. Jr. *Pioneer Prophetess Jemima Wilkinson: The Publick Universal Friend.* Ithaca: Cornell UP, 1964.

Eugene Zimmerman's Study, "Zim" House, Horseheads

Index

Mark Twain's Summer Home, East Hill, Elmira